The Student's **Shakespeare**

MACBETH

Introduction by Angela Sheehan

This edition published 2015 by Geddes & Grosset, an imprint of
The Gresham Publishing Company Ltd., Academy Park, Building 4000,
Gower Street, Glasgow, G51 1PR, Scotland, UK

First published 2014. Reprinted 2015.

ISBN: 978-1-84205-870-1

Printed and bound in Spain by Novoprint, SA.

Introduction

William Shakespeare (1564–1616) wrote three types of play: comedies, histories and tragedies. His understanding of human nature was so deep and his language so expressive, that after 400 years his plays are still performed, read and admired. Of his tragedies *Macbeth* is the most often performed. It is a play about ambition and evil. Its strange and murderous events are dramatised in matchless poetry, its unnerving characters depicted with seering psychological insight.

Shakespeare wrote *Macbeth* in about 1605 or 1606. It was first published in 1623. The play tells the story of a real King of the Scots who ruled in the eleventh century. He came to the throne in 1040 after defeating the ruling king, Duncan. He ruled for seventeen years but was then killed in battle in 1057 by Duncan's son, Malcolm. Shakespeare based the play loosely on accounts written by Raphael Holinshed in his *Chronicles of England, Scotland and Ireland*, published in 1577. This book was popular in Shakespeare's day and he took from it the stories of several English kings, and turned them into exciting plays. He did not always stick to the facts. He added incidents and altered characters to make the plays more interesting. He did this with *Macbeth*, who was not quite as evil as Shakespeare makes him out to be.

Conflict and kingship

Macbeth is about the overthrow of the rightful ruler of a country by a hero turned traitor. In the years before Shakespeare's birth and during his lifetime, there were many threats to England's rulers, including one from the then independent country of Scotland. There was fierce religious conflict and many innocent people were burnt at the stake, hanged or beheaded simply for their religious beliefs.

Good Queen Bess

When Shakespeare was born, Elizabeth I had been on the throne of England for six years. She succeeded her Roman Catholic sister Mary. Both of them were daughters of Henry VIII but of different religions. Elizabeth was a Protestant and head of the Church of England. She was clever and well educated and she became a strong ruler. The people loved her and called her Good Queen Bess.

Elizabeth loved to dress in magnificent clothes and jewels. She loved music and dancing, and enjoyed the attentions of handsome young men. She had many admirers and several 'favourites' but she refused to marry. This worried her advisers because the next in line to the throne was another Mary – Mary, Queen of Scots, and she was a Catholic.

Mary, Queen of Scots

Mary was the only child of James V of Scotland, and Elizabeth's cousin. She was married to the King of France but became a widow at eighteen. She returned to Scotland to take up her throne but there were many problems, not least her Catholic religion, for Scotland was now a Protestant country. Her personal relationships sparked her downfall. After several scandals, she was forced to abdicate. Her son became King James VI of Scotland. Mary fled to England and sought refuge from her cousin Elizabeth.

Elizabeth was wary of Mary. She kept her imprisoned, in comfort, but surrounded by courtiers and spies. For nineteen years, Mary plotted against Elizabeth but the English queen was reluctant to execute a fellow queen, anointed by God. In the end, there was so much evidence of Mary's involvement in a Catholic plot to murder her that, with much reluctance, Elizabeth, signed her death warrant, and in 1587 Mary was beheaded for treason.

The new English king, James I

Elizabeth was still childless, so she named Mary's son her successor. He was a popular choice because he was a Protestant, and a serious scholarly man, deeply committed to his religion. When Elizabeth eventually died, in 1603, James came to London to be crowned James I, the first Stuart King of England.

It did not at first appear that he would be a strong ruler. Because of this, in 1605, a group of Catholics, including the Spaniard Guy (Guido) Fawkes, plotted against him. They planned to blow up Parliament when James was opening the new session. Shakespeare's play *Macbeth* is about the wickedness of such plots to overthrow a rightful king. Macbeth is a traitor who deserves to die a horrible death. Banquo, the ancestor of the Stuart kings, is the most noble character in the play.

A new play for a new king

Shakespeare wrote *Macbeth* to please the new king. James had paid Shakespeare's company of actors the honour of being called 'The King's Men', and doubled their fees. Like most of Shakespeare's audience, James was interested in witchcraft and the supernatural. He even wrote a book on the subject called *Daemonologie*, and another book called *Newes from Scotland* about recent witch trials. One supposed witch, Agnis Sampson, was accused of attempting to wreck the ship on which James was sailing to Denmark to be married. The poor woman confessed and was sentenced to death. Shakespeare read about her in James's book and learned about witches' spells and chants and their ability to see into the future.

Ghosts and sprites and fairies appear in lots of Shakespeare's plays. Mostly they are good characters. The witches in *Macbeth* are horrible demonic hags, creatures of the devil, whose prophecies make a wicked man kill a king and a good man give rise to a dynasty of kings. Very few people people believe in witches and fairies today, but in Shakespeare's day most people believed in the devil and in supernatural beings that could infect a person with evil. Often the poor people who were accused of being witches were simply suffering from mental illnesses or were good women using herbs to try to help cure diseases. Their knowledge of medicine may have been no better or worse than those of the men who practised as doctors.

THE STORY OF *MACBETH*

Although *Macbeth* is based on the story of a real person, it powerfully dramatises the issues that were important to Shakespeare's audience and especially to the new king, James I. The trials of the conspirators who plotted to kill James were taking place, so treachery was in people's minds. With exceptional poetry and psychological insight, Shakespeare takes us into Macbeth's mind and explores his conscience as he descends into evil.

Act I Fair is foul and foul is fair
It is a stormy night on a wild heath. Three witches appear and arrange to meet later, with Macbeth, 'When the hurlyburley's done,/ When the battle's lost and won.' (Act I Sc i). Then they mysteriously disappear into the 'filthy air'.

The battle is between the army of Duncan, King of Scotland and those of some rebel Scottish lords, supported by the King of Norway and his forces. After fierce fighting, led by Macbeth, who is Duncan's kinsman and one of his bravest and most loyal generals, the battle is won. The rebels and foreign army have been defeated. The King learns that one of the rebel lords, the Thane of Cawdor, has been taken prisoner. (A thane was a Scottish baron.) The King orders the traitor to be put to death and declares that 'noble Macbeth' shall have his title. He sends two of his noblemen, Ross and Angus, to greet Macbeth with the news.

Macbeth and his fellow nobleman Banquo are returning from the battle. The witches are lying in wait for them. They talk of the evil spells they have cast on people. As the two men cross the heath, the mist suddenly clears and they see the witches, looking 'So withered, and so wild in their attire, … not like the inhabitants o' the earth.' (Act I Sc iii). Macbeth demands to know who they are. They greet him as Thane of Cawdor and prophesy that he will be king. They say Banquo is 'Lesser than Macbeth, and greater.' (Act I Sc iii). His heirs will be kings though he will not be king. The witches disappear and Banquo and Macbeth are left wondering what to make of the encounter.

At that moment, Ross and Angus arrive. They tell Macbeth that he has indeed been made Thane of Cawdor. Until then Macbeth was unaware of Cawdor's capture. The first of the witches' prophecies has come true. What about the second: that he will be king? Banquo warns him of the harm that belief in the 'instruments of darkness' can do. But Macbeth thinks that maybe he could also become king. For a moment, he imagines himself killing Duncan. Then he dismisses the 'horrible imaginings'. But the thought is in his mind. He is becoming ambitious.

At King Duncan's palace, the King hears from his son Malcolm that Cawdor has been executed. The King observes that, 'He was a gentleman on whom I built/ An absolute trust' (Act I Sc iv). At that moment, Macbeth (another man he trusts) arrives, with Banquo. The King greets them warmly and thanks them profusely. He announces that Malcolm is to be the heir to his throne. Then he declares his intention to visit Macbeth at his castle. This is a great honour, so Macbeth hurries off to prepare for the King's arrival. He will let his wife know that he is coming. As he leaves, he broods about Malcolm, another obstacle on his path to power. He tries to suppress his evil thoughts: 'Let not light see my black and deep desires.' (Act I Sc iv).

At Macbeth's castle, Lady Macbeth reads her husband's letter. It tells her of the witches' prophecies. Immediately she understands the 'nearest way' for Macbeth to ascend the throne but she fears that his nature is 'too full o' the milk of human kindness'. (Act I Sc v).

At that moment a messenger arrives telling her of the King's visit – the perfect opportunity to kill him. Alone, she voices her murderous thoughts, relishing them rather than trying to suppress them. She calls on the spirits to fill her 'from the crown to the toe top-full/ Of direst cruelty.' (Act I Sc v). The murder must be committed that night. When Macbeth arrives at the castle ahead of the King, she has arranged everything.

Duncan arrives on a lovely summer's day. He is full of good will and compliments: 'This castle hath a pleasant seat – the air/ Nimbly and sweetly recommends itself/ Unto our gentle senses.' (Act I Sc vi). Lady Macbeth greets him with exaggerated courtesy. Macbeth contemplates the murder. He fears the consequences and his conscience troubles him. Duncan is his cousin, he is a good king, he is Macbeth's guest. There is no reason for Macbeth to kill him, other than his own 'vaulting ambition' to be king. He tells Lady Macbeth that he has changed his mind. She accuses him of being a coward. She would kill her own child if she had promised to do so. Macbeth gives in completely. He agrees to go ahead with her plan.

Act II Most sacrilegious murder

Banquo and his son Fleance are also guests at the castle. It is after midnight but Banquo feels too uneasy to sleep. He tells Macbeth that he has been thinking of the witches, and how their predictions have come true. But Macbeth claims not to think about them. After Banquo and Fleance have gone, we hear what he is really thinking. He has a terrible vision of a dagger that he tries to grasp but cannot get hold of. He tells himself that he is imagining things because he is afraid. But the phantom dagger is still there, now with blood on it. Then he hears a bell ring. It is Lady Macbeth's signal. It is time to kill the King. 'I go and it is done. The bell invites me./ Hear it not, Duncan, for it is a knell/ That summons thee to heaven, or to hell.' (Act II Sc i).

Lady Macbeth has made sure that Duncan's two attendants are asleep by drugging their drinks. She has put out two daggers for Macbeth to use. She keeps watch outside, as Macbeth enters the King's chamber. When he comes out his arms are covered in blood. He is still holding the blood-stained daggers. In a state of shock, he describes the cries of the servants as he killed them: 'Methought I heard a voice cry "Sleep no more!/ Macbeth doth murder sleep" – the innocent sleep,/ Sleep that knits up the ravelled sleave of care,' (Act II Sc ii). Lady Macbeth attempts to calm him down. He must take the daggers back. But Macbeth cannot face the task. Impatiently, Lady Macbeth takes the daggers and smears the attendants with blood to make them seem guilty. Just then they hear knocking at the gates of the castle. Lady Macbeth knows that this might awaken the household. She urges Macbeth to return with her to their chamber, so that they can wash off the blood, put on their nightclothes, and appear to have been asleep.

The Porter has been slow to hear the knocking and open the gates. He too had fallen into a drunken sleep. Eventually he lets in the nobles, Lennox and Macduff, and greets them with some cheerfully irreverent banter. When Macbeth appears, they explain that the King asked them to call him early. While Macduff goes to waken Duncan, Lennox describes how their night was disturbed by 'Lamentings heard i' the air, strange screams of death,' (Act II Sc iii). Macduff returns, horror-stricken. Duncan has been murdered. He calls for the alarm bells to be rung, while Macbeth rushes off to 'investigate'. Lady Macbeth, Banquo and Duncan's sons hear the news as Macbeth returns. He confesses that he killed the 'murderers', the King's servants, in a fit of justifiable rage. Lady Macbeth faints – or pretends to faint – in horror.

Duncan's sons, Malcolm and Donalbain, are not convinced by Macbeth's feigned grief. They know they must now be in danger, so they decide to flee. But this makes them suspects in the murder.

Outside the castle, some time later, Ross and Macduff discuss what has happened. Macduff explains that Duncan's guards had been put up to the murders by his sons. Macbeth has been named king.

Act III Another murder and a Ghost at dinner

Macbeth is now living in the royal palace. Banquo suspects him of the murder, and thinks about the possibility that the witches' prophecy about his own son might come true. Macbeth invites Banquo to a formal banquet to be held that night. He envies Banquo because of the witches' prophecy that his heirs, not Macbeth's, will be kings. He takes a special interest in how Banquo and Fleance are to spend the afternoon because he has hired assassins to kill them – before the banquet.

He convinces the killers that Banquo is responsible for everything that is wrong in their lives, and is their enemy. He bullies and flatters them into agreeing to kill both father and son.

This time, Macbeth does not confide in the Queen. Meeting her husband after the murderers leave, Lady Macbeth thinks that he is still brooding about Duncan's murder. She tries to cheer him up by saying, 'What's done is done.' and encourages him to be 'bright and jovial' (Act III Sc ii) with his guests that night. In turn he tells her to be especially pleasant to Banquo. He does not tell her that he has already ordered his death.

As Banquo and Fleance ride towards the palace, they are waylaid by the murderers. Banquo is killed but Fleance escapes. The cut-throats have done only half their job. Macbeth receives this information just as the banquet begins. Lady Macbeth chides her husband for not welcoming their guests. As he goes to take his place at the table, Macbeth sees Banquo sitting in his seat, not really Banquo but the Ghost of Banquo, and only Macbeth can see the apparition. Macbeth cannot conceal his terror. Lady Macbeth tries to explain away his odd behaviour to the guests. He is not well, she says, and then quietly tries to bring him to his senses. When the Ghost disappears he recovers himself and passes his disturbance off as a 'strange affirmity'. But when it returns he speaks to the 'horrible shadow', to the astonishment of the guests. Lady Macbeth urges the guests to leave. Once they have gone, Macbeth relaxes but he resolves to see the witches next day. Now, there is no going back: 'I am in blood/ Stepped in so far that should I wade no more/ Returning were as tedious as go o'er.' (Act III Sc iv).

Act IV More murders and more prophecies

Macbeth finds the 'secret, black, and midnight hags' in their den, brewing up a cauldron of unsavoury ingredients: 'Eye of newt, and toe of frog,/ Wool of bat, and tongue of dog,/ Adder's fork, and blind-worm's sting,/ Lizard's leg, and howlet's wing,' (Act IV Sc i). He demands to know from them what will happen. They warn him to beware of Macduff. He is to be 'bloody, bold and resolute' for 'none of woman born/ Shall harm Macbeth.' And, further, he 'shall never vanquished be until/ Great Birnam wood to high Dunsinane hill/ shall come against him.' (Act IV Sc i). This means that he has no need to fear Macduff, but he decides to kill him anyway. And forests and trees do not move, so he need not worry about that. But what about Banquo? Will his descendants rule? In answer, the witches summon eight apparitions of future kings, all Banquo's heirs. (King James, one of them, would have seen a vision of himself.)

Macbeth has learned that Macduff has turned against him. He has fled to England to join Malcolm who is organising an army to march on Macbeth. In revenge he decides to kill Macduff's innocent family. Lady Macduff is at home with her children. She knows that she is in danger and laments the absence of her husband. A messenger arrives to tell her to flee but she has nowhere to go. She and her children are brutally murdered.

In England, Malcolm at first does not trust Macduff. He thinks he could be a spy for Macbeth. So he tests his loyalty by listing his own (pretended) faults. He paints an evil picture of himself. Macduff is devastated. Then Malcolm admits that he is lying, that he was just seeking proof of Macduff's loyalty to him. Macduff now learns that his wife and family have been slaughtered. His heart is broken. He vows to kill Macbeth.

Act V A tale told by an idiot

Back in Scotland, Lady Macbeth is behaving strangely. Her Gentlewoman tells the doctor how her mistress sleepwalks. They watch as she walks, rubbing her hands, and talking to herself about Duncan's murder: 'Out damned spot, out I say! … who would have thought the old man to have had so much blood in him? … What will these hands ne'er be clean? … All the perfumes of Arabia will not sweeten this little hand.' (Act V Sc i). In her mind she goes over what happened, and tries to wash the blood off, over and over again. Her guilt has driven her insane.

Macbeth, meanwhile, is busy fortifying the castle at Dunsinane. Most of his noblemen and soldiers have joined the other side. But he is certain he cannot be beaten – or not until the impossible happens, and Birnam forest comes to Dunsinane.

What he does not know is that his enemies have agreed to meet at Birnam wood. When the soldiers have assembled there, each man is given the branch of a tree to camouflage himself. As the men move forward to attack, they look like a moving forest. Macbeth is preparing for battle, when he is informed that his wife has taken her own life. He takes little notice. Now isolated, he thinks how meaningless life is: 'Life's but a walking shadow, a poor player/ That struts and frets his hour upon the stage,/ And then is heard no more: it is a tale/ Told by an idiot, full of sound and fury,/ Signifying nothing.' (Act V Sc v). Just then a messenger announces that Birnam wood seems to be on the move. The witches' prophecy has come true. Malcolm and Macduff have begun their attack. Macbeth fights bravely but his castle is taken. He meets Macduff on the battlefield, still believing that he cannot be killed by a man 'of woman born'. But Macduff reveals that he was not born in the normal way but by Caesarian section. They fight, and Macduff takes his revenge, killing Macbeth. Now, at last, peace is restored to Scotland and the rightful heir, Malcolm, is hailed as king.

THE PLAY'S CHARACTERS

Macbeth

At the beginning of the play, we hear that Macbeth is a brave soldier and supposedly a good man, loyal to the king. The king thinks highly of him. Only after he meets the witches does Macbeth begin to think evil thoughts, and at first he does not entertain them. He is ashamed of them: 'Let not light see my black and deep desires ...' (Act I Sc iv). His wife knows him well. They are a loving couple and she understands that deep down he would like to be king. But she thinks that he is too weak-willed to do anything about it. When accused by her of cowardice, he is keen to prove his manliness. He would assassinate the king willingly if he could escape the consequences. Against his better judgment, he lets his wife persuade him. But he wants it all to be over quickly: 'If it were done, when 'tis done, then 'twere well/ It were done quickly.' (Act I Sc vii). Before the murder, his fearful mind plays tricks on him. He sees a dagger that is not there. After the murder, he hears voices saying that he has 'murdered sleep'. He has a vivid imagination and a conscience that troubles him. He has killed an anointed monarch, a friend, and a fair ruler.

Once he is king, the immoral side of his nature takes over. He becomes a butcher and a tyrant without any feelings of remorse. He plans the murder of Banquo with cold-blooded relish. At first he had to be persuaded by his wife to kill. Now he does not even bother to tell her. His bravado is still tempered by cowardice. At the banquet he is unnerved by the Ghost, another figment of his imagination. But when the Ghost goes, his confidence returns.

He is now callous enough to order the murder of Lady Macduff and her children. When his wife goes mad, he shows little concern. He is concerned only for himself, foolishly believing that he cannot be defeated. His wife's suicide brings home to him the hopelessness of the path he has chosen. For the sake of ambition, he has thrown away the opportunity to live a happy life: '... that which should accompany old age,/ As honour, love, obedience, troops of friends,/ I must not look to have.' (Act V Sc iii). His spirit is broken but he carries on. In the end he dies bravely, a once good man corrupted by ambition.

Lady Macbeth

In his letter to his wife, Macbeth addresses her as 'my dearest partner of greatness' and later as 'dearest chuck'. She is a supportive wife, keen to help her husband realise his dreams. She is a good hostess, and makes excuses for her husband's strange behaviour at the banquet. Where he is weak and uncertain, she is strong-willed and ambitious – on his behalf – and unashamedly wicked. She is excited by the idea of the murder and calls on the 'spirits' to 'unsex' her, and suppress her maternal kindness. She hardly pauses to consider whether it is right or wrong to kill Duncan. She is more practical than Macbeth. It is she, not he, who works out the way to kill Duncan, and she who plans the cover-up. It is she who has the guts to return the daggers after the murder. She stays calm when Macbeth panics or sees hallucinations. Most of all, she is powerful. Her husband is a military commander in a patriarchal society, but he does as she says. She plays on his weakness, by goading him to prove his masculinity. Without her, it is unlikely that Macbeth would have translated the temptation to murder into the deed. For all her confidence and depravity, Lady Macbeth is not strong mentally. She finds that she has a conscience, and an imagination as haunting as her husband's. When her courage fails her, she cannot count on her husband. Once Macbeth becomes king, he no longer needs her support. It is as if her strength of character has been taken over by him – and his insecurity by her. She is now the person who broods about their horrific actions. She is frightened of the dark and continually washes her hands to wash off the blood. Eventually her guilty conscience drives her mad and she commits suicide.

Duncan

Shakespeare portrays Duncan as an ideal king, (perhaps wanting to flatter his own king), loved by his loyal kinsmen and nobles. Like James I, he has to cope with open and hidden hostility. But he is honest, humble and good; all that Macbeth is not. He administers justice to the rebel Cawdor and is saddened by his treachery but he does not revel in the sentence. He is trusting, but no fool. We feel he is not impressed with Lady Macbeth's fawning welcome, though he generously presents her with a diamond. He is a symbol of order. When he is murdered, the kingdom falls into dreadful disarray. Order can only be restored by the restitution of his son, the rightful ruler of Scotland.

Banquo

Like Macbeth, Banquo is a brave and loyal soldier. Unlike Macbeth he is wise and virtuous, the true hero of the play. Macbeth admires him for his nobility, wisdom and valour. He is the man Macbeth would like to be, a man fit to be king. Banquo is wary of the witches' prophecies. He knows, as does Macbeth, that they are evil creatures, and points out that 'to win us to our harm/ The instruments of darkness tell us truths–' (Act I Sc iii). He assumes that Macbeth shares his morality. When Macbeth hints at an honour to come for him, he welcomes the idea, so long as it does not bring dishonour. Because he is so honest and trusting, he does not suspect Macbeth until it is too late.

Macduff

Macduff is a gentleman. He tries to protect Lady Macbeth from hearing the details of Duncan's murder, perhaps thinking her as vulnerable as his own wife. He is immediately suspicious of Macbeth and courageous enough to take action against him. He goes to England to support Malcolm, the rightful king. He is a straightforward, honest man, deeply distressed at Malcolm's pretended depravity. His dutiful bravery, alas, leaves his wife and children unprotected, and they die. He takes his revenge on Macbeth, and in so doing restores peace to Scotland.

THEMES AND LANGUAGE

Shakespeare's finest plays are his great tragedies: *Hamlet* (1600–01), *King Lear* (1603–06), *Othello* (1604) and *Macbeth*. Each presents a dramatic and believable portrait of a prominent individual who is deeply flawed mentally and spiritually, in conflict with others, and with himself. In all the plays there are memorable characters and speeches, and expressions that have become part of our everyday language. All the plays deal with good and evil. *Macbeth* especially is about a man's conscience and the effect of guilt on his mind. It explores reality and illusion; witchcraft and the supernatural; ambition and kingship; the natural order; light and life, darkness and death; blood and dead babies.

Appearance and reality
In Shakespeare's day, many individuals were tried and found guilty of treason. Often the conspirators were loved and favoured at court. How is it possible to know where truth lies? When Duncan is betrayed, he ruefully observes that 'There's no art/ To find the mind's construction in the face.' (Act I Sc iv). This is one of the great themes of *Macbeth*: the difference between appearance and reality, between truth and falsehood. At first Macbeth has to be taught by his wife, how to hide his evil intentions: 'look like the innocent flower,/ But be the serpent under it.' (Act I Sc v). She is a master of deception. Even her home seems to lie. 'This castle hath a pleasant seat,' says Duncan as he arrives at his place of execution. By the use of soliloquies and 'asides', Shakespeare often tells us what is going on in his characters' minds and in their dreams. We know that the sleep-deprived Macbeths are a prey to their imaginations. Macbeth sees a dagger that is not there, and Lady Macbeth tries to wash a non-existent spot of blood off her hands. In Macbeth's final despair, when he compares the brevity of life to an hour on the stage, Shakespeare reminds us that we too are watching a play, not reality.

Superstition and the supernatural
James I was a religious man. He was also extremely superstitious. He believed in demons conjured by devils and wild women who could fly through the air, raise storms and tell the future. Their prime purpose was to create havoc and corruption. Whether or not Shakespeare shared all these beliefs, he made much of them in his play. From the first scene we know that the witches represent conflict: 'Fair is foul, and foul is fair,/ Hover through the fog and filthy air.' (Act I Sc i). They seem to delight in their wickedness. For them, planting the idea of being king in Macbeth's mind is a deadly game. Making him think he is invulnerable, is as cruel as it is clever. We owe our ideas of how witches behaved,

what they looked like, how they cast spells, and above all how they sounded almost entirely to Shakespeare. We do not know if Shakespeare believed in ghosts but he used them to spine-chilling effect in his plays. It is up to us to decide if the Ghost of Banquo is real or a figment of Macbeth's imagination.

Kingship and the natural order

Most people in Shakespeare's day believed in the natural order. God created the world and everything in it, good and bad, angels and demons. James I wrote a book called *The True Law of Free Monarchies* in which he expounded his belief that kings were ordained to rule by 'divine right'. Macduff says that the murder of Duncan 'hath broke ope/ The Lord's anointed temple, and stole thence/ The life of the building. (Act II Sc iii). Describing a man as a temple is an example of a figure of speech called metaphor. Shakespeare uses such powerful imagery (word pictures) to show how disruption of the natural order is reflected in the world of nature and to create a mood. The night of Duncan's murder is described as 'unruly', 'chimneys were blown down', 'lamentings heard i' the air', a bird 'clamoured', 'the earth was feverous and did shake.' (Act II Sc iii). The idea of nature being in harmony with dreadful deeds is familiar to us from horror films and novels. It is a literary device called 'pathetic fallacy'. That the heavens cried out against the murder of a king would have greatly appealed to James I.

Ambition and tyranny

Everyone thinks that Macbeth is an honourable man, loyal to his king – except his wife. She knows he 'wouldst be great' and is not 'without ambition' (Act I Sc v). He wants power. To make him seize it, all she has to do is rid him of his morality and his fear. To this end, she taunts him about his lack of manliness. He has to prove himself to her. Macbeth listens to the witches, who give him false hopes. Like many tyrants, he feels invincible, hardened to atrocity. To keep his power, he must keep on killing. Not content with becoming king himself, he wants to keep power in his family, so Banquo and Fleance must die. King James knew about treachery at first hand and must have feared ambitious men. His mother (Mary Queen of Scots) had been beheaded for plotting the death of Queen Elizabeth. His own right to the throne was challenged. Had he the foresight of the witches, he might have known that his own grandson, King Charles I, would be beheaded for insisting on his divine rights.

Bloody men and dead babies

Every page of *Macbeth* seems steeped in blood, real and imagined. Blood is a symbol of evil and guilt. The witches pour blood into their brew. Macbeth sees 'gouts of blood' on the dagger. After Duncan's murder he imagines that the blood on his hands would turn all first oceans blood-red: making the 'multitudinous seas incarnadine'. (Act II Sc ii). After Banquo's murder, he realises that one act of violence almost invariably begets another, 'It will have blood, they say: blood will have blood.' (Act III Sc iv). Lady Macbeth sleepwalks as she tries to remove the indelible stain of blood.

Images of babies abound in *Macbeth*. They are a symbol of innocence. Macbeth likens the pity that Duncan's meekness should arouse, to a 'naked new-born babe', (Act I Sc vii). Lady Macbeth tells him that, despite having breastfed her own son, she would have 'plucked the nipple from his boneless gums/ And dashed the brains out,' (Act I Sc vii). Macduff says that he was 'untimely ripped' from his mother's womb. The witches add the 'finger of birth-strangled babe' to their cauldron, and summon up an apparition of a bloody child. Poignantly, Macduff's wife and son chat playfully to each other. She explains to him what a traitor is, just before they are both slain. The shedding of blood in *Macbeth* takes place offstage; it is Shakespeare's genius that his words alone make the murders so visible to us.

Medicine and the mind
Hundreds of years before modern psychology, Shakespeare demonstrated a deep understanding of mental disorder. Psychologists document cases of Obsessive Compulsive Disorder, where sufferers continually wash their hands. We know too how stress and anxiety cause sleeplessness and nightmares. Both Macbeths have disturbed sleep and are afflicted with 'terrible dreams'. Lady Macbeth is terrified of the dark. Macbeth asks the Doctor if there is a cure for her but he cannot minister to a 'mind diseased': 'More she needs the divine than the physician.' (Act V Sc i). Unable to cope with the mental distress, she takes her own life. Shakespeare's audience would have believed that she and her husband were 'possessed' by the devil. But today we know that Macbeth has delusions of grandeur and symptoms of paranoia brought on by guilt. Today we would say his wife was traumatised.

The language of Shakespeare
Shakespeare wrote his plays mostly in verse, with rhyming or non-rhyming lines in a rhythm that closely resembles the pattern of normal speech. He matched his language to his characters. Duncan, Banquo and Macduff, for example, speak in eloquent verse. More lowly, or humorous, characters, such as the Porter, speak not in poetry but in prose. Lady Macbeth's vicious thoughts are voiced in powerful poetic images: 'The raven himself is hoarse/ That croaks the fatal entrance of Duncan/ Under my battlements.' (Act I Sc v). Shakespeare signals her decline into madness, by switching her language to prose. To make the witches appear other-worldly, he makes them speak like no other characters. They chant in short, sharp rhyming couplets (two lines) with a staccato rhythm: 'Double, double toil and trouble,/ Fire burn, and cauldron bubble.' (Act IV Sc i). For an audience that believed in witches, that must have been a hair-raising sound.

EXAMINING THE PLAY

If you have to write an essay or an exam question on *Macbeth*, make sure you understand what you are being asked for. Gather your thoughts and references, and put them in order. Make sure that everything you write is relevant to the question. You may know a lot more about some other topic but do not be tempted to show off your knowledge. You will get more marks for making a sound argument, and sticking to the point. Look at typical questions and practise answering them.

Suppose you are asked, 'Is Lady Macbeth more ambitious than Macbeth?' You need to make up your own mind by considering the evidence in the text. You can use Shakespeare's own words in your answer, not long quotations, but telling phrases that exemplify your point. Ask yourself questions and discuss them with your friends. Does Lady Macbeth seek power for herself? Does she want to be queen? Did Macbeth want the throne before he met the witches? How much is he swayed by them, and how much by his wife. Why does he not tell his wife about killing Banquo? Which of them regrets their actions more? Why does she commit suicide? The best answers to all these questions will be in the play, not in other books or on the internet.

Your own ideas will be as good as anybody else's

You might be asked to talk about the imagery in the play, in a question such as: 'What role does weather and the natural world play in Macbeth? Say how you think they enhance the action.' You know that the foul weather in the first scenes leads us to expect dreadful events. Go through the rest of the play and see how Shakespeare uses nature for dramatic effect. See what each of the characters says about the weather, about night and day, about darkness and the creatures of the dark. See how they talk about the birds and other animals. Compare Banquo's talk about the 'temple-haunting martlet' with Lady Macbeth's description of the raven. What do we learn about their characters? What do the animals symbolise? Show how Shakespeare associates darkness with evil, and light with goodness. Look at the language and poetry he uses to create an atmosphere and express a person's thought.

'Why was *Macbeth* relevant to Shakespeare's audience. Why is it still performed so often in our own times?' To answer this question you will need to know a little of the background to the plays. The examiners will not want to know the full history of the kings and queens of England and Scotland. But they will want to know what you understand from the play about kingship, and about tyranny, and about parallel conflicts in our own time. In your answer compare what is said about Duncan as a ruler, and about Macbeth when he has taken power. Think about ambitious people in our own times, and how they come to power. There are plenty of modern dictators. Describe what can happen to a country when a ruler is violently deposed.

Whatever the question, you will need to discuss the language of the play and give examples. Show how Shakespeare chooses words and images to contrast good and evil. Find instances of humour in the play. Find references to sleep and to blood and other themes. Pretend you are a director and think how you would stage your favourite scenes. Think of your own questions.

Most of all, read the play as often as you can. If you are lucky you may see it performed which will give you another means of finding new understanding of the text.

Angela Sheehan

Characters

DUNCAN: King of Scotland

| MALCOLM DONALBAIN | sons to the King |

| MACBETH BANQUO | Generals of the King's army |

| MACDUFF LENNOX ROSS MENTEITH ANGUS CAITHNESS | noblemen of Scotland (Thanes) |

LADY MACBETH: wife to Macbeth
FLEANCE: son to Banquo
SIWARD: Earl of Northumberland, General of the English forces
YOUNG SIWARD: his son
SEYTON: an officer attending on Macbeth
DOCTOR: one in England, one in Scotland
CAPTAIN
PORTER
OLD MAN
LADY MACDUFF: wife to Macduff
SON: son to Macduff
GENTLEWOMAN: attending on Lady Macbeth
WITCHES: three
HECATE
Lords, Gentlemen, Soldiers, Murderers, Attendants, Servants and Messengers
The Ghost of Banquo and other Apparitions

Scene: Scotland, except that the end of Act 4 is set in England (stage direction). Shakespeare was writing for an audience that generally believed in witchcraft and respected its formidable power. These witches are lieutenants of Satan, and the tempestuous atmosphere indicates the presence of evil forces, insurrection and war.

1–2   *When . . . rain?* Witches were believed to be able to raise storms at will. The question is, 'What weather should we create for our next meeting?' It establishes at once the extent of the witches' powers.

3–4   *When . . . won.* Already the witches begin to speak in riddles.

5   *That . . . sun.* The witches' prophetic powers, so important to the play, are established with a casual remark.

7   *There . . . Macbeth.* The witches here predetermine the meeting with Macbeth.

8   *Greymalkin,* a grey cat. 'The familiars of witches do most ordinarily appear in the shape of cats, which is an argument that this beast is dangerous in soul and body.' (Topsell, *History of Four-footed beasts,* 1607). The cat (and the toad in 1.9) call from off-stage.

9   *Paddock,* a toad, regarded as venomous. Another familiar.

10   *Anon!* Coming!

11–12   *Fair . . . air.* The first sign of the anarchic reversal of values, the confusion between reality and appearance, good and evil, which breaks natural, social and moral order. The 'fog' was produced by burning resin under the main stage.

Scene Two

(stage direction) Alarum within. An alarum was a trumpet-call to action or a warning of danger, and 'within' means that it was sounded off-stage, where the engagement has taken place.

1   *bloody.* References to blood recur more often in *Macbeth* than in any other Shakespeare play, reiterating violence.

1–3   *He . . . state.* His battle-scarred condition suggests that he can tell us the latest news of the fight/The broken syntax expresses the confused excitement of Duncan's situation.

3   *sergeant,* i.e. the Captain. Rank was not precisely designated by title in Shakespeare's day.

5   *'Gainst my captivity,* to prevent my capture.

Act One · Scene One

A heath

Thunder and lightning. Enter three WITCHES

1 WITCH   When shall we three meet again?
In thunder, lightning, or in rain?

2 WITCH   When the hurlyburly's done,
When the battle's lost and won.

3 WITCH   That will be ere the set of sun.   5

1 WITCH   Where the place?

2 WITCH   Upon the heath.

3 WITCH   There to meet with Macbeth.

1 WITCH   I come Greymalkin!

2 WITCH   Paddock calls.

3 WITCH   Anon!   10

ALL   Fair is foul, and foul is fair;
Hover through the fog and filthy air.   [*Exeunt*

Scene Two

A camp

Alarum within. Enter DUNCAN · MALCOLM · DONALBAIN · LENNOX ·
with Attendants, meeting a bleeding CAPTAIN

DUNCAN   What bloody man is that? He can report,
As seemeth by his plight, of the revolt
The newest state.

MALCOLM   This is the sergeant
Who like a good and hardy soldier fought
'Gainst my captivity . . . Hail brave friend!   5

6   *broil*, struggle.

8   *spent*, exhausted.

9   *art*, skill.

10–12   *Worthy . . . upon him*, just right for treachery, since to that end all the infamous deeds to which human nature is prone have occupied his soul and redoubled there, until evil overwhelmed him/The words, spoken of the rebel Macbeth defeats, ironically foreshadow Macbeth's own development, with evil, once admitted, breeding evil.

13   *kerns and gallowglasses*, rough Irish infantry and mounted retainers.

14–15   *And fortune . . . whore*. Fortune was personified as a fickle woman. She appeared to favour Macdonwald's evil cause, but ultimately revealed her true nature by deserting him as a prostitute might.

15   *all's too weak*. Macdonwald and fortune cannot match Macbeth.

17   *Disdaining fortune*, i.e. disregarding the fact that fortune seemed against him. The existence of arbitrary, untrustworthy supernatural powers is hinted at in the references to fortune and her favourites. At the beginning of the play, Macbeth the warrior, truly himself and self-fulfilled in active service to his King, is immune to such influences.

19   *minion*, favourite.

21   *Which . . . hands*. Part of the text seems to be missing before this phrase. If 'which' refers to Macbeth it is a grim jest.

22   *unseamed . . . chops*, ripped him open from the navel to the jaw-bone/The violence of language reflects an attitude to rebellion that we hardly share.

24   *cousin*. Often a courtesy title or term of affection; but Duncan and Macbeth were cousins, grandsons of King Malcolm.

25   *whence . . . reflection*, from that quarter where the sun begins to shine/All this for 'the east.' The Captain has delivered his main news, and having regained his breath begins to speak with a mannered, courtly flourish. The whole style of his narrative now changes. The developed, over-done similes here (ll.25–43) are common in heroic speeches in Elizabethan drama. The style contrasts absolutely with the spontaneously generated imagery of Shakespeare's normal dialogue.

26   *direful*, ominous, dreadful.

28   *Discomfort*, discouragement.   *swells*, rises.

31   *the Norweyan lord*, Sweno, King of Norway.
     surveying vantage, 'seeing an opportunity' (Wilson).

32   *furbished*, well-prepared.

36   *sooth*, truth.

37   *overcharged . . . cracks*, primed with an excessive charge.

41   *memorize another Golgotha*, make the battlefield as unforgettable as another Golgotha.

Say to the King the knowledge of the broil
As thou didst leave it.

CAPTAIN   Doubtful it stood,
As two spent swimmers that do cling together
And choke their art. The merciless Macdonwald
(Worthy to be a rebel, for to that   10
The multiplying villainies of nature
Do swarm upon him) from the Western Isles
Of kerns and gallowglasses is supplied,
And fortune on his damned quarrel smiling
Showed like a rebel's whore. But all's too weak,   15
For brave Macbeth (well he deserves that name)
Disdaining fortune, with his brandished steel,
Which smoked with bloody execution,
Like valour's minion carved out his passage
Till he faced the slave;   20
Which ne'er shook hands, nor bade farewell to him,
Till he unseamed him from the nave to the chops
And fixed his head upon our battlements.

DUNCAN   O valiant cousin, worthy gentleman!

CAPTAIN   As whence the sun 'gins his reflection   25
Shipwracking storms and direful thunders break,
So from that spring whence comfort seemed to come
Discomfort swells. Mark, King of Scotland, mark!
No sooner justice had, with valour armed,
Compelled these skipping kerns to trust their heels,   30
But the Norweyan lord, surveying vantage,
With furbished arms and new supplies of men
Began a fresh assault.

DUNCAN   Dismayed not this
Our captains, Macbeth and Banquo?

CAPTAIN   Yes,
As sparrows eagles, or the hare the lion.   35
If I say sooth, I must report they were
As cannons overcharged with double cracks.
So they
Doubly redoubled strokes upon the foe.
Except they meant to bathe in reeking wounds,   40
Or memorize another Golgotha,

44–5   *So well . . . both,* both your words and your wounds become you. There is honour in both.

48   *seems to,* is about to.

50   *flout,* mock. The event in the past, prior to Macbeth's intervention, is described vividly in the historic present, underlining the Scots' initial 'cold' dread of the enemy, and enhancing Macbeth's achievement.

52   *Norway himself,* the Norwegian King himself.

54   *a dismal conflict,* a disastrous onslaught.

55   *Bellona's bridegroom.* Bellona was the Roman goddess of war. *lapped in proof,* clad in strong armour.

56   *Confronted . . . comparisons,* faced him (Sweno) with courage and skill to match his own.

58   *lavish,* overweening.

60   *That now,* so that now/Ross continues the sentence broken by Duncan's exclamation.

61   *craves composition,* sues for terms.

62   *deign,* allow.

63   *disbursed,* paid out.   *Saint Colme's Inch,* Inchcolm, an island in the Firth of Forth.

66   *bosom interest,* close trust.   *present death,* immediate execution.

I cannot tell . . .
But I am faint, my gashes cry for help.

DUNCAN   So well thy words become thee as thy wounds,
They smack of honour both. Go get him surgeons.   45
Who comes here?   [*Exit* CAPTAIN, *attended*

Enter ROSS *and* ANGUS

MALCOLM   The worthy Thane of Ross.

LENNOX   What a haste looks through his eyes! So should he look
That seems to speak things strange.

ROSS   God save the King!

DUNCAN   Whence camest thou, worthy Thane?

ROSS   From Fife, great King,
Where the Norweyan banners flout the sky   50
And fan our people cold.
Norway himself, with terrible numbers
Assisted by that most disloyal traitor,
The Thane of Cawdor, began a dismal conflict,
Till that Bellona's bridegroom, lapped in proof,   55
Confronted him with self-comparisons,
Point against point, rebellious arm 'gainst arm,
Curbing his lavish spirit. And to conclude,
The victory fell on us—

DUNCAN   Great happiness!

ROSS   That now   60
Sweno, the Norways' King, craves composition.
Nor would we deign him burial of his men
Till he disbursed, at Saint Colme's Inch,
Ten thousand dollars to our general use.

DUNCAN   No more that Thane of Cawdor shall deceive   65
Our bosom interest. Go pronounce his present death,
And with his former title greet Macbeth.

ROSS   I'll see it done.

DUNCAN   What he hath lost, noble Macbeth hath won   [*Exeunt (stage direction) Enter . . . Witches.* The witches arranged to meet 'when the battle's lost and won,' and they now appear as Duncan echoes their phrase.

2   *Killing swine.* A favourite pastime of witches.

6   *Aroint,* get out.   *ronyon,* mangy wretch.

7   *the Tiger.* A common name for a ship. The vindictive incantation of the witch contrasts dramatically with Ross's affected, ingratiating manner in the previous scene.

9   *like,* in the form of.   *without a tail.* While a witch could assume what animal shape she wished, she could not acquire a tail. Hence, an animal without a tail was evidence of witchcraft.

11   *I'll . . . a wind.* Marco Polo and others related that witches were prepared 'to sell winds to mariners, and cause tempests.'

14   *the other,* the other winds.

15   *the very . . . blow.* The witch controls entry to the ports, by controlling the particular wind that makes each port inaccessible.

16   *quarters,* i.e. of the compass.

17   *shipman's card,* the mariner's compass card.

18–19   *drain him . . . day.* By depriving him of drinking water and by keeping him out of port.

20   *penthouse lid,* eyelid, which is like the sloping roof of a penthouse.

21   *forbid,* cursed.

22   *sev'n-nights,* weeks.   *nine times nine.* Nine was a magic number.

23   *dwindle . . . pine,* shrink, waste away and become emaciated.

30   *A drum!* As most editors notice, Macbeth is without attendants to sound a drum. But it makes a dramatic first entry, and I take it that Macbeth is 'drummed up' by the witches' servants and that the sound we hear is ghostly. At the signal they turn from gossip to their incantation, aimed to bewitch Macbeth.

Scene Three

A heath

Thunder. Enter the three WITCHES

1 WITCH   Where hast thou been, sister?

2 WITCH   Killing swine.

3 WITCH   Sister, where thou?

1 WITCH   A sailor's wife had chestnuts in her lap,
  And munched, and munched, and munched. 'Give me,'   **5**
  quoth I.
  'Aroint thee witch,' the rump-fed ronyon cries.
  Her husband's to Aleppo gone, master o' the *Tiger*,
  But in a sieve I'll thither sail,
  And like a rat without a tail
  I'll do, I'll do, and I'll do.   **10**

2 WITCH   I'll give thee a wind.

1 WITCH   Th' art kind.

3 WITCH   And I another.

1 WITCH   I myself have all the other,
  And the very ports they blow,   **15**
  All the quarters that they know
  I' the shipman's card.
  I'll drain him dry as hay—
  Sleep shall neither night nor day
  Hang upon his penthouse lid.   **20**
  He shall live a man forbid.
  Weary sev'n-nights nine times nine
  Shall he dwindle, peak, and pine.
  Though his bark cannot be lost,
  Yet it shall be tempest-tossed.   **25**
  Look what I have.

2 WITCH   Show me, show me.

1 WITCH   Here I have a pilot's thumb,
  Wracked as homeward he did come. [*drum within*]

3 WITCH   A drum, a drum!   **30**
  Macbeth doth come.

32   *Weird,* ominous, fateful/Holinshed calls them 'the weird sisters, that is (as ye would say) the goddesses of destiny.' The *Tiger* episode has demonstrated the range and malice of their power.

33   *Posters,* swift travellers.

37   *wound up,* complete, all set.

38   *So . . . seen.* Macbeth's first words recalling to our minds the witches' own (Act1 Sc.1,l.11) bring an uncomfortable suspicion of demonic affinity. His paradoxical remark, seemingly so innocently explained by the victory and foul weather, is to mean more than it says.

39   *How . . . Forres?* The contrast is complete between this matter-of-fact uncommitted question and Macbeth's remark. Banquo goes on to seek to identify the witches in an objective way. From the beginning the difference between the two attitudes to the witches is clearly distinguished. Macbeth's silence is itself expressive of a frame of mind that is the devil's best ally.   *called,* reckoned to be.

42-3 *Live . . . question?* Are you flesh and blood, or at least are you beings it is lawful to address?

44-5 *By . . . lips.* They motion Banquo to be silent, turning to Macbeth.

44   *choppy,* chapped.

46   *beards.* Witches were usually bearded. cf. Beaumont & Fletcher, *Honest Man's Fortune,* ii, 1:

And the women that
Come to us for disguises must wear beards,
And that's (they say) a token of a witch.

47   *Speak.* Wilson points out that 'spirits might not speak unless first addressed,' and refers to Hamlet who has to speak first to the Ghost (*Hamlet,* Act1 Sc.1,l.45 and Act1 Sc.4,l.43). Significantly, it is Macbeth not Banquo who asks them to speak.

49   *Thane of Cawdor.* The effect of the next prophecy is enhanced by our knowledge that this promise is already fulfilled by Duncan.

51   *start.* Macbeth may be already guilty in thought, or afraid of a revelation of his plans.   *seem.* Again we have this word, drawing reality into question.

53   *fantastical,* imaginary.

53-4 *or . . . show,* or do you actually exist as your appearance indicates?/It is the doubt again about appearance and reality, here put in terms of form (the outward shape of a thing) and substance (its physical existence), a question to which the old philosophers gave much thought.

55-6 *present grace, noble having, royal hope,* i.e. the titles Glamis, Cawdor and King.

58   *seeds of time.* Much the same as 'nature's germens' in Act4 Sc.1,l.59. All nature was thought to develop from latent invisible seeds implanted by the Creator, cf. *Henry the Fourth, Part 2* Act3 Sc.1:

the main chance of things
As yet not come to life, which in their seeds
And weak beginnings lie intreasured.

ALL   The Weird Sisters, hand in hand,
    Posters of the sea and land,
    Thus do go about, about,
    Thrice to thine and thrice to mine,   **35**
    And thrice again to make up nine.
    Peace, the charm's wound up.

Enter MACBETH *and* BANQUO

MACBETH   So foul and fair a day I have not seen.
BANQUO   How far is't called to Forres? . . . What are these,
    So withered, and so wild in their attire,   **40**
    That look not like the inhabitants o' the earth
    And yet are on't? Live you? or are you aught
    That man may question? You seem to understand me,
    By each at once her choppy finger laying
    Upon her skinny lips. You should be women,   **45**
    And yet your beards forbid me to interpret
    That you are so.
MACBETH   Speak if you can. What are you?
1 WITCH   All hail Macbeth, hail to thee, Thane of Glamis!
2 WITCH   All hail Macbeth, hail to thee, Thane of Cawdor!
3 WITCH   All hail Macbeth, thou shalt be King hereafter!   **50**
BANQUO   Good sir, why do you start and seem to fear
    Things that do sound so fair? . . . In the name of truth
    Are ye fantastical, or that indeed
    Which outwardly ye show? My noble partner
    You greet with present grace and great prediction   **55**
    Of noble having and of royal hope,
    That he seems rapt withal. To me you speak not.
    If you can look into the seeds of time
    And say which grain will grow and which will not,
    Speak then to me, who neither beg nor fear   **60**
    Your favours nor your hate.
1 WITCH   Hail!
2 WITCH   Hail!
3 WITCH   Hail!
1 WITCH   Lesser than Macbeth, and greater.   **65**
2 WITCH   Not so happy, yet much happier.

67   *get*, beget.

72–3   *The Thane . . . gentleman.* That Macbeth seemingly knows
         nothing of Cawdor's treachery has been a constant talking
         point among editors. Ross has spoken (Act1 Sc.2, l.53) of
         Cawdor's league with Sweno whom Macbeth defeated. And
         Angus' explanation later in this scene (l.111) that the help
         was secret is a little tardy to be convincing. Most editors
         plead textual cuts or Shakespeare's forgetfulness. But it is
         not what Macbeth knows or does not know that is important,
         but how we react. The effect of knowing the prophecy to
         have been fulfilled as we hear it made is startling; and
         suspense and expectation depend upon our knowledge of the
         fulfilment of the Cawdor prophecy, as Macbeth speaks his
         disbelief in this and the promise of the crown. By mani-
         pulating time and ignoring irrelevant logic Shakespeare
         involves us in a complex, fascinating set of relationships.

74   *Stands . . . belief*, is an incredible prospect.

76   *owe*, have.   *strange intelligence*, surprising news.

77   *blasted*, blighted.

78   *charge*, command.

80   *of them*, of the same nature as bubbles, ephemeral.

81   *corporal*, corporeal, solid flesh.

84   *the insane root*. Either hemlock or henbane, both thought to
         cause insanity. Banquo seeks a physical explanation for the
         phenomena; Macbeth hardly listens.

88   *To . . . words*. Wilson points out the quibble in Macbeth's 'went'
         in a musical sense, and that Banquo speaks lightly.

92–3   *His . . . or his*. The usual explanation is that Duncan, torn
         between amazement and a desire to praise Macbeth, is lost
         for words. This ignores the vital clause 'which should be
         thine or his,' and fails to convey the irony of Duncan's
         generous implication that Macbeth has earned and deserved
         something of the dues of kingship. If 'wonders' means
         admiration, the plural is odd. If 'his praises' means the
         praises due to Macbeth we should expect '*thy* praises,' as in
         l.99. And it is difficult to see praise and admiration in conflict
         ('do contend'). For 'contend', cf. Act2 Sc.2, l.7.

         The passage becomes clear if we remember that Duncan is
         reported to be reading an account of the battle. I take 'his'
         (twice) in l.92 to have the commonplace meaning 'its,' and
         to refer to the account of the 'personal venture in the
         rebels' fight.' 'Wonders' means 'incredible events.' The lines
         then mean: the incredible events and expressions of praise
         contained in the account set up such a conflict in his mind,
         that he feels that he himself should have achieved the feats
         or should relinquish the dues of kingship to Macbeth.

         This sense of inadequacy is much more likely to 'silence'
         him, and is powerfully dramatic.

94   *viewing o'er*, reading about/The emphasis is still on the
         written report.

96–7   *Nothing . . . of death*, utterly fearless of joining your victims,
         who wear the unnatural masks of death.

98   *post with post*, messenger after messenger.

3 WITCH   Thou shalt get kings, though thou be none.
    So all hail Macbeth and Banquo!

1 WITCH   Banquo and Macbeth, all hail!

MACBETH   Stay you imperfect speakers, tell me more!   70
    By Sinel's death I know I am Thane of Glamis,
    But how of Cawdor? The Thane of Cawdor lives
    A prosperous gentleman, and to be king
    Stands not within the prospect of belief,
    No more than to be Cawdor. Say from whence   75
    You owe this strange intelligence, or why
    Upon this blasted heath you stop our way
    With such prophetic greeting? Speak, I charge you!   [WITCHES *vanish*

BANQUO   The earth hath bubbles as the water has,
    And these are of them. Whither are they vanished?   80

MACBETH   Into the air, and what seemed corporal
    Melted as breath into the wind . . . Would they had stayed.

BANQUO   Were such things here as we do speak about?
    Or have we eaten on the insane root
    That takes the reason prisoner?   85

MACBETH   Your children shall be kings.

BANQUO   You shall be King.

MACBETH   And Thane of Cawdor too—went it not so?

BANQUO   To the selfsame tune and words. Who's here?

Enter ROSS *and* ANGUS

ROSS   The King hath happily received, Macbeth,
    The news of thy success; and when he reads   90
    Thy personal venture in the rebels' fight,
    His wonders and his praises do contend,
    Which should be thine or his. Silenced with that,
    In viewing o'er the rest o' the selfsame day,
    He finds thee in the stout Norweyan ranks,   95
    Nothing afeard of what thyself didst make,—
    Strange images of death. As thick as hail
    Came post with post, and every one did bear
    Thy praises in his kingdom's great defence
    And poured them down before him.

104   *earnest*, pledge.

106   *addition*, title.

107   *can . . . true.* The devil speaks true, it was thought, only to mislead us. Cf. Act5Sc.1, ll.122–6.

108–9 *dress . . . robes.* Images relating to ill-fitting and borrowed clothes are frequent in the play, and express Macbeth's treachery and usurpation.

110   *heavy judgment*, death sentence.

112   *line*, reinforce.

113   *vantage*, support.

114   *wrack*, destruction.

115   *capital*, carrying the death penalty.

117   *is behind*, is yet to come.

120   *home*, utterly, to the finish.

121   *enkindle . . . unto*, incite you to covet/Banquo's light-hearted spontaneous reply contrasts with the clumsy device of Macbeth's leading question.

123–6 *oftentimes . . . consequence.* Banquo goes on to reiterate common knowledge, which Macbeth neglects because it denies his wishes. Macbeth's thoughts in his next speech catch at the word 'truths,' and develop the lines of Banquo's warning in a revealing manner. Banquo is not simply a good character acting as a foil to Macbeth. His presence and what he says intensifies the uncertainty of Macbeth's position and preoccupation.

123   *to win*, to coax.

124   *instruments of darkness*, powers of evil.

128–9 *As happy . . . theme*, as welcome introductions to the unfolding drama on the theme of royalty/In imagination, Macbeth is already dressed for the part of King.

130   *supernatural soliciting*, prompting by the spirits.

131–3 *If ill . . . truth*, if evil, why has it offered me a pledge of my succession to the throne, by beginning with something proved true.

131   *ill*, evil.

132   *success*, succession. The ordinary modern sense for 'success' seems to me impossible after 'if ill,' as Macbeth is here considering himself as the passive recipient of good fortune. He does not turn to consider the success of an action till the next lines.

ANGUS   We are sent   100
  To give thee from our royal master thanks,
  Only to herald thee into his sight,
  Not pay thee.

ROSS   And for an earnest of a greater honour,
  He bade me, from him, call thee Thane of Cawdor.   105
  In which addition, hail most worthy Thane!
  For it is thine.

BANQUO   [aside]   What, can the devil speak true?

MACBETH   The Thane of Cawdor lives. Why do you dress me
  In borrowed robes?

ANGUS   Who was the Thane lives yet,
  But under heavy judgment bears that life   110
  Which he deserves to lose. Whether he was combined
  With those of Norway, or did line the rebel
  With hidden help and vantage, or that with both
  He laboured in his country's wrack, I know not.
  But treasons capital, confessed and proved,   115
  Have overthrown him.

MACBETH   [aside]   Glamis, and Thane of Cawdor . . .
  The greatest is behind. [to ROSS and ANGUS] Thanks for your pains.
  [to BANQUO] Do you not hope your children shall be kings,
  When those that gave the Thane of Cawdor to me
  Promised no less to them?

BANQUO   That, trusted home,   120
  Might yet enkindle you unto the crown,
  Besides the Thane of Cawdor. But 'tis strange,
  And oftentimes to win us to our harm
  The instruments of darkness tell us truths—
  Win us with honest trifles, to betray us   125
  In deepest consequence . . .
  Cousins, a word I pray you.   [goes to ROSS and ANGUS]

MACBETH   [aside]   Two truths are told
  As happy prologues to the swelling act
  Of the imperial theme. [aloud] I thank you gentlemen.
  [aside] This supernatural soliciting   130
  Cannot be ill, cannot be good. If ill,
  Why hath it given me earnest of success,

134   *suggestion*, incitement to foul deeds, temptation of the devil/It is questionable if what the witches have said amounts to 'suggestion'. Rather Macbeth's thought (1.139) has read this into their words, meeting the devil more than half way.

134–5   *why . . . my hair*, why do I yield to that bewitching temptation that brings to my mind's eye a vision so fearsome that it uproots my hair?

136   *seated*, firm-set.

137   *Against . . . nature*, in an unnatural way.

137–8   *Present . . . imaginings*, imminent and real perils are less fearful than the horrors imagination breeds.

139–42   *My thought . . . not*, though murder still exists only in my imagination, the purpose shaping in my mind so undermines my self-control that all constructive action is lost in speculation, and fantasies of kingship obsess me/Again, a bare paraphrase conveys little of Shakespeare's full meaning. His language says this but also refers Macbeth's observation to the developing theme of the play.

139   *thought*, half-formed purpose.

140   *single state of man*, poor little world of man. A man's being was seen as a small replica (microcosm) of a kingdom, the world, or the universe (macrocosm). In *Macbeth* evil undermines human beings, the state and all nature alike, and the strands of these themes interweave.

145   *cleave . . . mould*, fit the body/The clothing image again.

147   *Time . . . day*. There is already a weariness in the fatalistic acceptance that things will run their course. The phrase 'time and the hour' introduces another dimension in the play, the hyper-sensitivity to time, and time measured.

148   *stay*, wait.

149   *Give . . . favour*, pardon me.   *wrought*, burdened.

151–2   *Are registered . . . them*, i.e. in his memory.

154   *The interim . . . it*, when in the meantime we have considered the matter.

155   *Our free hearts*, our hearts freely.

Scene Four

    (stage direction) Flourish. A fanfare for the King.

2   *in commission*, charged with the duty.

Commencing in a truth? I am Thane of Cawdor.
If good, why do I yield to that suggestion
Whose horrid image doth unfix my hair,   135
And make my seated heart knock at my ribs,
Against the use of nature? Present fears
Are less than horrible imaginings.
My thought, whose murder yet is but fantastical,
Shakes so my single state of man that function   140
Is smothered in surmise, and nothing is
But what is not.

BANQUO   Look how our partner's rapt.

MACBETH [aside] If chance will have me king, why, chance may
  crown me
  Without my stir.

BANQUO   New honours come upon him,
  Like our strange garments, cleave not to their mould   145
  But with the aid of use.

MACBETH [aside]   Come what come may,
  Time and the hour runs through the roughest day.

BANQUO Worthy Macbeth, we stay upon your leisure.

MACBETH Give me your favour. My dull brain was wrought
  With things forgotten. Kind gentlemen, your pains   150
  Are registered where every day I turn
  The leaf to read them. . . . Let us toward the King.
  [aside to BANQUO] Think upon what hath chanced, and at more time,
  The interim having weighed it, let us speak
  Our free hearts each to other.

BANQUO   Very gladly.   155

MACBETH Till then enough. . . . Come friends.   [Exeunt

Scene Four

Forres · A room in the palace

Flourish. Enter DUNCAN · MALCOLM · DONALBAIN · LENNOX · *and Attendants*

DUNCAN Is execution done on Cawdor? Are not
  Those in commission yet returned?

9   *been studied*, rehearsed the part he had to play.
10   *owed*, possessed.
11–12   *There's . . . face.* Both the innocence and the nature of the
         remark immediately preceding Macbeth's entry (on the cue
         'absolute trust') make it superbly ironic. But Duncan is
         saying much more than 'it is impossible to discover a man's
         thoughts in his looks.' The word 'art' is loaded, and meant
         skill, sublety, knowledge, and even artifice, or magic (*ars
         magica*). The last meaning makes cruel sense.
16–18   *Thou . . . overtake thee*, your merits so far outstrip mine that even
         the most prompt reward fails to meaure up to your deserts.
19–20   *That . . . been mine*, that I might have been able to balance your
         deserts with due gratitude and reward.
21   *all*, all my possessions/Duncan is ominously repeating more
         or less what Ross reported in Act1 Sc.3,ll.92–3.
23   *pays itself*, is its own reward/The involved syntax and
         elaborate emphasis reflect Macbeth's strain and hypocrisy
         in this speech.
25   *children and servants*, i.e. as children and servants.
27   *Safe toward*, with a steadfast regard for.
28–9   *I have . . . growing.* The image of natural growth and nurture
         used by Duncan helps to identify the frank sincerity that
         Macbeth is to destroy.
31   *infold*, embrace.

MALCOLM   My liege,
They are not yet come back. But I have spoke
With one that saw him die, who did report
That very frankly he confessed his treasons,   5
Implored your Highness' pardon, and set forth
A deep repentance. Nothing in his life
Became him like the leaving it. He died
As one that had been studied in his death,
To throw away the dearest thing he owed   10
As 'twere a careless trifle.

DUNCAN   There's no art
To find the mind's construction in the face.
He was a gentleman on whom I built
An absolute trust—

Enter MACBETH · BANQUO · ROSS · *and* ANGUS

                     O worthiest cousin!
The sin of my ingratitude even now   15
Was heavy on me. Thou art so far before,
That swiftest wing of recompense is slow
To overtake thee. Would thou hadst less deserved,
That the proportion both of thanks and payment
Might have been mine! Only I have left to say,   20
More is thy due than more than all can pay.

MACBETH   The service and the loyalty I owe,
In doing it, pays itself. Your Highness' part
Is to receive our duties; and our duties
Are to your throne and state, children and servants,   25
Which do but what they should by doing everything
Safe toward your love and honour.

DUNCAN   Welcome hither.
I have begun to plant thee, and will labour
To make thee full of growing . . . Noble Banquo,
That hast no less deserved, nor must be known   30
No less to have done so, let me infold thee
And hold thee to my heart.

BANQUO   There if I grow,
The harvest is your own.

34	*Wanton in fulness,* blossoming without restraint.
36	*you . . . nearest,* you who are close to the succession.
37–9	*We will . . . Cumberland.* By establishing the succession on Malcolm, Duncan excludes the possibility that 'chance' may crown Macbeth as he had wished.
41	*signs of nobleness,* titles and honours.
42	*Inverness,* i.e. Macbeth's castle. The King addresses Macbeth.
43	*bind . . . you,* makes us even more deeply indebted to you.
44	*The rest . . . you,* the leisure hours not used in your service seem filled with tedious labour.
45	*harbinger.* An outrider, who preceded the King.
50–51	*Stars . . . desires.* Though it is still daylight, Macbeth's imagination transfers the outrageous deed to its appropriate setting. Darkness is constantly invoked for the murder throughout the play.
52	*The eye . . . hand,* let the eye disregard what the hand does. It is as if Macbeth dissociates his will from the action of his hands. *yet . . . be,* yet let the hand's deed be done.
53	*Which . . . to see.* His eye was not afraid to look death in the face on the battlefield; yet the idea of Duncan murdered at once fascinates and terrifies his sight. The nomination of Malcolm as heir has roused his furiously acquisitive instinct and, in a frustrated way, his conscience. The witches are now not in his mind.
54	*He,* i.e. Macbeth. *so,* as you say. Banquo and Duncan have been conversing while Macbeth spoke words aside.
55	*And . . . fed,* and I am sustained by compliments paid to him.
56	*It,* i.e. Macbeth, as in l. 58.
57	*Whose . . . before,* who has so considerately gone ahead.
58	*kinsman.* Macbeth was Duncan's first cousin.

Scene Five

2	*by the perfectest report,* from the most reliable source/Macbeth has very quickly enquired about the validity of the supernatural powers of the witches, indicating his intense interest in the reliability of the prophecies.
2–3	*more . . . than mortal,* supernatural.

DUNCAN   My plenteous joys,
   Wanton in fulness, seek to hide themselves
   In drops of sorrow . . . Sons, kinsmen, thanes,   35
   And you whose places are the nearest, know,
   We will establish our estate upon
   Our eldest, Malcolm, whom we name hereafter
   The Prince of Cumberland, which honour must
   Not unaccompanied invest him only,   40
   But signs of nobleness, like stars, shall shine
   On all deservers . . . From hence to Inverness,
   And bind us further to you.

MACBETH   The rest is labour, which is not used for you.
   I'll be myself the harbinger, and make joyful   45
   The hearing of my wife with your approach—
   So humbly take my leave.

DUNCAN   My worthy Cawdor!

MACBETH   [aside] The Prince of Cumberland—that is a step
   On which I must fall down, or else o'erleap,
   For in my way it lies. Stars hide your fires,   50
   Let not light see my black and deep desires.
   The eye wink at the hand; yet let that be,
   Which the eye fears (when it is done) to see.

DUNCAN   True worthy Banquo. He is full so valiant,
   And in his commendations I am fed;   55
   It is a banquet to me. Let's after him,
   Whose care is gone before to bid us welcome.
   It is a peerless kinsman.   [flourish, Exeunt

Scene Five

Macbeth's castle

Enter LADY MACBETH, *with a letter*

LADY MACBETH   [reads] 'They met me in the day of success, and I have
   learned by the perfectest report, they have more in them than
   mortal knowledge. When I burned in desire to question them
   further, they made themselves air, into which they vanished.

5   *missives,* messengers.

9   *deliver thee,* report to you.

10   *dues of rejoicing,* anything that might please you.

11   *Lay . . . heart,* consider it closely and keep it to yourself/In the part of the letter we hear Lady Macbeth reading, Shakespeare suppresses any mention of Banquo's participation in the prophecy. The reaction of Lady Macbeth and the audience's participation is thus limited to Macbeth's interest, an effective dramatic concentration.

15–16 *It is . . . nearest way,* it is too governed by pale compassion for you to take the shortest cut to the throne/In *King Lear,* Act1Sc.4, l.319 Goneril castigates Albany's 'harmful mildness' as 'This milky gentleness and course of yours.' The idea of 'milk' implying natural kindness is taken up later in the play in opposition to the unnatural forces of evil.

       The phrase 'the milk of human kindness' has been endlessly debated, especially taken as a strange assessment of Macbeth as we have seen him already. There is a hint of what she means in Macbeth's remark at Act1Sc.3, l.140 however, and in any case it is quite uncritical to consider Lady Macbeth here as a character intimately observing Macbeth and speaking truth. This is the beginning of a new conflict in the play, and her words are written to that end, not as an expression or exemplification of 'character.' What she says is essentially slanted, biased, tendentious.

15   *human.* Both 'human' and 'humane'.   *kindness.* A powerful word, meaning positive human instincts for good.

18   *illness,* unscrupulous streak. The general meaning in Shakespeare's day was 'evil', 'wickedness'. The age expected and required ruthlessness in matters of state, and it was an indispensable weapon in the struggle for power; yet ambition was also sinful.

18–19 *What . . . holily,* though you deeply desire the crown, you want to remain innocent while achieving it/The counterbalancing of good with evil that Lady Macbeth sees in her husband fits the equivocal values so prominent in the play.

21   *That, it,* i.e. the crown.

22–3   *And that . . . undone,* i.e. the murder. Cf. Act1Sc.4, ll.52–3, where Macbeth has admitted this precisely.   *Hie,* hurry.

25   *chastise,* correct by whipping.   *valour,* boldness.

26–8   *All . . . withal,* all that prevents you from achieving the crown which fate and supernatural intervention seem about to set on your head.

27   *doth seem,* is about to, as in Act1Sc.2, l.48.

29   *Thou'rt . . . say it.* Lady Macbeth in her preoccupation with thoughts of the murder is taken off guard. She soon recovers.

30   *were't so,* if it were so.

33   *had . . . of him,* outstripped him.

35   *Give him tending,* look after him/With little justice, messengers were treated well or ill according to nature of the news they delivered. Lady Macbeth's elation is scarcely concealed.

36–8   *The raven . . . battlements.* 'The sad presaging raven' was a bird of deadly omen, and Lady Macbeth would make death so cer-

Whiles I stood rapt in the wonder of it, came missives from the   5
King, who all-hailed me "Thane of Cawdor", by which title,
before, these weird sisters saluted me and referred me to the
coming on of time with "Hail King that shalt be!" This have I
thought good to deliver thee, my dearest partner of greatness,
that thou mightst not lose the dues of rejoicing by being ignorant   10
of what greatness is promised thee. Lay it to thy heart, and fare-
well.'
Glamis thou art, and Cawdor, and shalt be—
What thou art promised. Yet do I fear thy nature.
It is too full o' the milk of human kindness   15
To catch the nearest way. Thou wouldst be great,
Art not without ambition, but without
The illness should attend it. What thou wouldst highly
That wouldst thou holily—wouldst not play false
And yet wouldst wrongly win. Thou'dst have, great Glamis,   20
That which cries 'Thus thou must do', if thou have it—
And that which rather thou dost fear to do
Than wishest should be undone. Hie thee hither,
That I may pour my spirits in thine ear,
And chastise with the valour of my tongue   25
All that impedes thee from the golden round,
Which fate and metaphysical aid doth seem
To have thee crowned withal.

Enter ATTENDANT

                      What is your tidings?

ATTENDANT   The King comes here tonight.

LADY MACBETH   Thou'rt mad to say it.
Is not thy master with him, who were't so   30
Would have informed for preparation?

ATTENDANT   So please you, it is true. Our Thane is coming.
One of my fellows had the speed of him
Who, almost dead for breath, had scarcely more
Than would make up his message.

LADY MACBETH   Give him tending,   35
He brings great news.   [*Exit* ATTENDANT
            The raven himself is hoarse

B

tain that he would croak himself hoarse announcing Duncan.

38–48   *Come . . . nature's mischief.* A deliberate and seriously phrased invocation to the power of evil to possess her body and soul. It was accepted that the devil 'being a slender incomprehensible spirit, can easily insinuate and wind himself into human bodies.'

39   *tend . . . thoughts,* wait upon murderous designs.   *unsex me here,* destroy my woman's nature here and now.

41–4   *Make . . . purpose.* According to Jacobean medicine, one function of the blood was to convey 'spirit,' 'a most subtle vapour . . . the instrument of the soul, a common tie or medium betwixt the body and the soul' to the brain, where the spirits arrive 'brought hither by the arteries from the heart, and are there refined to a more heavenly nature to perform the actions of the soul.' (Robert Burton, *The Anatomy of Melancholy*, 1628). The effect of thickening blood to 'stop up the access and passage to remorse' from heart to brain is obvious. This terrifying prayer is literally for a breach between body and soul, a negation of human divinity, spoken in anatomical terms not available today.

43   *compunctious . . . nature,* natural impulses of pity and remorse, generated in the heart.

44–5   *nor keep . . . it,* nor come between my purpose and its fulfilment.

46   *gall.* An excess of gall was thought to breed wrath. *ministers,* spirits.

47   *sightless,* invisible.

48   *You . . . mischief,* you wait to intervene in a universe of evil.

50   *That . . . makes.* She sees herself as directing both Macbeth and the knife. Again we have the dissociation of will from action.

51–2   *Nor . . . hold!* Again the invocation of darkness, as if this will mask her conscience from the deed. The homely word 'blanket' has a claustrophobic effect, and hints at Duncan the sleeper crying out in heaven's name.

54–6   *Thy letters . . . instant,* your letter has carried me out of the present time with its ignorance of the future, and I sense our future shaping at this moment.

56–8   *My dearest . . . purposes.* Macbeth's words beg a reaction from Lady Macbeth. He must know an attendant went ahead of him.

61   *To beguile the time,* to deceive the world.

62   *Look like the time,* fashion your looks as the occasion demands. The irony of Duncan's remark at Act1Sc.4,l.11 becomes frightening.

65   *provided for.* The ugly quibble shows how completely Lady Macbeth's prayer 'unsex me here' is already fulfilled.

66   *dispatch,* management, with a pun on 'sending off'.

67–8   *Which . . . masterdom.* This hope proves absolutely ('solely') barren as the play goes on.

69   *We . . . further,* We'll see about it/Macbeth reacts to Lady Macbeth's assertiveness by hesitating. The irresolution is psychologically true, and heightens the suspense.

That croaks the fatal entrance of Duncan
Under my battlements . . . Come you spirits
That tend on mortal thoughts, unsex me here,
And fill me from the crown to the toe top-full   40
Of direst cruelty. Make thick my blood,
Stop up the access and passage to remorse,
That no compunctious visitings of nature
Shake my fell purpose, nor keep peace between
The effect and it. Come to my woman's breasts   45
And take my milk for gall, you murdering ministers,
Wherever in your sightless substances
You wait on nature's mischief. Come thick night,
And pall thee in the dunnest smoke of hell,
That my keen knife see not the wound it makes,   50
Nor heaven peep through the blanket of the dark,
To cry 'Hold, hold!'

Enter MACBETH

                    Great Glamis, worthy Cawdor,
Greater than both, by the all-hail hereafter!
Thy letters have transported me beyond
This ignorant present, and I feel now   55
The future in the instant.

MACBETH   My dearest love.
Duncan comes here tonight.

LADY MACBETH   And when goes hence?

MACBETH Tomorrow, as he purposes.

LADY MACBETH   O never
Shall sun that morrow see.
Your face, my Thane, is as a book where men   60
May read strange matters. To beguile the time,
Look like the time, bear welcome in your eye,
Your hand, your tongue; look like the innocent flower,
But be the serpent under it. He that's coming
Must be provided for; and you shall put   65
This night's great business into my dispatch,
Which shall to all our nights and days to come
Give solely sovereign sway and masterdom.

MACBETH We will speak further.

69 *clear,* with a clear conscience.

70 *To alter . . . fear,* let your looks change like that and we'll always be afraid/Again she forces him to put on an appearance, and reality is again disguised.

Scene Six

 (*stage direction*) *Hautboys and torches.* 'Hautboy' meant oboe. The words were also used for the instrument player and the torch-bearer. The torches are not necessarily at present alight in this daylight scene, simply in attendance as evening approaches.

1 *seat,* situation.

2 *Nimbly,* freshly. The clarity of the line contrasts with the closeness of the last scene. It is the contrast between heaven and hell, clarity and conspiracy, the natural and the devilish.

3 *Unto our gentle,* gently to our.

4 *temple-haunting martlet,* the martin that frequents churches. The air of true holiness, natural regeneration, love and gentleness in these speeches identify Duncan before the murder and contrast absolutely with the murderous darkness which Macbeth and Lady Macbeth wish into their habitation and which destroys not only Duncan but with him all the grace here exemplified. *approve,* demonstrate.

5 *By . . . mansionry,* by choosing this place for so many nests.

7 *coign of vantage,* convenient projecting corners.

8 *pendent,* suspended. *procreant cradle,* nest for fledgelings.

11–14 *The love . . . trouble.* Duncan turns from relaxation with Banquo to the tortuous courtesies of greeting Lady Macbeth. It is also ironic: 'The love people bear to me sometimes makes them tiresomely attentive, and yet I always acknowledge it as love. And so I show you how you should pray God to reward me for the trouble I am putting you to and how you should thank me for the visit, which, though inconvenient, springs from my loving regard.'

16 *single,* paltry. *contend,* set.

18 *house,* family.

19 *heaped . . . them,* with which they have been augmented.

20 *We . . . hermits,* we shall always offer dutiful prayers for you. The hermit (or beadsman) said prayers in return for his patron's protection. Lady Macbeth's obsequious manner, too fulsome even by the standards of King James's court, is patently insincere. Beautifully conceived is Duncan's indifferent (perhaps cold, even unfriendly) reception of it throughout the scene.

21 *We . . . heels,* we followed close on his heels.

22 *purveyor.* An official who went ahead to arrange for the King's lodging and provision.

23 *holp,* helped.

LADY MACBETH   Only look up clea ·
  To alter favour ever is to fear.   70
  Leave all the rest to me.   [*Exeunt*

Scene Six

Before Macbeth's castle

Hautboys and torches. Enter DUNCAN · MALCOLM · DONALBAIN · BANQUO ·
LENNOX · MACDUFF · ROSS · ANGUS · *and Attendants*

DUNCAN This castle hath a pleasant seat—the air
  Nimbly and sweetly recommends itself
  Unto our gentle senses.

BANQUO   This guest of summer,
  The temple-haunting martlet, does approve
  By his loved mansionry that the heaven's breath   5
  Smells wooingly here. No jutty, frieze,
  Buttress, nor coign of vantage, but this bird
  Hath made his pendent bed and procreant cradle.
  Where they most breed and haunt, I have observed
  The air is delicate.

Enter LADY MACBETH

DUNCAN   See, see our honoured hostess!   10
  The love that follows us sometime is our trouble,
  Which still we thank as love. Herein I teach you
  How you shall bid God 'ild us for your pains,
  And thank us for your trouble.

LADY MACBETH   All our service
  In every point twice done, and then done double,   15
  Were poor and single business to contend
  Against those honours deep and broad wherewith
  Your Majesty loads our house. For those of old,
  And the late dignities heaped up to them,
  We rest your hermits.

DUNCAN   Where's the Thane of Cawdor?   20
  We coursed him at the heels, and had a purpose
  To be his purveyor. But he rides well,
  And his great love, sharp as his spur, hath holp him

26–7   *in compt . . . audit*, in trust, to be disposed.
28   *Still . . . own*, always to return to you what are really your own possessions.

Scene Seven

(stage direction) Enter . . . stage. The Sewer was the official in charge of serving the meal. The sound of hautboys, and the procession of servants indicates that the King is being given a formal banquet from which Macbeth has excused himself (ll.29–30). The order and ceremonious duty of a banquet offsets the destructive treachery of Macbeth's intentions.

1–7   *If . . . to come*, if the business was finished with at the first blow, then it would be best to get on with it at once. If the assassination could itself prevent all other after-effects, and achieve the succession conclusively with Duncan's death—if only this one blow put an end to what it started, here only here in this uncertain, superficial life, we'd risk eternity.

3   *trammel up.* A trammel was a fishing or fowling net. The idea is developed and turned in typically Shakespearean fashion in the word 'catch.'

4   *his surcease.* 'His' could mean 'its.' So we have an ambiguity, probably intentional, where the words may refer either to Duncan ('his death') or the murder ('its conclusion').
         success. Either 'success,' or the 'succession' (to the throne).

7   *cases.* As well as 'affairs,' the word could equally mean 'bodies.' And also there is a hint of legal matters.

8–10   *that . . . inventor*, in that we only demonstrate techniques of murder, which are then turned against their originator.

10   *To plague.* Frequently used with special reference to divine retribution, a half-thought extended into the next sentence.

17   *faculties*, powers and liberties conferred by law/Divine retribution has already occurred to Macbeth; now begins the powerfully subconscious identification in his mind of Duncan with divine law, and the horror of 'sacrilegious murder' appals him.

18   *clear*, immaculate.   *office*, duties and obligations. The word implies service rather than authority, and has strong religious undertones. Duncan's saintly humility is recollected.
         virtues, grace of character. A powerful word, especially in this context. One meaning was the power invested in a divine being.

20   *The deep . . . off.* Macbeth's imagination identifies the murder inseparably with damnation, generating this most powerful prolepsis.

21–5   *And pity . . . wind.* The confused apocalyptic metaphors express the breakdown of control in Macbeth's mind, when he imagines the murder of 'renown and grace' exemplified in Duncan. This is the symbolic core of the play, and the enormity of the issue is expressed in its shattering impact on Macbeth's conscience.

22   *cherubin.* One of the angelic orders.

To his home before us. Fair and noble hostess,
We are your guest tonight.

LADY MACBETH   Your servants ever   25
  Have theirs, themselves, and what is theirs, in compt,
  To make their audit at your Highness' pleasure,
  Still to return your own.

DUNCAN   Give me your hand.
  Conduct me to mine host. We love him highly,
  And shall continue our graces towards him . . .   30
  By your leave hostess.   [*Exeunt*

Scene Seven

Macbeth's castle

Hautboys and torches. Enter a Sewer, and divers Servants with dishes and service, and pass over the stage. Then enter MACBETH

MACBETH If it were done, when 'tis done, then 'twere well
  It were done quickly. If the assassination
  Could trammel up the consequence, and catch,
  With his surcease, success; that but this blow
  Might be the be-all and the end-all . . . here,   5
  But here, upon this bank and shoal of time,
  We'd jump the life to come. But in these cases
  We still have judgment here, that we but teach
  Bloody instructions, which being taught return
  To plague the inventor. This even-handed justice   10
  Commends the ingredients of our poisoned chalice
  To our own lips. He's here in double trust:
  First, as I am his kinsman and his subject,
  Strong both against the deed; then, as his host,
  Who should against his murderer shut the door,   15
  Not bear the knife myself. Besides, this Duncan
  Hath borne his faculties so meek, hath been
  So clear in his great office, that his virtues
  Will plead like angels, trumpet-tongued against
  The deep damnation of his taking-off.   20
  And pity, like a naked new-born babe,
  Striding the blast, or heaven's cherubin, horsed

23 *sightless*, invisible. *couriers*, messengers, i.e. the winds.

25–8 *I have . . . other*, I have nothing to urge on my purpose but my own overweening ambition, which like a horseman rushing his fences, falls to disaster/Lady Macbeth's entry interrupts the sentence.

29 *almost supped*, almost finished supper.

30 *Know . . . has?* It implies that the King has asked for Macbeth—as he did on arrival at the castle, during Lady Macbeth's flattery (Act1 Sc.6,ll.20,28). This running accompaniment of a natural affinity between Macbeth and the King is hardly noticed till Lady Macbeth's question here so credibly motivates his retraction from the conspiracy.

32 *bought*, won.

34 *would be*, should be. *newest gloss*, glossy newness.

35 *Was . . . drunk*, was it only a drunken hope?

38 *freely*, readily.

39 *Such*, so changeable.

41–2 *Wouldst . . . life*. 'The ornament of life' is commonly taken to mean the crown. But Lady Macbeth catches and turns the ideas in ll.33–4 in 'chastising' 'all that impedes' Macbeth from the crown—that is his desire for a clear conscience. 'The ornament of life' is 'that which is not corruptible, even the ornament of a meek and quiet spirit.' (The text of *1 Peter*, Ch. 3 v.4, used in the marriage service, concerns 'men being won by the conversation of their wives.') In Act3 Sc.1, ll.64–8 Macbeth calls his soul 'mine eternal jewel,' an associated image in a highly relevant sequence of ideas. The importance of 'a quiet spirit' as 'the ornament of life' is central to all Macbeth has been saying, and Lady Macbeth's speech develops the theme in a typical way. Macbeth's loss of his 'quiet spirit' under his wife's persuasion is at the heart of the play, and to take the phrase to mean the crown ignores the equivocation on conscience and cowardice, and drains the situation of all its ironic depth.

43 *in thine own esteem*, in your self-esteem/The sneer in the repetition of 'esteem' depends for its bite on the interpretation of l.42.

44 *wait upon*, always follow.

45 *Like . . . adage*. 'The cat would eat fish and would not wet his feet.'

47 *is none*, is not a man.

50 *And to . . . you were*, i.e. by fulfilling your boast, and becoming King.

51–2 *Nor time . . . adhere*, neither time nor place was then convenient.

Upon the sightless couriers of the air,
Shall blow the horried deed in every eye,
That tears shall drown the wind . . . I have no spur   25
To prick the sides of my intent, but only
Vaulting ambition, which o'erleaps itself,
And falls on the other—

Enter LADY MACBETH

                              How now? What news?
LADY MACBETH He has almost supped. Why have you left the
  chamber?
MACBETH Hath he asked for me?
LADY MACBETH   Know you not he has?   30
MACBETH We will proceed no further in this business.
  He hath honoured me of late, and I have bought
  Golden opinions from all sorts of people,
  Which would be worn now in their newest gloss,
  Not cast aside so soon.
LADY MACBETH   Was the hope drunk   35
  Wherein you dressed yourself? Hath it slept since?
  And wakes it now to look so green and pale
  At what it did so freely? From this time
  Such I account thy love. Art thou afeard
  To be the same in thine own act and valour   40
  As thou art in desire? Wouldst thou have that
  Which thou esteem'st the ornament of life,
  And live a coward in thine own esteem,
  Letting 'I dare not' wait upon 'I would,'
  Like the poor cat i' the adage?
MACBETH   Prithee peace.   45
  I dare do all that may become a man;
  Who dares do more is none.
LADY MACBETH   What beast was't then
  That made you break this enterprise to me?
  When you durst do it, then you were a man,
  And to be more than what you were, you would   50
  Be so much more the man. Nor time nor place
  Did then adhere, and yet you would make both.
  They have made themselves, and that their fitness now

54   *unmake you,* make you less than a man/The whole passage distorts what Macbeth said.

54–9 *I have . . . to this.* Coleridge: 'though usually thought to prove a merciless and unwomanly nature, (this) proves the direct opposite: she brings it as the most solemn enforcement to Macbeth of the solemnity of his promise . . . Had *she* so sworn, she would have done—"that which was most horrible to her feelings, rather than break the oath." ' It succeeds with Macbeth, the brutal force of the language shocking him into re-acceptance of the project. And despite the logic of Coleridge's point, the audience is similarly shocked, Lady Macbeth being identified in her proposition, which also reveals her self-imposed strain.

60   *to the sticking-place,* till it is firm set.

64   *convince,* overcome.

65–6 *That . . . fume.* The memory was thought to be lodged 'in the back part of the brain' whence it acted as 'warder' against vapours rising from the stomach along the spine to cause sleep or drunkenness.

66–7 *the receipt . . . only.* The common explanation that the brain, and therefore reason itself becomes confused 'like a still' is unacceptable because (a) reason was not one of 'the inner senses' (common-sense, phantasy, and memory) lodged solely 'within the brain-pan', (b) reason was thought to remain 'free' during sleep as 'commander' of phantasy, and (c) reason, unlike memory, is unaffected by drink once sobriety is regained.

    In a still the 'limbeck' was the retort in which liquids were mixed and heated (therefore confused) and the 'receipt' was the vessel into which the distilled drops passed.

    Memory 'lays up all the species which the senses have brought in, and records them as a good register, that they may be forthcoming when they are called for by phantasy and reason' (Burton). Hence memory was 'the receipt of reason' (of=belonging to, controlled by). Lady Macbeth is concerned with memory as (a) a guard to consciousness and (b) as the receptacle for impressions—as indeed she amplifies in the rest of her speech. And incidentally, 'to limbeck one's brain' meant to rack one's memory for things forgotten.

68   *drenched,* drowned, or medicined with a draught as an animal.

70   *put upon,* falsely ascribe to.

72   *quell,* murder.

74   *received,* accepted. The fawning, obvious cunning of this remark shows how completely Macbeth is dominated.

77–9 *Who . . . death,* who will dare to take it any other way, considering the noisy show of grief we will put on at his death?

79–80 *bend up . . . agent,* strain all my faculties.

81   *mock . . . show,* deceive the world with a show of friendship. He weakly repeats back her advice.

Does unmake you. I have given suck, and know
How tender 'tis to love the babe that milks me.   55
I would while it was smiling in my face
Have plucked my nipple from his boneless gums,
And dashed the brains out, had I so sworn as you
Have done to this.

MACBETH   If we should fail?

LADY MACBETH   We fail?
But screw your courage to the sticking-place,   60
And we'll not fail. When Duncan is asleep
(Whereto the rather shall his day's hard journey
Soundly invite him) his two chamberlains
Will I with wine and wassail so convince,
That memory, the warder of the brain,   65
Shall be a fume, and the receipt of reason
A limbeck only. When in swinish sleep
Their drenched natures lie as in a death,
What cannot you and I perform upon
The unguarded Duncan? What not put upon   70
His spongy officers, who shall bear the guilt
Of our great quell?

MACBETH   Bring forth men-children only,
For thy undaunted mettle should compose
Nothing but males . . . Will it not be received,
When we have marked with blood those sleepy two   75
Of his own chamber, and used their very daggers,
That they have done't?

LADY MACBETH   Who dares receive it other,
As we shall make our griefs and clamour roar
Upon his death?

MACBETH   I am settled and bend up
Each corporal agent to this terrible feat.   80
Away, and mock the time with fairest show—
False face must hide what the false heart doth know.   [*Exeunt*

1–9   *How . . . sword.* The atmosphere is ominous as we approach the time of murder. The darkness, the measuring of time, the sense of oppression, the familiar domestic imagery, the presence of evil thoughts and the edginess all add to the suspense.

4   *Hold*, wait.   *husbandry*, economy.

5   *that.* Probably dagger and belt. He is disarming for bed.

6   *heavy summons*, an overpowering call to give way to sleep.

7   *would not*, do not want to.

7–9   *Merciful Powers . . . repose.* The Powers (the sixth order of Angels) were particularly responsible to God for restraining demons.

9   *Give . . . sword!* The recollection of his dreams puts him on edge, and he reacts to a noise.

11   *A friend.* Banquo stands guard in the castle where he should instinctively feel secure, and Macbeth gives the conventional response to a challenge in his own house, without a second thought. None of this is explicable in terms of characters. The speakers are simultaneously reacting to, and creating, the tension.

14   *great largess*, generous gifts.   *offices*, servants' quarters.

15   *withal*, with.

16   *shut up*, ended the day.

17–19   *Being . . . wrought*, our lack of preparation meant that our desire to give generous hospitality only served to expose our shortcomings.

20   *I . . . Weird Sisters.* The 'cursed thoughts' he mentioned in 1.8, and he does not tell Macbeth what evil visions revealed themselves to him.

22   *entreat . . . serve*, find a convenient moment.

Act Two · Scene One
A courtyard in Macbeth's castle

Enter BANQUO · *and* FLEANCE *bearing a torch before him*

BANQUO   How goes the night, boy?

FLEANCE   The moon is down; I have not heard the clock.

BANQUO   And she goes down at twelve.

FLEANCE   I take't 'tis later sir.

BANQUO   Hold—take my sword . . . There's husbandry in heaven,
Their candles are all out . . . Take thee that too.   5
A heavy summons lies like lead upon me,
And yet I would not sleep. Merciful Powers,
Restrain in me the cursed thoughts that nature
Gives way to in repose . . . Give me my sword!
Who's there?   10

Enter MACBETH, *and a* SERVANT *with a torch*

MACBETH   A friend.

BANQUO   What sir, not yet at rest? The King's abed.
He hath been in unusual pleasure, and
Sent forth great largess to your offices.
This diamond he greets your wife withal,   15
By the name of most kind hostess, and shut up
In measureless content.

MACBETH   Being unprepared,
Our will became the servant to defect,
Which else should free have wrought.

BANQUO   All's well.
I dreamt last night of the three Weird Sisters.   20
To you they have showed some truth.

MACBETH   I think not of them.
Yet when we can entreat an hour to serve,

24   *At . . . leisure*, when you are graciously pleased to find it con-
      venient/Perhaps Banquo's polite formality measures his
      respect and also suggests his uncertainty about Macbeth.

25-6 *If you . . . for you.* Macbeth is deliberately obscure. Banquo can
      take it to mean 'If you will follow my advice . . . ' or 'If you
      give me your support when the time comes, it will mean
      titles for you.' 'When 'tis' is especially open to interpretation.

26-9 *So I . . . counselled,* provided I lose no honour in seeking to
      increase my honours, but always keep my conscience free
      and my loyalty unblemished, I am prepared to listen to
      your suggestions/Banquo's directness contrasts with the
      deviousness of Macbeth.

31-2 *Go . . . bell.* The homely instruction signals murder.

33-49 *Is this . . . eyes.* Macbeth is tormented by the vision of the
      dagger, and by his inability to decide whether his own
      heated imagination is responsible for the vision, or whether
      the dagger is a demonic representation. If the latter is true,
      the powers of darkness have subverted his reason and are
      controlling his phantasy. On the one hand we have the
      working of conscience and its suppression of the will and
      reason to the devil. Shakespeare need not answer the ques-
      tion which is the greater evil; he simply raises it.

35   *still,* constantly.

36   *fatal,* ominous.

36-7 *sensible To,* perceptible by.

38   *false,* counterfeit.

39   *heat-oppressed,* fevered.

40-43 *I see . . . use.* Perhaps now, as he is induced almost subcon-
      sciously to draw his dagger, and the vision 'marshals' him
      towards Duncan's room, he decides that the devil is present.

44-5 *Mine . . . rest,* either my eyes are deceived while my other
      senses are in the right, or the dagger is a reality that my eyes
      alone can comprehend.

46   *dudgeon,* hilt.   *gouts,* splashes. This glance into the future
      suggests demonic intervention.

47-9 *There's . . . eyes.* The attempt to reassure himself turns cruelly
      against him, as it invites the supposition that witchcraft is at
      work.   *informs Thus,* manifests itself in this shape.

50   *Nature . . . dead,* all natural (good) things seem dead.

50-51 *wicked . . . sleep,* malign dreams violate the security of sleep.

52   *Pale Hecate.* Goddess of witchcraft.   *offerings,* rituals.

53   *Alarumed,* roused.   *the wolf.* Associated with murder from
      time immemorial.

54   *his watch.* The watch (watchman) cried out the time as he
      patrolled the streets. The wolf gives murder the signal, and
      Macbeth's mind goes from that to Tarquin and himself.

55   *Tarquin's . . . strides.* Tarquin ravished Lucretia, wife of one of
      his kinsmen. See Shakespeare's *The Rape of Lucrece,* in which
      there are many parallels with *Macbeth.*   *design,* purpose.

57-8 *which way . . . whereabout.* The phrase 'which way they walk' is
      important. He does not fear that his footsteps will be over-
      heard, but that their direction will make the very stones
      talk. It is a fear of his own guilt.

We would spend it in some words upon that business,
If you would grant the time.

BANQUO   At your kindest leisure.

MACBETH If you shall cleave to my consent, when 'tis,   25
It shall make honour for you.

BANQUO   So I lose none
In seeking to augment it, but still keep
My bosom franchised and allegiance clear,
I shall be counselled.

MACBETH   Good repose the while.

BANQUO Thanks sir, the like to you.   [*Exeunt* BANQUO *and* FLEANCE 30

MACBETH Go bid thy mistress, when my drink is ready,
She strike upon the bell . . . Get thee to bed . . .   [*Exit* SERVANT
Is this a dagger which I see before me,
The handle toward my hand? Come let me clutch thee.
I have thee not, and yet I see thee still.   35
Art thou not, fatal vision, sensible
To feeling as to sight? Or art thou but
A dagger of the mind, a false creation
Proceeding from the heat-oppressed brain?
I see thee yet, in form as palpable   40
As this which now I draw.
Thou marshall'st me the way that I was going,
And such an instrument I was to use.
Mine eyes are made the fools o' the other senses,
Or else worth all the rest. I see thee still,   45
And on thy blade and dudgeon gouts of blood,
Which was not so before . . . There's no such thing.
It is the bloody business which informs
Thus to mine eyes . . . Now o'er the one half-world
Nature seems dead, and wicked dreams abuse   50
The curtained sleep . . . Witchcraft celebrates
Pale Hecate's offerings, and withered murder,
Alarumed by his sentinel the wolf,
Whose howl's his watch, thus with his stealthy pace,
With Tarquin's ravishing strides, towards his design   55
Moves like a ghost. Thou sure and firm-set earth,
Hear not my steps which way they walk, for fear
Thy very stones prate of my whereabout,

59–60   *And take . . . it*, and postpone the impending horrible deed
from this hour that suits it so well/In his traumatic self-
dramatization he is concerned with the loss of effect post-
ponement would bring, and darkness obsesses and cloaks
him.

62   *The bell invites me.* Another macabre use of a familiar word,
'invites'.

Scene Two

1   *That . . . bold.* Her bed-time drink, and a reminder of the plot.

3   *the fatal bellman*, death's bellman/The owl's cries were associated with death. The bellman went before a corpse to the
grave, and also visited the condemned before execution.

4   *stern'st*, most grim.

5–6   *the surfeited . . . snores*, the snores of the drunken gentlemen of
the bedchamber make a mockery of their duties of guarding
the King.

6   *possets*. A drink of hot milk, wine, spices etc.

7–8   *That . . . die*, so that the powers of life and death seem to be
struggling for possession of them/The notion that the
sleeping and the dead are simply unreal counterfeits of the
living is repeated in the play, and is part of the deceptive
ambiguity between appearance and reality.

10–11   *The attempt . . . us*, an unsuccessful attempt will ruin us.

12–13   *Had . . . had done't.* This should be remembered, because she
returns to the chamber. Her attitude to murder is different
from Macbeth's, and not necessarily harsher.

13   *My husband.* The only point in the play where she calls Macbeth 'husband.' The anxiety and relief break through her
sense of position, and create a momentary sympathy.

16   *As I descended?* Macbeth makes sure that it was his own shout
Lady Macbeth heard, not the cry mentioned in l. 22, and at
once loses interest. The dialogue delicately reflects Macbeth's
preoccupation, and establishes this as dominating the Scene.

And take the present horror from the time
Which now suits with it. Whiles I threat, he lives.   60
Words to the heat of deeds too cold breath gives. [*A bell rings*]
I go, and it is done. The bell invites me.
Hear it not Duncan, for it is a knell
That summons thee to heaven, or to hell.   [*Exit*

Scene Two

A courtyard in Macbeth's castle

Enter LADY MACBETH

LADY MACBETH   That which hath made them drunk hath made me
bold,
What hath quenched them hath given me fire. Hark! Peace!
It was the owl that shrieked—the fatal bellman
Which gives the stern'st good night. He is about it.
The doors are open, and the surfeited grooms   5
Do mock their charge with snores. I have drugged their possets,
That death and nature do contend about them,
Whether they live or die.

MACBETH   [*within*]   Who's there? What ho!

LADY MACBETH   Alack, I am afraid they have awaked,
And 'tis not done. The attempt and not the deed   10
Confounds us. Hark! I laid their daggers ready—
He could not miss 'em. Had he not resembled
My father as he slept, I had done't.

Enter MACBETH

                                My husband!

MACBETH   I have done the deed. Didst thou not hear a noise?

LADY MACBETH   I heard the owl scream and the crickets cry.   15
Did not you speak?

MACBETH   When?

LADY MACBETH   Now.

MACBETH   As I descended?

LADY MACBETH   Ay.

19   *second chamber*, next room.

20   *a sorry sight*, a sight appalling in its grief/'Sorry' is a powerful
        word, and the line begins the panic in Macbeth's imagina-
        tion, which Lady Macbeth tries to halt with her realistic curt
        rejoinders.

22–4   *There's . . . to sleep.* On reflection this seems to refer to Malcolm
        and Donalbain 'in the second chamber,' because the grooms
        are 'drunk.' Maybe; but it accords with the infernal atmos-
        phere if the grooms cried out despite their drugged possets,
        especially as one laughed—in a room infested with evil.
        There is no apparent reason for the princes to laugh. More-
        over as the word 'they' is spoken (l. 23) our minds are with
        Macbeth in the chamber and we think of the grooms. And
        Macbeth would hardly be aware of prayers and the occu-
        pants' preparing for sleep in an adjacent room. It seems all
        too intimately close, as do the details that follow, ll.26–32.
        And if they were involved, it is odd that the princes do not
        recollect this shattering disturbance. See note on Act 2 Sc.3,
        ll.94, 112.

25   *There . . . together.* Either the princes, or the grooms lodged in
        the same room, but apart from the King.

27   *hangman's hands.* Blood stained the hangman's hands when he
        drew and quartered his victim alive.

33–4   *These . . . mad.* The remark is ominous, suggesting that Lady
        Macbeth's calculating self-control is unsure. The future is
        anticipated. Macbeth in his frenzy does not hear her.

36   *Macbeth . . . sleep.* As if the sleeping King personified natural
        and healing sleep, which henceforth will be lost to Macbeth
        and Lady Macbeth.

37   *knits . . . care*, smooths out the tangled threads of anxiety and
        fear.   *sleave*, filaments of silk.

38   *The death . . . life.* The idea of 'death' as welcome is intrusive
        in the list of refreshing and comforting associations for
        sleep, and psychologically important—preferable to Mac-
        beth's 'life.'

39   *second course.* After wakefulness sleep is the second cycle of
        life; and after life, death the second cycle of being. Also the
        'second course' was the main part of a meal, which suggests
        the next line.

41   *Still*, ceaselessly.

42–3   *Glamis . . . no more.* How much of this is spoken by an external
        voice addressing Macbeth's conscience and how much is his
        comment is difficult to say.

45   *unbend*, slacken.

47   *witness*, evidence.

MACBETH Hark!
  Who lies i' the second chamber?
LADY MACBETH   Donalbain.
MACBETH This is a sorry sight. [*looks at his hands*]   20

LADY MACBETH A foolish thought, to say a sorry sight.

MACBETH There's one did laugh in's sleep, and one cried 'Murder!'
  That they did wake each other. I stood and heard them.
  But they did say their prayers, and addressed them
  Again to sleep.
LADY MACBETH   There are two lodged together.   25

MACBETH One cried 'God bless us!' and 'Amen' the other,
  As they had seen me with these hangman's hands.
  Listening their fear, I could not say 'Amen'
  When they did say 'God bless us'.

LADY MACBETH Consider it not so deeply.   30

MACBETH But wherefore could not I pronounce 'Amen'?
  I had most need of blessing, and 'Amen'
  Stuck in my throat.
LADY MACBETH   These deeds must not be thought
  After these ways; so, it will make us mad.

MACBETH Methought I heard a voice cry 'Sleep no more!   35
  Macbeth does murder sleep'—the innocent sleep,
  Sleep that knits up the ravelled sleave of care,
  The death of each day's life, sore labour's bath,
  Balm of hurt minds, great nature's second course,
  Chief nourisher in life's feast—
LADY MACBETH   What do you mean?   40

MACBETH Still it cried 'Sleep no more!' to all the house,
  'Glamis hath murdered sleep, and therefore Cawdor
  Shall sleep no more. Macbeth shall sleep no more.'

LADY MACBETH Who was it that thus cried? Why worthy Thane,
  You do unbend your noble strength to think   45
  So brainsickly of things. Go get some water,
  And wash this filthy witness from your hand.
  Why did you bring these daggers from the place?
  They must lie there. Go carry them, and smear
  The sleepy grooms with blood.

55   *painted devil*, the picture of a devil, or the actor made up as the
      devil in a show. But Shakespeare often used 'painted' to
      mean 'bloodstained' and also 'counterfeit.'

56-7 *I'll gild . . . guilt.* The cynical pun is 'a sign of the immense
      effort of will needed by Lady Macbeth to visit the scene of the
      crime.' (Muir) 'Red' was an epithet often applied to gold.
      and red and gold look alike in semi-darkness. Cf. Act2Sc.3,l.30.

57   *(stage direction) Knocking within*, i.e. off-stage. This is the knocking
      of which De Quincey wrote his famous essay 'On the knock-
      ing at the gate in *Macbeth*,' pointing out that the knocking
      ends an interlude in hell, and that the abrupt 're-establish-
      ment of the goings-on of the world in which we live first
      makes us profoundly sensible of the awful parenthesis that
      had suspended them.'

62   *multitudinous*, countless.   *incarnadine*, dye blood-red.

63   *Making . . . one red.* Not 'making the green sea red,' but 'turn-
      ing the green of the sea totally red.' A comma after 'one' in
      the Folio seems to argue against this, but simply indicates
      stress.

65   *I hear a knocking.* Macbeth has been (and remains) spell-bound
      beyond the threat of discovery.

68-9 *Your constancy . . . unattended*, your self-control has deserted you.

70   *nightgown*, dressing-gown.   *lest . . . call us*, in case we are
      wanted.

71   *watchers*, still awake and about.

73   *To know . . . myself.* The expression 'he seems not to know him-
      self' is still a common colloquialism for 'he seems to act
      distractedly.' Macbeth says: 'If I am bound to comprehend
      my deed, it is best that I remain distracted.' Macbeth's words,
      though answered by Lady Macbeth's conscious voice, often
      seem to lodge in her subconscious mind and find a terrifying
      answer there in her subsequent loss of reason. This sentence,
      seemingly innocent, is perhaps the most pointed of all.

Scene Three 2   *old*, more than enough.

MACBETH   I'll go no more.   50
  I am afraid to think what I have done.
  Look on't again I dare not.

LADY MACBETH   Infirm of purpose!
  Give me the daggers. The sleeping and the dead
  Are but as pictures. 'Tis the eye of childhood
  That fears a painted devil. If he do bleed,   55
  I'll gild the faces of the grooms withal,
  For it must seem their guilt.   [*Exit. Knocking within*

MACBETH   Whence is that knocking?
  How is't with me, when every noise appals me?
  What hands are here? ha! they pluck out mine eyes!
  Will all great Neptune's ocean wash this blood   60
  Clean from my hand? No, this my hand will rather
  The multitudinous seas incarnadine,
  Making the green one red.

Enter LADY MACBETH

LADY MACBETH   My hands are of your colour; but I shame
  To wear a heart so white. I hear a knocking   65
  At the south entry. Retire we to our chamber.
  A little water clears us of this deed.
  How easy is it then! Your constancy
  Hath left you unattended. Hark, more knocking!
  Get on your nightgown, lest occasion call us   70
  And show us to be watchers. Be not lost
  So poorly in your thoughts.

MACBETH   To know my deed, 'twere best not know myself.
  Wake Duncan with thy knocking! I would thou couldst.   [*Exeunt*

Scene Three

A courtyard in Macbeth's castle

Enter a PORTER *to loud knocking*

PORTER   Here's a knocking indeed! If a man were porter of hell-
  gate, he should have old turning the key.
  Knock, knock, knock! Who's there, i' the name of Beelzebub?

4   *hanged . . . plenty*, i.e. because the price would drop.

5   *time-server.* Wilson's inspired suggestion for the Folio 'time,'
to parallel the 'equivocator' and 'tailor' later. As Wilson says
'time-server' applies to all farmers who wait on the seasons,
and as 'server' also means a waiter at table it links with the
otherwise unrelated words 'napkins' and 'farmer.'

7   *equivocator.* One who evades the truth by using words subject
to more than one interpretation. Equivocation was a burning topic at the time, and the Jesuit Garnet, hanged on May 3,
1606 after the Gunpowder Plot, defended himself by equivocation. He went by the name Farmer, and a punning
topical connection between the equivocator and the farmer
is possible.

7–8   *that . . . either scale,* that could swear in such an ambiguous
way, that if challenged with having said one thing he could
maintain that he meant the opposite.

8–9   *treason . . . God's sake.* Garnet would claim that treason 'for
God's sake' was no treason.

11   *for stealing . . . hose.* French hose were breeches reaching below
the knee. The tailor cheated by stealing cloth and skimping
his garments.

12   *roast your goose,* heat your smoothing iron.

19   *the second cock,* about three a.m.

22   *Lechery,* lust.

24–5   *to be an equivocator with,* to deceive.

25   *him,* it—lechery.

28   *equivocates . . . sleep,* cheats him into sleep and with mere
dreams.

30   *i' the very throat on me.* 'He lies in his throat' meant 'he is a down-
right liar.'   *requited him,* made him answer for (as in a duel).

32   *took . . . sometime,* lifted my legs off the ground/He sees his
struggle to stay sober as a wrestling match with drink.
made a shift, contrived.   *cast.* Could mean both 'throw,' as
in wrestling, and also 'vomit,' 'throw up.'

The Porter scene, with its coarse humour, relaxes the
tension and at the same time provides a commentary at
common level with its references to hell, retribution,
equivocation, and human duplicity.

Here's a farmer that hanged himself on the expectation of plenty.
Come in time-server, have napkins enow about you, here you'll   5
sweat for't. Knock, knock! Who's there, i' the other devil's name?
Faith here's an equivocator, that could swear in both the scales
against either scale, who committed treason enough for God's
sake, yet could not equivocate to heaven. O come in, equivocator.
Knock, knock, knock! Who's there? Faith here's an English tailor   10
come hither, for stealing out of a French hose. Come in tailor,
here you may roast your goose. Knock, knock! Never at quiet.
What are you? But this place is too cold for hell. I'll devil-porter
it no further. I had thought to have let in some of all professions,
that go the primrose way to the everlasting bonfire. Anon, anon!   15
I pray you remember the porter. [*opens the gate*]

Enter MACDUFF *and* LENNOX

MACDUFF   Was it so late, friend, ere you went to bed,
    That you do lie so late?

PORTER   Faith sir, we were carousing till the second cock, and drink,
    sir, is a great provoker of three things.   20

MACDUFF   What three things does drink especially provoke?

PORTER   Marry sir, nose-painting, sleep, and urine. Lechery, sir, it
    provokes, and unprovokes; it provokes the desire, but it takes
    away the performance. Therefore much drink may be said to be
    an equivocator with lechery; it makes him, and it mars him; it   25
    sets him on, and it takes him off; it persuades him, and disheartens
    him; makes him stand to, and not stand to; in conclusion,
    equivocates him in a sleep, and, giving him the lie, leaves him.

MACDUFF   I believe drink gave thee the lie last night.

PORTER   That it did sir, i' the very throat on me. But I requited   30
    him for his lie, and I think, being too strong for him, though he
    took up my legs sometime, yet I made a shift to cast him.

MACDUFF   Is thy master stirring?
    Our knocking has awaked him, here he comes.

Enter MACBETH

LENNOX   Good morrow noble sir.

MACBETH   Good morrow both.   35

MACDUFF   Is the King stirring, worthy Thane?

37   *timely*, early.

38   *slipped the hour*, missed the time.

40   *'tis one*, it is a trouble.

41   *The labour . . . pain.* A proverbial saying, which is all Macbeth
      can say.   *physics*, alleviates.

43   *limited service*, appointed duty.

44   *He does—he did.* The instinctive 'guilty self-correction' in-
      dicates how completely the deed has overwhelmed Macbeth.

45–52 *The night . . . shake.* The storms and disorders of the first three
      lines reflect in natural and supernatural terms the affront
      to order of Macbeth's deed, and the next three lines foretell
      the effect of the unnatural deed upon society and human
      relationships.

47   *strange*, unaccountable.

49–50 *Of dire . . . time*, of dreadful civil strife and anarchic con-
      sequences just initiated in a time of distress.

50   *The obscure bird*, the owl. Muir refers to Pliny: 'The screech owl
      always betokeneth some heavy news and is most execrable
      and accursed, and namely in the presages of public affairs . . .
      and . . . fearful misfortune.' With Muir, I take 'the obscure
      bird' to be 'prophesying.' Most editors put a full stop after
      'time.'

51–2   *Some say . . . shake.* 'An earthquake is a shaking of the earth,
      which is caused by means of wind and . . . the pestilent
      exhalations.' (William Fulke). This animalist view of the earth
      was commonplace to Shakespeare, and gave him a natural
      link in cause and effect between human actions and the
      universe of nature. The idea of earth as an animal did not
      survive Newtonian physics.

53–4   *My . . . to it*, my young memory cannot recall another night
      like it.

55   *O . . . horror!* Spoken off stage as he approaches.

57   *Confusion*, ruin, chaos.

58–60 *Most sacrilegious . . . building.* Kings were held to rule from God,
      and James I assiduously fostered this theory of Divine Right.
      Since the King was viceroy of God, regicide was sacrilegious.

60   *What . . . life?* The word 'life' in relation to Duncan confounds
      Macbeth. He seems momentarily to take Macduff to say that
      Duncan has been removed, and perhaps fears further super-
      natural intervention. Lennox speaks simultaneously.

63   *Gorgon.* In classical myth all who looked upon the Gorgons
      were turned to stone.

MACBETH   Not yet.

MACDUFF   He did command me to call timely on him.
   I have almost slipped the hour.

MACBETH   I'll bring you to him.

MACDUFF   I know this is a joyful trouble to you,
   But yet 'tis one.   40

MACBETH   The labour we delight in physics pain.
   This is the door.

MACDUFF   I'll make so bold to call,
   For 'tis my limited service.   [*Exit*

LENNOX   Goes the King hence today?

MACBETH   He does—he did appoint so.

LENNOX   The night has been unruly. Where we lay   45
   Our chimneys were blown down, and as they say,
   Lamentings heard i' the air, strange screams of death,
   And, prophesying with accents terrible,
   Of dire combustion, and confused events
   New hatched to the woeful time, the obscure bird   50
   Clamoured the livelong night. Some say the earth
   Was feverous and did shake.

MACBETH   'Twas a rough night.

LENNOX   My young remembrance cannot parallel
   A fellow to it.

Re-enter MACDUFF

MACDUFF   O horror! horror! horror! Tongue nor heart   55
   Cannot conceive nor name thee!

MACBETH, LENNOX   What's the matter?

MACDUFF   Confusion now hath made his masterpiece!
   Most sacrilegious murder hath broke ope
   The Lord's anointed temple, and stole thence
   The life o' the building!

MACBETH   What is't you say? the life?   60

LENNOX   Mean you his Majesty?

MACDUFF   Approach the chamber, and destroy your sight
   With a new Gorgon. Do not bid me speak.

65   *the alarum-bell*, the great bell sounded in case of attack.

69   *The great doom's image*, picture of the horror of Judgment Day.

70   *As . . . rise up.* The idea of 'judgment day' caught up in a way typical of Shakespeare; and again, the analogy between sleep and death, always horrifyingly present.   *sprites*, ghosts.

71   *To countenance*, in keeping with.   *business.* A strangely controlled word in the circumstances, reflecting Lady Macbeth's guarded coolness. It is also the euphemism they used for the murder, and one that Shakespeare repeatedly recollects for its commonplace effect.

75   *repetition*, mention of it.

81–6   *Had I . . . of.* The words, to be taken as a formal expression of grief at Duncan's death, are sombrely applicable to his own situation. Macbeth speaks with 'the equivocation of the fiend That lies like truth,' though not with full conscious command here, any more than at l.44 and l.60. The ironic sincerity of the language is appalling and profound.

83   *mortality*, human existence. But it also means 'death on a vast scale.'

84   *toys*, triviality.

85   *lees*, dregs.

86   *vault.* Primarily the cellar, but suggesting the earth under the vault of the sky.

See, and then speak yourselves.   [*Exeunt* MACBETH *and* LENNOX
                              Awake, awake!
Ring the alarum-bell! Murder and treason!   65
Banquo and Donalbain! Malcolm awake!
Shake off this downy sleep, death's counterfeit,
And look on death itself! Up, up and see
The great doom's image! Malcolm! Banquo!
As from your graves rise up, and walk like sprites,   70
To countenance this horror! [*bell rings*]

Enter LADY MACBETH

LADY MACBETH   What's the business,
That such a hideous trumpet calls to parley
The sleepers of the house? Speak, speak.
MACDUFF   O gentle lady,
'Tis not for you to hear what I can speak.
The repetition in a woman's ear   75
Would murder as it fell.

Enter BANQUO

                        O Banquo, Banquo,
Our royal master's murdered!
LADY MACBETH   Woe, alas!
What, in our house?
BANQUO   Too cruel anywhere.
Dear Duff, I prithee contradict thyself,
And say it is not so.   80

Re-enter MACBETH *and* LENNOX

MACBETH   Had I but died an hour before this chance,
I had lived a blessed time, for from this instant
There's nothing serious in mortality.
All is but toys. Renown and grace is dead.
The wine of life is drawn, and the mere lees   85
Is left this vault to brag of.

Enter MALCOLM *and* DONALBAIN

DONALBAIN   What is amiss?
MACBETH   You are, and do not know't.

88–9   *The spring . . . stopped.* His feigned agitation is all so desperately
       sincere. Macduff interrupts him; and Macduff's acquired
       calmness contrasts with his initial horror, and Macbeth's
       apparent distress.

88   *the head, the fountain,* the fountain head, the source.

92   *badged,* plainly marked.

94   *stared . . . distracted.* Usually taken to be the effects of the
       possets. Lady Macbeth said she had 'made them drunk'
       Act2Sc.2,l.1. But 'distracted' is not 'drunk' and (especially
       after 'stared') implies the bewilderment of mental dis-
       turbance, which is the commonplace meaning. Fearsome
       visions and the satanic atmosphere would be more likely to
       make them 'distracted' than drink, and this line has a bearing
       on Act2Sc.2, ll.22–4.

98   *amazed,* bewildered.   *temperate,* under self-control.
       furious, mad for revenge.

100–1 *The expedition . . . Reason,* the impetuosity of my overwhelming
       love slipped the restraint of reason/Again the sentence is
       equivocal. Macbeth's 'love' for Duncan was indeed 'violent.'
       Reason was the supreme, God-given faculty in mankind
       that controlled the will, desire, etc. and 'violent love' un-
       controlled by Reason was not love at all.

101–8 *Here lay . . . known.* Johnson pointed out the 'forced unnatural
       metaphors,' 'a mark of artifice and dissimulation,'—the
       whole speech 'a remarkable instance of judgment, as it
       consists entirely of antithesis and metaphor.' It also begins and
       ends with twisted emphasis on Macbeth's 'love,' associated
       with an odd courage (for Macbeth the great warrior) ex-
       pressed against two grooms.

103–4 *a breach . . . entrance.* Nature is seen as a fortress. Again, it is
       equivocal.

106   *Unmannerly breeched,* indecently covered with breeches. 'Mac-
       beth's hyperbole topples to absurdity.' (Wilson)

108   *Help me hence, ho!* Probably a timely diversion (Macbeth is
       saying too much), possibly a real faint.

110   *That most . . . ours,* who have most right to speak.
       argument, theme.

112   *an auger-hole,* a hole made with an auger, a spy-hole. Most
       editors see a hint at witchcraft, because witches could 'go in
       and out at auger-holes.' But is this relevant here? The
       princes are singularly calm, neither shows the slightest
       recollection of the demonic revelation Macbeth heard in the
       night (Act2,Sc.2, ll.22–4), and they fear being spied on and
       'rushed', not spell-bound. They do not believe the fiction
       of the grooms' guilt (ll.109, 110). They represent the
       forces of social authority, which at this point makes the first
       move against Macbeth's treason. Their fears are circumspect
       and their actions politic. They are unaware of witchcraft,
       let alone afraid of it, as their function in the play requires.

114   *Our tears.* With the emphasis on 'our'.

115   *Upon . . . motion,* yet really underway.

116   *naked frailties,* our poor ill-clad bodies.   *hid,* covered.

The spring, the head, the fountain of your blood
Is stopped, the very source of it is stopped.

MACDUFF   Your royal father's murdered.

MALCOLM   O, by whom?   90

LENNOX   Those of his chamber, as it seemed, had done't.
  Their hands and faces were all badged with blood,
  So were their daggers, which unwiped we found
  Upon their pillows. They stared and were distracted—
  No man's life was to be trusted with them.   95

MACBETH   O yet I do repent me of my fury,
  That I did kill them.

MACDUFF   Wherefore did you so?

MACBETH   Who can be wise, amazed, temperate and furious,
  Loyal and neutral, in a moment? No man.
  The expedition of my violent love   100
  Outrun the pauser, Reason. Here lay Duncan,
  His silver skin laced with his golden blood,
  And his gashed stabs looked like a breach in nature
  For ruin's wasteful entrance; there the murderers,
  Steeped in the colours of their trade, their daggers   105
  Unmannerly breeched with gore. Who could refrain,
  That had a heart to love, and in that heart
  Courage to make's love known?

LADY MACBETH   Help me hence, ho!

MACDUFF   Look to the lady.

MALCOLM   [aside to DONALBAIN] Why do we hold our tongues,
  That most may claim this argument for ours?   110

DONALBAIN   [aside to MALCOLM] What should be spoken here, where
  our fate,
  Hid in an auger-hole, may rush and seize us?
  Let's away.
  Our tears are not yet brewed.

MALCOLM   [aside to DONALBAIN]   Nor our strong sorrow
  Upon the foot of motion.

BANQUO   Look to the lady . . .   115
                                   [LADY MACBETH is carried out
  And when we have our naked frailties hid,
  That suffer in exposure, let us meet,

118	*question,* hold an inquest on.
119	*scruples,* doubts.
121	*undivulged pretence,* concealed plot.
122	*treasonous malice,* treacherous enemies. It is crucial that from the very beginning Banquo associates the fight against treason with 'the great hand of God.'
123	*briefly,* quickly. *put . . . readiness,* arm for action, like men.
126	*office,* business.
130–31	*the near . . . bloody,* the closer kinsman is the likelier murderer. Macbeth was their uncle.
131	*shaft,* arrow.
132	*lighted,* hit its mark.
134	*dainty,* particular.
135–6	*There's warrant . . . itself,* we have justification for stealing away. A quibble on 'steal.' cf. *All's Well,* Act2Sc.1:

        BERTRAM I'll steal away.

        FIRST LORD There's honour in the theft.

Scene Four

This scene, like the Porter scene, brings a relaxation of tension. It offers a commentary on the unnatural deed by marshalling the omens in evidence. The language of Ross and the Old Man is carefully distinguished. The Old Man shows the precise-minded interest of old age in the strange phenomena, and compares them rather fussily, but directly enough with his recollections. The selfconscious, balanced, cleverly affected imagery used by Ross is near to the language typical of mannered society on the Elizabethan stage. It dresses out the observations rather than communicating tension. It is sophisticated with strained metaphors and over-emphasis, that express Ross's shocked insincerity. His curiosity is appropriately satisfied with the 'obvious' conclusion of the princes' guilt, which he acts upon and joins Macbeth. Macduff, by contrast, is more circumspect and his misgivings are roused. So the theme moves forward, as the first seeds of opposition to Macbeth begin to show.

4	*Hath . . . knowings,* has made all earlier experiences seem trivial.
5	*as,* as if.

And question this most bloody piece of work,
To know it further. Fears and scruples shake us.
In the great hand of God I stand, and thence   120
Against the undivulged pretence I fight
Of treasonous malice.

MACDUFF   And so do I.

ALL   So all.

MACBETH   Let's briefly put on manly readiness,
  And meet i' the hall together.

ALL   Well contented.
                              [*Exeunt all but* MALCOLM *and* DONALBAIN

MALCOLM   What will you do? Let's not consort with them.   125
  To show an unfelt sorrow is an office
  Which the false man does easy. I'll to England.

DONALBAIN   To Ireland, I. Our separated fortune
  Shall keep us both the safer. Where we are
  There's daggers in men's smiles—the near in blood,   130
  The nearer bloody.

MALCOLM   This murderous shaft that's shot
  Hath not yet lighted, and our safest way
  Is to avoid the aim. Therefore to horse,
  And let us not be dainty of leave-taking,
  But shift away. There's warrant in that theft   135
  Which steals itself, when there's no mercy left.   [*Exeunt*

Scene Four

Outside Macbeth's castle

Enter ROSS *and an* OLD MAN

OLD MAN   Threescore and ten I can remember well,
  Within the volume of which time I have seen
  Hours dreadful, and things strange; but this sore night
  Hath trifled former knowings.

ROSS   Ha, good father,
  Thou seest the heavens, as troubled with man's act,   5
  Threatens his bloody stage. By the clock 'tis day,

7   *travelling lamp,* journeying sun.

8   *Is't . . . shame,* does night predominate because of the dark deed, or does the day hide with shame?

12   *towering . . . place.* The Old Man is reporting accurately in the technical terms of falconry. 'Towering' meant rising to a great height, and its 'place' was the pitch attained by the falcon before it stooped.

15   *minions,* most manageable darlings.   *race,* breed.

24   *What . . . pretend?* What did they think to gain by it?
      suborned, bribed.

27   *'Gainst nature still.* Cf. "'Tis unnatural,' l. 10. The unnatural prodigies that have been quoted by Ross and the Old Man reflect the threat to natural order of the regicide. Ross's remark focuses the casual conversation on the central deed.

28–9   *Thriftless . . . means,* unprofitable ambition, that will devour even the being that brought it to life.

31   *named,* elected.   *Scone,* the royal palace where the ancient Scottish Kings were crowned, 2½ miles north of Perth.

33–5   *Carried . . . bones.* Colme-kill, now Iona, is sacred as the Isle of St. Columba, and was the burial ground of Scottish Kings.

And yet dark night strangles the travelling lamp.
Is't night's predominance, or the day's shame,
That darkness does the face of earth entomb,
When living light should kiss it?

OLD MAN   'Tis unnatural,   10
Even like the deed that's done. On Tuesday last,
A falcon towering in her pride of place
Was by a mousing owl hawked at and killed.

Ross   And Duncan's horses (a thing most strange and certain)
Beauteous and swift, the minions of their race,   15
Turned wild in nature, broke their stalls, flung out,
Contending 'gainst obedience, as they would make
War with mankind.

OLD MAN   'Tis said they eat each other.

Ross   They did so, to the amazement of mine eyes
That looked upon't. Here comes the good Macduff.   20

Enter MACDUFF

How goes the world sir, now?

MACDUFF   Why, see you not?

Ross   Is't known who did this more than bloody deed?

MACDUFF   Those that Macbeth hath slain.

Ross   Alas the day,
What good could they pretend?

MACDUFF   They were suborned.
Malcolm and Donalbain, the King's two sons,   25
Are stolen away and fled, which puts upon them
Suspicion of the deed.

Ross   'Gainst nature still.
Thriftless ambition, that will ravin up
Thine own life's means! Then 'tis most like
The sovereignty will fall upon Macbeth.   30

MACDUFF   He is already named, and gone to Scone
To be invested.

Ross   Where is Duncan's body?

MACDUFF   Carried to Colme-kill,
The sacred storehouse of his predecessors,

C

36   *to Fife.* A pointed departure to his own castle.
37   *Well . . . well.* Muir points out the ironical repetition of
      Ross's 'well'.
40–41 *God's . . . foes.* The couplet may be an ordinary pious prayer.
      On the other hand, the play on the contraries of good and
      evil, friends and foes may be a scornful dismissal of Ross, the
      time-server.

And guardian of their bones.

Ross   Will you to Scone?   35

MACDUFF   No cousin, I'll to Fife.

Ross   Well, I will thither.

MACDUFF   Well, may you see things well done there. Adieu!
Lest our old robes sit easier than our new!

Ross   Farewell father.

OLD MAN   God's benison go with you, and with those   40
That would make good of bad, and friends of foes.   [*Exeunt*

(stage direction) Enter Banquo. He meditates and it is as if the audience overhears him. In the Elizabethan theatre, he has no need to address the audience. If he stands at the front of the apron the audience surrounds him on three sides, and those standing near can almost touch him.

1–3   *Thou . . . foully for't.* The conversation of the last scene and the coolness of Macduff lead naturally into this speech.

4   *stand . . . posterity,* pass to your descendants.

5–6   *root . . . kings.* Banquo was recognized as the first ancestor of the Stuarts and therefore of James I. The presentation of successful insurrection against an anointed king, even a tyrant, would be dubiously received by James. This genealogical point helped make Macbeth's overthrow palatable.

7   *shine,* radiate splendour.

8   *the verities . . . good,* the truths made manifest in your case.

10   *(stage direction) Sennet.* A long flourish on the trumpet, heralding royalty.

11–13   *If he . . . unbecoming.* By addressing Macbeth in these formal terms in Banquo's presence before he has been greeted, Lady Macbeth is at once regally distant and coldly ingratiating to Banquo. Shakespeare reflects developing relationships in apparently quite unimportant pronouncements.

13   *all-thing,* totally.

14   *solemn supper,* state banquet.

15   *I'll.* 'I'll,' where we might expect the royal 'we' (as in l. 21), implies 'I, personally.' The limp gesture of comradeship is gainsaid by the phraseology.

15–18   *Let . . . knit.* Banquo's promise of loyalty is strained and wordy. The natural ease of their earlier conversation is gone. Macbeth enters playing the king, and already he has lost a friend and gained a courtier.

22   *still,* always.   *grave,* influential.   *prosperous,* advantageous.

Act Three · Scene One

Enter BANQUO

BANQUO Thou hast it now, King, Cawdor, Glamis, all,
    As the weird women promised, and I fear
    Thou play'dst most foully for't. Yet it was said
    It should not stand in thy posterity,
    But that myself should be the root and father   5
    Of many kings. If there come truth from them
    (As upon thee Macbeth, their speeches shine)
    Why by the verities on thee made good
    May they not be my oracles as well,
    And set me up in hope? But hush, no more.   10

Sennet sounded. Enter MACBETH *as* KING · LADY MACBETH *as* QUEEN · LENNOX ·
ROSS · LORDS · LADIES · *and* ATTENDANTS

MACBETH Here's our chief guest.

LADY MACBETH   If he had been forgotten,
    It had been as a gap in our great feast,
    And all-thing unbecoming.

MACBETH
    Tonight we hold a solemn supper sir,
    And I'll request your presence.

BANQUO   Let your Highness   15
    Command upon me, to the which my duties
    Are with a most indissoluble tie
    For ever knit.

MACBETH Ride you this afternoon?

BANQUO Ay, my good lord.   20

MACBETH We should have else desired your good advice,
    Which still hath been both grave and prosperous,

23   *we'll take tomorrow,* we'll arrange it tomorrow.

24   *Is't far you ride?* The question that really interests Macbeth is put directly and clearly (as in ll. 18, 36) if seemingly casually, offset by the hypocritical, courtly phrased arrangements for a council of state. From the outset Macbeth is reduced to petty intrigue, hardly becoming for a king.

26   *Go . . . the better,* if my horse does not go faster (than to make it necessary).

28–9   *Fail . . . will not.* The bland callousness of the royal injunction is capped by the irony of Banquo's promise.

30   *bloody cousins,* murderous kinsmen.

33   *strange invention,* fantastic stories (concerning Macbeth's guilt).

34–5   *When . . . jointly,* when, moreover, we shall have state affairs requiring our mutual attention.

35   *Hie,* Hurry.

36   *Goes . . . with you?* The vital information is sought as if in an afterthought. The murder and his accession have hardened Macbeth's powers of dissimulation.

41   *be mast . . . time,* occupy his time as he wishes.

43   *To make . . . welcome,* to make the company of our guests the more welcome and pleasing.

45–6   *Sirrah . . . pleasure.* After declaring his intention to remain alone in anticipation of pleasant company, and having blessed his companions, Macbeth sends for the murderers. Appearance and reality are once more at odds in this sinister transition.

46   *Attend . . . pleasure,* are those men waiting for us to send for them?

48   *To be . . . safely thus,* to look like a king is nothing, unless I am secure in the trappings.

50–51   *and in . . . feared,* and his kingly qualities threaten my safety. Macbeth's fear of the 'royalty of nature' in Banquo acknowledges that his own nature is the antithesis of royalty.

52–4   *And to . . . safety.* Macbeth sees in Banquo the man he would wish to be, and he has to destroy the image. The resentment against Banquo gradually builds up from this initial recognition of his own inadequacy.

55–6   *under him . . . rebuked.* Macbeth's guardian spirit is over-awed by Banquo's. 'Genius' meant originally the deity allotted to a man at birth to guide him through life. *rebuked,* thwarted.

In this day's council. But we'll take tomorrow.
Is't far you ride?

BANQUO   As far, my lord, as will fill up the time   25
'Twixt this and supper. Go not my horse the better,
I must become a borrower of the night
For a dark hour or twain.

MACBETH   Fail not our feast.

BANQUO   My lord, I will not.

MACBETH   We hear our bloody cousins are bestowed   30
In England and in Ireland, not confessing
Their cruel parricide, filling their hearers
With strange invention. But of that tomorrow,
When therewithal we shall have cause of state
Craving as jointly. Hie you to horse. Adieu,   35
Till you return at night . . . Goes Fleance with you?

BANQUO   Ay my good lord. Our time does call upon's.

MACBETH   I wish your horses swift and sure of foot,
And so I do commend you to their backs.
Farewell.   [*Exit* BANQUO   40
Let every man be master of his time
Till seven at night.
To make society the sweeter welcome
We will keep ourself till supper-time alone.
While then, God be with you.   [*Exeunt all but* MACBETH *and* SERVANT
                          Sirrah, a word with you.   45
Attend those men our pleasure?

SERVANT   They are, my Lord,
Without the palace gate.

MACBETH   Bring them before us.   [*Exit* SERVANT
To be thus is nothing, but to be safely thus.
Our fears in Banquo
Stick deep, and in his royalty of nature   50
Reigns that which would be feared. 'Tis much he dares,
And to that dauntless temper of his mind,
He hath a wisdom that doth guide his valour
To act in safety. There is none but he
Whose being I do fear, and under him   55
My Genius is rebuked as it is said

56–7   *as . . . Caesar*. It was common knowledge that Mark Antony's
        'good angel and spirit' became 'fearful and timorous' when
        near to Caesar's 'genius.'

57   *chid*, rebuked.

61   *fruitless*, barren.

62   *gripe*, grip.

63   *with . . . hand*, by someone not descended from me.

64   *No . . . succeeding*. The witches said nothing of this in their
        promise to Banquo. The present soliloquy shows this inter-
        pretation of the prophecy developing in Macbeth's mind
        from his admiration and jealousy of Banquo. Having arrived
        at the idea, Macbeth's mind floods with malice to the end of
        the speech.

65   *filed*, defiled.

67   *Put rancours . . . peace*, surrendered my peace of mind to poison-
        ous malice. Cf. Act1Sc.7,l.11. Macbeth is already aware of the
        effects of his deed.

68   *eternal jewel*, immortal soul.

69   *the common . . . man*, the devil. Macbeth knows the extent of his
        forfeit to the devil.

72   *champion . . . utterance*, challenge me to mortal combat/The
        attempt on Fleance's life is in effect a challenge against fate,
        an attempt to turn aside the prophecy. And again, Macbeth's
        wish destroys him in the fulfilment.

        (stage direction) two murderers. Possibly wearing masks. The
        change of tone, compared with the Macbeth-Banquo con-
        versation, is most noticeable.

77–8   *he . . . under fortune*, he (Banquo) who in the past kept you in
        disfavour.

79   *made . . . you*, demonstrated to you.

80   *passed in probation*, proved point by point.

81   *borne in hand*, hoodwinked.   *crossed*, thwarted.
        the instruments, the means he used.

83   *half a soul*, a half wit.   *a notion crazed*, an unsound mind.

88–9   *Are you . . . man*. He sneers at the gospel teaching, 'pray for
        them which hurt you and persecute you.' 'Good man' is of
        course, sarcastic. As if by reflection, the sarcasm only helps
        to establish the righteousness of Banquo.

Mark Antony's was by Caesar. He chid the sisters
When first they put the name of king upon me,
And bade them speak to him. Then, prophet-like,
They hailed him father to a line of kings.   60
Upon my head they placed a fruitless crown
And put a barren sceptre in my gripe,
Thence to be wrenched with an unlineal hand,
No son of mine succeeding. If't be so,
For Banquo's issue have I filed my mind,   65
For them the gracious Duncan have I murdered,
Put rancours in the vessel of my peace
Only for them, and mine eternal jewel
Given to the common enemy of man
To make them kings—the seed of Banquo kings!   70
Rather than so, come fate into the list
And champion me to the utterance. Who's there?

Re-enter SERVANT, *with two* MURDERERS

Now go to the door, and stay there till we call.   [*Exit* SERVANT
Was it not yesterday we spoke together?

1 MURDERER   It was, so please your Highness.

MACBETH   Well then, now   75
Have you considered of my speeches? Know
That it was he in the times past which held you
So under fortune, which you thought had been
Our innocent self. This I made good to you
In our last conference, passed in probation with you,   80
How you were borne in hand, how crossed; the instruments,
Who wrought with them; and all things else that might
To half a soul and to a notion crazed
Say 'Thus did Banquo'.

1 MURDERER   You made it known to us.

MACBETH   I did so. And went further, which is now   85
Our point of second meeting. Do you find
Your patience so predominant in your nature,
That you can let this go? Are you so gospelled
To pray for this good man and for his issue,
Whose heavy hand hath bowed you to the grave   90
And beggared yours for ever?

91   *We are men.* Usually taken to mean 'we are men enough to pursue revenge.' Rather, I think, 'we are human enough to want revenge.' See note on l. 103.

92   *catalogue,* general register.

94   *Shoughs,* shaggy dogs.   *water-rugs,* rough-haired water-dogs. *clept,* called.

95   *valued file,* classified index.

96   *subtle,* cunning.

97   *housekeeper,* watchdog.

99   *Hath . . . closed,* has endowed him with.

99–101   *whereby . . . all alike,* which entitles him to a description under a separate heading, as distinct from the general list that enters them indiscriminately.

101   *And so of men.* The curt sentence after its tortuous preamble makes its point: You can divide men up like dogs.

103   *Not . . . manhood.* The long comparison with dogs, intended to bind the murderers to their deed is a taunting insult, un-intentional perhaps, but instinctive. Through it Macbeth unknowingly reveals his implicit evaluation of mankind.

        'Manhood' means 'human nature'. As dogs prove their qualities, so the men are taunted to prove themselves distinguished in humanity—by murdering. Murder becomes a virtue of status. Such reversal of values is a main theme in the play. Though 'manhood' cannot simply mean 'courage' or this appalling point is lost, this sense inevitably crosses the mind. The same two ideas interweave in Lady Macbeth's taunt in Act1 Sc.7, ll.36–51, of which this passage is possibly a subconscious, twisted recollection. So deeply is Macbeth's being destroyed?

107–8   *Who . . . perfect,* whose position is unhealthy while he lives, which could be perfect were he dead/Again, the image of clothing.

108–14   *I am . . . on't.* They kill out of spite, despair, and subservience.

111   *to spite the world.* The killing of Banquo will spite mankind in general. The enmity is not even directed at Banquo in particular. It makes the murder even more petty.

112   *disasters,* evil luck.   *tugged,* buffeted.

113   *set,* stake.

116   *bloody distance,* murderous enmity.

118   *nearest of life,* vital parts.

120   *bid . . . avouch it,* justify it as my whim/The phrase is most telling. It is a revelation of casual tyranny, a negation of the Elizabethan concept of order, where a sovereign's actions should be 'avouched' (find their authority) in the great controlling force of reason, certainly not in the unbridled 'will' (desire, whim, humour). And Macbeth speaks of his will as if it were an agent independent of himself, that could be commanded to justify a convenient killing.

122   *loves,* affections.   *drop,* discard.   *but wail,* but I must lament.

124   *make love,* entreat. His explanation is devious and politic, his approach hardly regal. He is uncertain.

1 MURDERER   We are men, my liege.

MACBETH   Ay, in the catalogue ye go for men,
As hounds and greyhounds, mongrels, spaniels, curs,
Shoughs, water-rugs and demi-wolves are clept
All by the name of dogs. The valued file   95
Distinguishes the swift, the slow, the subtle,
The housekeeper, the hunter—every one
According to the gift which bounteous nature
Hath in him closed, whereby he does receive
Particular addition, from the bill   100
That writes them all alike. And so of men.
Now if you have a station in the file,
Not i' the worst rank of manhood, say't,
And I will put that business in your bosoms
Whose execution takes your enemy off,   105
Grapples you to the heart and love of us,
Who wear our health but sickly in his life,
Which in his death were perfect.

2 MURDERER   I am one, my liege,
Whom the vile blows and buffets of the world
Have so incensed, that I am reckless what   110
I do to spite the world.

1 MURDERER   And I another
So weary with disasters, tugged with fortune,
That I would set my life on any chance,
To mend it or be rid on't.

MACBETH   Both of you
Know Banquo was your enemy.

BOTH MURDERERS   True my lord.   115

MACBETH   So is he mine, and in such bloody distance
That every minute of his being thrusts
Against my nearest of life, and though I could
With barefaced power sweep him from my sight,
And bid my will avouch it, yet I must not,   120
For certain friends that are both his and mine,
Whose loves I may not drop, but wail his fall
Who I myself struck down. And thence it is,
That I to your assistance do make love,

Scene One (continued)

128 *Your . . . through you* A king even flatters his murderous hench-
men.
129 *advise*, inform.
130 *the perfect . . . time.* A phrase that has been much discussed, and
for which many emendations have been suggested. Johnson
thought it referred to the third murderer. Macbeth seems
however to be saying something like 'I will let you know the
exact place and time.' He elaborates in the next two lines,
and is most concerned with the time and place of the deed.
If we emended the phrase to read 'perfect espy and the time'
(espy=hiding-place, ambush) it would fit the subsequent
lines. As the event showed there was one quite particular
spot 'something from the palace' where the deed had to be
done. Lady Macbeth was similarly concerned with time and
place in Act1Sc.7, ll.51–2, which this could clumsily echo.
132 *something*, some distance.
132–3 *Always thought . . . clearness*, keep it in mind that I want no
incriminating evidence.
134 *To . . . work*, to finish off the job properly/A 'rub' was evidence
of bad craftsmanship in a piece of work and we still speak of
a clumsy job as 'botched.'
138 *Resolve . . . apart*, go away and make up your minds.
141 *straight*, right away. *within*, indoors.

Scene Two 4 *Nought's . . . spent*, nothing is gained, and all is lost.
5 *content*, peace of mind.
6–7 *'Tis safer . . . joy.* Macbeth elaborates this at l.19. In these lines
it may be that Lady Macbeth's mind is on her husband as
much as herself. Her concern for Macbeth, though mis-
guided, is real and one saving grace.
7 *doubtful*, full of suspicious fears, The revelation of her true
feelings, expressed in soliloquy but concealed from Macbeth,
enhance her stature, and the tragedy of her misjudgment.

Masking the business from the common eye 125
For sundry weighty reasons.

2 MURDERER   We shall, my lord,
Perform what you command us.

1 MURDERER   Though our lives—

MACBETH   Your spirits shine through you. Within this hour at most,
I will advise you where to plant yourselves,
Acquaint you with the perfect spy o' the time— 130
The moment on't, for't must be done tonight,
And something from the palace. Always thought
That I require a clearness. And with him
(To leave no rubs nor botches in the work)
Fleance his son, that keeps him company, 135
Whose absence is no less material to me
Than is his father's, must embrace the fate
Of that dark hour. Resolve yourselves apart,
I'll come to you anon.

BOTH MURDERERS   We are resolved, my lord. 140

MACBETH   I'll call upon you straight. Abide within.   [*Exeunt* MURDERERS
It is concluded. Banquo, thy soul's flight,
If it find heaven, must find it out tonight.   [*Exit*

Scene Two

The palace

Enter LADY MACBETH *and a* SERVANT

LADY MACBETH   Is Banquo gone from Court?

SERVANT   Ay madam, but returns again tonight.

LADY MACBETH   Say to the King, I would attend his leisure
For a few words.

SERVANT   Madam I will.   [*Exit*

LADY MACBETH   Nought's had, all's spent,
Where our desire is got without content. 5
'Tis safer to be that which we destroy
Than by destruction dwell in doubtful joy.

Enter MACBETH

9   *sorriest fancies,* most painful delusions.

12   *without regard,* not contemplated.

13   *scorched,* slashed, as with a knife/The line shows how completely Macbeth's mind is occupied with Banquo and Fleance, and refers to the whole unfinished business of finding 'content.'

14–15   *whilst . . . tooth,* while we, after our malicious half-measures, are open to the same deadly threat as before.

16   *the frame of things,* the established universe/Shakespeare has in mind the planetary spheres, which suggest a settled 'framework.'   *both the worlds,* all creation and the Kingdom of heaven. 'World' could mean either the earth, or this life, or the universe.   *suffer,* perish.

18   *the affliction of,* the agony inflicted by.

19   *shake,* convulse. 'Shake' was the medical term for the rigors of fever (Falstaff was 'shaked' by a burning fever when dying).   *nightly,* nightlong—not 'each night.'

21   *Than . . . lie.* The line suggests that the tortured mind is a rack causing physical agony. It is an example of the particular quality of Shakespeare's writing, in that it catches up an idea already suggested, and turns the abstract idea of torture itself into the bed of pain, identifying both with the mind, with intense physical concentration.

22   *ecstasy,* delirium. It was the standard medical term for the delirium accompanying fever.

24   *his,* its—as often in Shakespeare.

25   *foreign levy.* Already his fears stretch into the future.

27   *Gentle,* noble.   *sleek o'er,* smooth. Her self-control gives no hint of the devastating effect on her of Macbeth's words.

29   *So . . . be you.* The sudden transition from morbid preoccupations to instinctive deception is ominous and implies mental derangement—in Elizabethan terms, possession by the devil.

30–31   *Let . . . tongue,* give all your consideration to Banquo, regard him and address him with due deference/He knows that Banquo is away and will be dead by supper time so that Lady Macbeth cannot possibly have to flatter him again. The fierce irony in the light of the ghost's appearance is obvious.

32–3   *Unsafe . . . streams,* in our present insecurity, we must sink our greatness in a show of flattery.

34   *vizards,* masks.

38   *But . . . eterne,* they are not built to an immortal pattern.

42   *shard-borne,* borne on scaly wings/In this speech and the next the imagery is wrenched into that unhealthy cohesion typical of Macbeth's chaotic mind. Reason is excluded, and the imagery conveys the pathological depth of his obsession with satanic atmosphere and needless violence.

43   *yawning,* soporific. But the bat, the beetle, Hecate, the darkness and the pealing bell all have associations with death. The fleeting idea of yawning graves is inevitable, and the whole passage links death with sleep again, at a subconscious level.

44   *of dreadful note.* For most editors 'note' means 'notoriety'. But setting aside the simple meaning (of note=of importance) deprives Macbeth of his ironic, inverted sense of values.

How now my lord? Why do you keep alone,
Of sorriest fancies your companions making,
Using those thoughts which should indeed have died   10
With them they think on? Things without all remedy
Should be without regard. What's done is done.

MACBETH We have scorched the snake, not killed it.
She'll close and be herself, whilst our poor malice
Remains in danger of her former tooth.   15
But let the frame of things disjoint, both the worlds suffer,
Ere we will eat our meal in fear and sleep
In the affliction of these terrible dreams
That shake us nightly. Better be with the dead,
Whom we, to gain our peace, have sent to peace,   20
Than on the torture of the mind to lie
In restless ecstasy. . . Duncan is in his grave.
After life's fitful fever he sleeps well,
Treason has done his worst. Nor steel, nor poison,
Malice domestic, foreign levy, nothing,   25
Can touch him further.

LADY MACBETH   Come on.
Gentle my lord, sleek o'er your rugged looks.
Be bright and jovial among your guests tonight.

MACBETH So shall I, love, and so I pray be you.
Let your remembrance apply to Banquo,   30
Present him eminence both with eye and tongue—
Unsafe the while that we
Must lave our honours in these flattering streams,
And make our faces vizards to our hearts,
Disguising what they are.

LADY MACBETH   You must leave this.   35

MACBETH O full of scorpions is my mind, dear wife.
Thou know'st that Banquo and his Fleance lives.

LADY MACBETH But in them nature's copy's not eterne.

MACBETH There's comfort yet—they are assailable.
Then be thou jocund. Ere the bat hath flown   40
His cloistered flight, ere to black Hecate's summons
The shard-borne beetle with his drowsy hums
Hath rung night's yawning peal, there shall be done
A deed of dreadful note.

45   *Be . . . chuck.* He would spare her the terrible thoughts that guilty knowledge would bring.

46   *seeling.* In falconry the eyes of a hawk in training were blind-folded ('scarfed up'), then its eyelids sewn together ('seeled') to make it tractable.

48–9   *And with . . . pieces.* Again Macbeth dissociates himself from the hand that will kill.

49   *that great bond,* i.e. the lives of Banquo and Fleance, and the promise the witches made for Banquo.

50   *crow,* rook.

55   *ill,* evil.

Scene Three

     (stage direction) three murderers. The third is usually taken to have been sent by Macbeth, who trusts nobody, to make sure of the others. He seems to some extent to take charge.

2   *He needs . . . mistrust,* we need not suspect him.

3   *offices,* duties.

4   *To . . . just,* exactly as Macbeth directed.

6   *lated,* belated.

7   *the timely inn,* the inn in time/Again, the homely thoughts before a ghastly deed.

9–10   *The rest . . . expectation,* all the other guests expected.

LADY MACBETH   What's to be done?

MACBETH   Be innocent of the knowledge dearest chuck,   45
    Till thou applaud the deed. Come seeling night,
    Scarf up the tender eye of pitiful day,
    And with thy bloody and invisible hand
    Cancel and tear to pieces that great bond
    Which keeps me pale. Light thickens, and the crow   50
    Makes wing to the rooky wood.
    Good things of day begin to droop and drowse,
    Whiles night's black agents to their preys do rouse.
    Thou marvell'st at my words. But hold thee still,
    Things bad begun make strong themselves by ill.   55
    So prithee, go with me.   [*Exeunt*

Scene Three

A park near the palace

Enter three MURDERERS

1 MURDERER   But who did bid thee join with us?

3 MURDERER   Macbeth.

2 MURDERER   He needs not our mistrust, since he delivers
    Our offices, and what we have to do,
    To the direction just.

1 MURDERER   Then stand with us.
    The west yet glimmers with some streaks of day.   5
    Now spurs the lated traveller apace
    To gain the timely inn, and near approaches
    The subject of our watch.

3 MURDERER   Hark! I hear horses.

BANQUO   [*within*] Give us a light there, ho!

2 MURDERER   Then 'tis he. The rest
    That are within the note of expectation   10
    Already are in the court.

1 MURDERER   His horses go about.

3 MURDERER   Almost a mile, but he does usually,

18   *(stage direction) he dies.* There is no indication that Banquo's body is removed from the stage, yet he dies on stage. He cannot be visible as Macbeth enters for the banquet scene. Around the main stage was a railing to protect it when the yard was used for bear baiting (see J. W. Saunders, *Shakespeare Survey*, no. 7). The space between the stage and the railing was used as an alley by the actors. If Banquo fell from the stage into the alley it solves the problem of his *Exit*, and he is realistically 'safe in a ditch' as the first murderer later reports to Macbeth.

Scene Four

(stage direction) A banquet. The feast is presented with full ceremonial, at the climax of Macbeth's apparent triumph. Prudence, order and formal relationships are repeatedly noticed, and the occasion should contrast with the chaos of the preceding scene, until the impossibility of an usurper's establishing true order is demonstrated in the intrusion of the murderer and his victim's ghost.

1–2   *At first . . . last,* from beginning to end.

3   *society,* the guests.

4   *play . . . host.* The word 'play' is especially telling. Macbeth speaks so often in terms of pretence, even here when it is not needed. It speaks the self-consciousness of the King about his royalty; he has no natural grace.

5   *keeps her state,* remains in her chair of state.   *state,* a chair of state with a canopy.

6   *require . . . welcome,* ask her to express her welcome.

So all men do, from hence to the palace gate
Make it their walk.

Enter BANQUO · *and* FLEANCE *with a torch*

2 MURDERER   A light, a light!

3 MURDERER   'Tis he.   15

1 MURDERER   Stand to't.

BANQUO   It will be rain tonight.

1 MURDERER   Let it come down.
                           [*They set upon* BANQUO]

BANQUO   O treachery! Fly good Fleance, fly, fly, fly!
    Thou mayst revenge . . . O slave!   [*He dies.* FLEANCE *escapes*

3 MURDERER   Who did strike out the light?

1 MURDERER   Was't not the way?

3 MURDERER   There's but one down; the son is fled.

2 MURDERER   We have lost   20
    Best half of our affair.

1 MURDERER   Well let's away, and say how much is done.   [*Exeunt*

Scene Four

The palace

A banquet prepared. Enter MACBETH · LADY MACBETH · ROSS · LENNOX ·
LORDS · *and Attendants*

MACBETH   You know your own degrees. Sit down. At first
    And last the hearty welcome.

LORDS   Thanks to your Majesty.

MACBETH   Ourself will mingle with society,
    And play the humble host.
    Our hostess keeps her state, but in best time   5
    We will require her welcome.

LADY MACBETH   Pronounce it for me sir, to all our friends,
    For my heart speaks they are welcome.

Enter FIRST MURDERER *to the door*

MACBETH   See, they encounter thee with their hearts' thanks.

10   *Both . . . midst,* the table is evenly occupied on each side; I will sit here among you.

11   *a measure,* a toast.

14   *'Tis . . . within,* it is better outside you than inside him/It could have got on his face from his hand when he removed his mask.

18   *nonpareil,* paragon.

20   *fit.* A critical mental seizure. Macbeth's disorder is expressed in the highly excited lines that follow. He has spoken like this before in other 'fits.'

21   *founded,* secure.

22   *broad and general,* free and untrammelled.   *casing,* encompassing.

23   *cribbed,* boxed in.

24   *saucy,* nagging.

25   *bides,* waits.

26   *trenched,* deeply cut.

27   *a . . . nature,* a mortal blow.

28   *worm,* serpent.

31   *We'll . . . again,* we'll talk more fully.

32–6 *The feast . . . it,* if we neglect to acknowledge our guests throughout a feast, we are no better than caterers. The whole point of giving a banquet is to welcome guests. Mere eating is best done at home. Away from home, gracious entertainment gives food its savour. A social occasion would be lacking without it.

36   *(stage direction) The Ghost . . . seat.* The Folio indicates the entry of the Ghost at this point. Most editors put the entry after l.39, some at various points down to l.45. The astrologer Simon Forman saw the play on Saturday 20 April 1611, and wrote that the ghost 'came and sat down in his chair behind' Macbeth who was standing ready to 'drink a carouse to him.'

Both sides are even. Here I'll sit in the midst.   10
Be large in mirth! Anon we'll drink a measure
The table round. [*goes to the door*]
There's blood upon thy face.

MURDERER   'Tis Banquo's then.

MACBETH 'Tis better thee without than he within.
    Is he dispatched?

MURDERER   My lord, his throat is cut,   15
    That I did for him.

MACBETH   Thou art the best o' the cut-throats.
    Yet he's good that did the like for Fleance.
    If thou didst it, thou art the nonpareil.

MURDERER Most royal sir . . . Fleance is scaped.

MACBETH Then comes my fit again. I had else been perfect,   20
    Whole as the marble, founded as the rock,
    As broad and general as the casing air.
    But now I am cabined, cribbed, confined, bound in
    To saucy doubts and fears. But Banquo's safe?

MURDERER Ay my good lord, safe in a ditch he bides   25
    With twenty trenched gashes on his head,
    The least a death to nature.

MACBETH   Thanks for that.
    There the grown serpent lies. The worm that's fled
    Hath nature that in time will venom breed,
    No teeth for the present . . . Get thee gone, tomorrow   30
    We'll hear ourselves again.   [*Exit* MURDERER

LADY MACBETH   My royal lord,
    You do not give the cheer. The feast is sold
    That is not often vouched, while 'tis a-making,
    'Tis given with welcome. To feed were best at home.
    From thence the sauce to meat is ceremony—   35
    Meeting were bare without it.

The GHOST OF BANQUO *enters, and sits in Macbeth's seat*

MACBETH   Sweet remembrancer!
    Now, good digestion wait on appetite,
    And health on both.

LENNOX   May't please your Highness sit?

39   *our . . . honour.* Banquo himself, in whom Macbeth with extravagant flattery identifies all Scotland's honour.
roofed, under one roof.

40   *graced,* full of grace.

41-2   *Who . . . mischance,* whom I hope I may have to censure for
lack of due regard, rather than pity for some accident that
has befallen him.

42-3   *His . . . promise,* he is to blame for not keeping his promise to
attend.

47   *moves,* perturbs.

48   *done this?* i.e. murdered Banquo. Macbeth has taken care
this time not to soil his own hands with blood, and so to
avoid the haunting thoughts that followed Duncan's killing.
The visitation is therefore not only terrifying but bewildering.
The question is a desperate cover for himself, followed up in
the next line.

49   *Thou . . . did it.* Said to the Ghost, but at this stage I think
Macbeth still has half his mind on the rest of the company,
and so far he does not know he is alone in experiencing the
visitation.   *shake,* nod.

54   *upon a thought,* in a moment.

56   *You . . . passion,* you will make him worse and prolong his
disorder/'Offend' meaning 'harm' is commonplace. Most
editors take 'offend' to mean 'vex', but I cannot see how
Lady Macbeth can pretend that Macbeth may be annoyed
and also that he is lost in a fit.

57-83   *Are you . . . forget.* All this is spoken aside, at the front of the
stage, while the guests behind obey Lady Macbeth and
silently go on eating, their forced preoccupation in this
commonplace action providing a grotesque contrast to the
dialogue. This background augments the horror with
tension, as they gradually stop eating to 'muse at' him.

60   *very painting . . . fear,* spurious vision bred of your cowardice.
Cf. Act1 Sc.2, l.54.

61   *air-drawn,* drawn in and through the air.

62   *flaws and starts,* sudden outbursts and fits.

63   *to,* compared with.

65   *Authorized,* vouched for.

70   *charnel-houses,* vaults where the bones of the dead are stored.

MACBETH   Here had we now our country's honour roofed
   Were the graced person of our Banquo present,   **40**
   Who may I rather challenge for unkindness,
   Than pity for mischance.

ROSS   His absence sir,
   Lays blame upon his promise. Please't your Highness
   To grace us with your royal company.

MACBETH   The table's full.

LENNOX   Here is a place reserved, sir.   **45**

MACBETH   Where?

LENNOX   Here my good lord ... What is't that moves your Highness?

MACBETH   Which of you have done this?

LORDS   What, my good lord?

MACBETH   Thou canst not say I did it, never shake
   Thy gory locks at me.   **50**

ROSS   Gentlemen rise, his Highness is not well.

LADY MACBETH   Sit worthy friends. My lord is often thus
   And hath been from his youth. Pray you keep seat.
   The fit is momentary—upon a thought
   He will again be well. If much you note him   **55**
   You shall offend him, and extend his passion.
   Feed, and regard him not ... Are you a man?

MACBETH   Ay, and a bold one, that dare look on that
   Which might appal the devil.

LADY MACBETH   O proper stuff!
   This is the very painting of your fear.   **60**
   This is the air-drawn dagger which you said
   Led you to Duncan. O these flaws and starts,
   (Impostors to true fear) would well become
   A woman's story at a winter's fire,
   Authorized by her grandam ... Shame itself!   **65**
   Why do you make such faces? When all's done,
   You look but on a stool.

MACBETH   Prithee, see there!
   Behold! look! lo! how say you?
   Why what care I? If thou canst nod, speak too.
   If charnel-houses and our graves must send   **70**

71–2   *our . . . kites,* we shall have to leave the dead to be safely disposed of by kites.

72   *quite . . . folly.* Possibly 'such a coward in your madness!' but probably 'so mad that you're not fit for company!' Lady Macbeth is not taunting him for foolish behaviour.

    unmanned. 'Turned coward' is the sense usually taken. However in falconry 'unmanned' referred to a hawk unready for human company. This sense (? suggested by Macbeth's reference to kites) suits the context, expresses Lady Macbeth's primary concern with the effect on the company, and seems to make better sense with 'folly,' meaning 'madness'.

75   *Ere . . . weal,* before civilized laws gave us a healthy and peaceful society/Macbeth is horrified at the unnatural consequences of murder, in which the present state contrasts with both civilized society and the barbarous past. His state is unique in its reversal of natural order.

80   *twenty mortal murders,* twenty deadly wounds. In his brooding Macbeth recollects the precise number given him by the murderer in l.26.

83   *do lack you,* miss your company.

84   *muse at,* wonder at.

87   *(stage direction)* The Folio gives the Ghost's entry here. Some editors mark the entry at various points between this line and l.91.

90   *thirst,* desire to drink.

91   *And all to all,* all good health to all.   *Our . . . pledge,* we offer you our loyalty and a toast!

92   *Avaunt,* Be off!

94   *speculation,* comprehension.

96   *a thing of custom,* a matter of habit.

98   *What . . . dare.* Macbeth continues his last speech, not hearing his wife in his mental seizure.

99   *rugged,* shaggy.

100   *Hyrcan.* Hyrcania was a province of the Persian empire on the Black Sea renowned (through Virgil) for the ferocity of its tigers.

Those that we bury back, our monuments
Shall be the maws of kites.   [GHOST *disappears*

LADY MACBETH   What, quite unmanned in folly?

MACBETH   If I stand here, I saw him.

LADY MACBETH   Fie for shame!

MACBETH   Blood hath been shed ere now, in the olden time,
Ere humane statute purged the gentle weal,   75
Ay, and since too, murders have been performed
Too terrible for the ear. The time has been,
That when the brains were out the man would die,
And there an end. But now they rise again
With twenty mortal murders on their crowns,   80
And push us from our stools. This is more strange
Than such a murder is.

LADY MACBETH   My worthy lord,
Your noble friends do lack you.

MACBETH   I do forget . . .
Do not muse at me, my most worthy friends,
I have a strange infirmity which is nothing   85
To those that know me. Come, love and health to all,
Then I'll sit down . . . Give me some wine . . . fill full.

Re-enter GHOST

I drink to the general joy o' the whole table.
And to our dear friend Banquo, whom we miss.
Would he were here. To all, and him, we thirst,   90
And all to all.

LORDS   Our duties, and the pledge!

MACBETH   Avaunt, and quit my sight! let the earth hide thee!
Thy bones are marrowless, thy blood is cold,
Thou hast no speculation in those eyes
Which thou dost glare with!

LADY MACBETH   Think of this good peers,   95
But as a thing of custom. 'Tis no other,
Only it spoils the pleasure of the time.

MACBETH   What man dare, I dare.
Approach thou like the rugged Russian bear,
The armed rhinoceros, or the Hyrcan tiger—   100

101 *Take . . . that.* Macbeth will face anything (even the supernatural) except the sight of his murdered victim. It has the
same effect as the dreams that 'shake' him, but is a more
devastating manifestation. *nerves,* sinews. Macbeth is
shaking physically.

103 *dare . . . desert,* challenge me to a fight to the death.

104 *If . . . then,* if I then harbour fear. The phrase has been much
discussed and many emendations suggested, but the basic
meaning is clear, and 'inhabit' could mean 'house.'
protest me, proclaim me.

105 *The . . . girl,* a slip of a girl. (A phrase like 'a giant of a man',
'a brute of a boy'.)

106 *Unreal mockery,* counterfeit shadow. Macbeth tries to dismiss
the Ghost as an insubstantial creation of his own imagination, to deny the visitation.

108 *displaced,* banished.

109 *admired disorder,* astonishing and frenzied behaviour.

110 *overcome us,* come over us.

111–2 *You . . . owe,* you make me feel a stranger to myself/He still
thinks Lady Macbeth, who has shared his guilt for Duncan's
murder, can also see the Ghost. He has forgotten that he
told her 'be innocent of the knowledge.' *owe,* possess.

115 *mine,* i.e. the natural ruby of my cheeks.

118–9 *Stand . . . once,* do not wait to leave in order of precedence,
but break up at once.

122 *Stones . . . move,* i.e. to reveal the corpse of a victim concealed
beneath them.

123 *Augures,* i.e. auguries: the interpretation of omens seen in the
behaviour of birds, and in their entrails after sacrifice.
understood relations, the expert interpretation of the relationship between signs and omens and what they portend.

124 *magot-pies,* magpies. *choughs,* jackdaws, or any of the smaller chattering birds in the crow family. All these birds had
ominous associations. For instance, seven magpies meant the
devil was present, four meant death; rooks gathered around
the house of a dying man 'because they smell a corpse.' All
these birds are 'gossips.'

126 *Almost . . . which.* Lady Macbeth answers Macbeth's weary
question in a voice that is spent. Wilson sees the line as 'a
symbolical timing of the central moment of the play; borne
out by the immediate reference to Macduff who is to usher
in the dawn.'

127–8 *How . . . bidding.* What do you say to this—Macduff will not
present himself at our command/So Macduff affronts
Macbeth's authority, and a new development, the challenge
that re-establishes order and natural royalty, is initiated.

Take any shape but that, and my firm nerves
Shall never tremble. Or be alive again,
And dare me to the desert with thy sword;
If trembling I inhabit then, protest me
The baby of a girl. Hence horrible shadow,   105
Unreal mockery, hence!   [GHOST *disappears*
                 Why, so . . . being gone,
I am a man again . . . Pray you sit still.

LADY MACBETH You have displaced the mirth, broke the good
   meeting
With most admired disorder.

MACBETH   Can such things be,
And overcome us like a summer's cloud,   110
Without our special wonder? You make me strange
Even to the disposition that I owe,
When now I think you can behold such sights,
And keep the natural ruby of your cheeks,
When mine is blanched with fear.

ROSS   What sights, my lord?   115

LADY MACBETH I pray you speak not, he grows worse and worse.
Question enrages him. At once, good night . . .
Stand not upon the order of your going,
But go at once.

LENNOX   Good night, and better health
Attend his Majesty.

LADY MACBETH   A kind good night to all.   120
           [*Exeunt all but* MACBETH *and* LADY MACBETH

MACBETH It will have blood, they say: blood will have blood.
Stones have been known to move, and trees to speak.
Augures and understood relations have
By magot-pies and choughs and rooks brought forth
The secretest man of blood . . . What is the night?   125

LADY MACBETH Almost at odds with morning, which is which.

MACBETH How say'st thou that Macduff denies his person
At our great bidding?

LADY MACBETH   Did you send to him sir?

MACBETH I hear it by the way; but I will send.
There's not a one of them but in his house   130

131   *a servant fee'd*, a paid spy. The simple statement indicates the disorder in the realm, and the fact that Macduff is not alone in being suspected.

134   *the worst . . . good*. The punctuation is Sisson's, and points the fundamental contradiction of 'worst' and 'good.' Most editions have 'the worst. For mine own good . . .'

135   *causes*, considerations.

137   *Returning . . . go o'er*. The dull weariness, which develops into despair, exists in all alternatives.   *as go o'er*, as struggling on.

138–9   *Strange . . . scanned*, I have in my mind remarkable things that demand to be resolved in action before they can be examined by me/Again Macbeth speaks as if his intentions and his hands have wills of their own and he is not answerable for their actions.

140   *season . . . sleep*, sleep, by which all human life is preserved/ Burton wrote: 'Sleep is a rest or binding of the outward senses . . . for the preservation of body and soul . . . The phantasy alone is free, and his commander, reason, as appears by those imaginary dreams which are of diverse kinds, natural, divine, demoniacal, etc.' It is important that for Shakespeare 'reason' was alert during sleep, and the 'terrible dreams' indicate the overpowering of reason by evil forces.

141   *strange and self-abuse*, remarkable delusions.

142   *initiate*, novice's.   *wants hard use*, needs toughening with practice.

Scene Five

This scene, different in style and conception from the rest of *Macbeth*, was probably not written by Shakespeare, but added about 1616 to lead into the songs, 'Come away, come away' here, and 'Black Spirits' in Act4 Sc.1, which had been introduced into *Macbeth* from Thomas Middleton's play, *The Witch*. *The Witch* (not printed till 1778) still exists in a copy made by Ralph Crane, one of the scriveners to the King's Men after Shakespeare's death, who provided the copy from which some of the plays in the first Folio were printed. The author of the Hecate scenes is unknown.

2   *beldams*, old hags.

3   *saucy*, presumptuous.

7   *close*, secret.

11   *wayward son*. Intractable, possibly because he has tried to frustrate the prophecies about Banquo.

15   *pit of Acheron*. In Elizabethan literature, hell. Acheron was a river in Hades in ancient mythology.

I keep a servant fee'd. I will tomorrow,
(And betimes I will) to the Weird Sisters.
More shall they speak, for now I am bent to know
By the worst means, the worst, for mine own good.
All causes shall give way. I am in blood   135
Stepped in so far that should I wade no more
Returning were as tedious as go o'er.
Strange things I have in head that will to hand,
Which must be acted ere they may be scanned.

LADY MACBETH   You lack the season of all natures, sleep.   140

MACBETH   Come, we'll to sleep. My strange and self-abuse
Is the initiate fear that wants hard use.
We are yet but young in deed.   [*Exeunt*

Scene Five

The heath

Thunder. Enter the three WITCHES *meeting* HECATE

1 WITCH   Why how now Hecate, you look angerly.

HECATE   Have I not reason, beldams as you are,
Saucy and overbold? How did you dare
To trade and traffic with Macbeth
In riddles and affairs of death,   5
And I, the mistress of your charms,
The close contriver of all harms,
Was never called to bear my part,
Or show the glory of our art?
And, which is worse, all you have done   10
Hath been but for a wayward son,
Spiteful, and wrathful, who, as others do,
Loves for his own ends, not for you.
But make amends now. Get you gone,
And at the pit of Acheron   15
Meet me i' the morning; thither he
Will come to know his destiny.
Your vessels and your spells provide,
Your charms and every thing beside.

21 *dismal*, disastrous.

23–4 *Upon . . . profound*. 'A foam which the moon was supposed to shed . . . when strongly solicited by enchantment.' (Steevens) Called the *virus lunare*.

27 *artificial sprites*, i.e. the apparitions in Act4Sc.1.
   artificial, ingenious.

28 *illusion*, deception.

29 *confusion*, ruin.

32 *security*, over-confidence.

35 *little spirit*, familiar spirit.

36 *foggy cloud*. Hecate makes her exit in a stage car drawn up through a trap in the 'heavens' by pulleys, and concealed in a 'cloud' of draperies. (Wilson)

Scene Six 1–2 *My . . . further*, what I have already said has only confirmed your own thoughts, and you can draw your own conclusions/Again this scene relieves the tension, this time with an exposition and commentary. The mood of the country is clearly conveyed, together with the suspicion of Macbeth, and the mustering of the powers of good against him.

3 *borne*, managed.

4 *marry*, well, of course.

5 *right-valiant*. He is cynically quoting Macbeth's opinion.

7 *Men . . . late*. A bitter echo of the cynical reason a murderer gives for his deed in *The Spanish Tragedy*, by Thomas Kyd, one of the most popular Elizabethan revenge plays.

8 *Who . . . thought*, who can help thinking. Logically the sense required 'Who *can* want the thought.' But the line as it stands carries with it an implication of '*I* cannot want the thought . . . ,' the idea at the back of the speaker's mind, from which the question surely derives.

10 *fact*, deed.

12 *pious rage*, passionate devotion. The phrase glances ironically at the divinity of the King, Duncan. *delinquents*, shirkers who failed in their duty. *tear*, lacerate.

13 *thralls*, captives.

I am for the air; this night I'll spend   20
Unto a dismal and a fatal end.
Great business must be wrought ere noon.
Upon the corner of the moon
There hangs a vaporous drop profound.
I'll catch it ere it come to ground;   25
And that distilled by magic sleights,
Shall raise such artificial sprites,
As, by the strength of their illusion,
Shall draw him on to his confusion.
He shall spurn fate, scorn death, and bear   30
His hopes 'bove wisdom, grace, and fear;
And you all know security
Is mortals' chiefest enemy.
                    [*song within*, 'Come away, come away,' etc.]
Hark! I am called; my little spirit, see,   35
Sits in a foggy cloud, and stays for me.   [*Exit*
1 WITCH   Come, let's make haste, she'll soon be back again.   [*Exeunt*

Scene Six

Somewhere in Scotland

Enter LENNOX *and another* LORD

LENNOX   My former speeches have but hit your thoughts,
        Which can interpret further. Only I say
        Things have been strangely borne. The gracious Duncan
        Was pitied of Macbeth—marry he was dead!
        And the right-valiant Banquo walked too late,   5
        Whom you may say, if't please you, Fleance killed,
        For Fleance fled. Men must not walk too late.
        Who cannot want the thought how monstrous
        It was for Malcom and for Donalbain
        To kill their gracious father? Damned fact!   10
        How it did grieve Macbeth! Did he not straight
        In pious rage the two delinquents tear,
        That were the slaves of drink and thralls of sleep?
        Was not that nobly done? Ay and wisely too,
        For 'twould have angered any heart alive   15

17   *borne . . . well*, settled everything well.

19   *an't*, if it.

20   *What t'were*, what it meant.

21   *broad words*, unguarded talk

22   *tyrant's*. The word meant 'usurper' as well as 'oppressor.' Macbeth here first acquires this title.

23   *disgrace*, disfavour.

24–37   *The son . . . for now*. Macbeth, though a murderer, is nonetheless crowned King, and to satisfy contemporary assumptions Shakespeare had to justify insurrection, even against a Macbeth, in the clearest terms. In this passage, he does this almost incidentally, as he propounds the developing conflict of good versus evil. At the outset he contrasts Malcolm's true lineage ('son of Duncan') with the 'tyrant' who usurped his birthright. Macduff's prayers, the holiness of Edward the Confessor, and the blessing of the Almighty are with Malcolm. The reference to sleep, banquets and knives recall directly the terms in which Shakespeare has conveyed the chaotic effect of Macbeth's sin against God and nature. By making Malcolm the agent of God and natural order against the dark disease of Macbeth's Scotland, Shakespeare identifies true royalty in him and authorizes the deposition of Macbeth.

25   *holds*, withholds.

28–9   *That . . . respect*, that his extreme misfortune in no way detracts from the respect he is shown.

30   *upon his aid*, on his behalf.

31   *wake*, call to arms.

35   *Free . . . knives*, rid our feasts and banquets of the threat of murder.

36   *free honours*, titles untainted with corruption.

38   *exasperate*, incensed.   *the King*, i.e. Macbeth.

40   *with . . . not I*, having got a point blank refusal from Macduff.

41   *cloudy*, sullen.   *turns me*, turns. 'Me' is the ethic dative which Shakespeare often used.

42   *hums*, mutters to himself.

43   *clogs*, burdens. The messenger knows that Macbeth will react violently to ill tidings.

44–5   *Advise . . . provide*, induce him to safeguard himself by prudently setting as great a distance as possible between himself and Macbeth.

48–9   *suffering . . . Under*, i.e. country suffering under.

To hear the men deny it. So that I say
He has borne all things well. And I do think
That had he Duncan's sons under his key
(As, an't please heaven, he shall not) they should find
What 'twere to kill a father. So should Fleance.   20
But peace—for from broad words, and 'cause he failed
His presence at the tyrant's feast, I hear
Macduff lives in disgrace. Sir, can you tell
Where he bestows himself?

LORD   The son of Duncan,
From whom this tyrant holds the due of birth,   25
Lives in the English court, and is received
Of the most pious Edward with such grace,
That the malevolence of fortune nothing
Takes from his high respect. Thither Macduff
Is gone to pray the holy king, upon his aid   30
To wake Northumberland and warlike Siward,
That by the help of these (with Him above
To ratify the work) we may again
Give to our tables meat, sleep to our nights,
Free from our feasts and banquets bloody knives,   35
Do faithful homage, and receive free honours,
All which we pine for now. And this report
Hath so exasperate the King, that he
Prepares for some attempt of war.

LENNOX   Sent he to Macduff?

LORD   He did; and with an absolute 'Sir, not I',   40
The cloudy messenger turns me his back,
And hums, as who should say, 'You'll rue the time
That clogs me with this answer.'

LENNOX   And that well might
Advise him to a caution, to hold what distance
His wisdom can provide. Some holy angel   45
Fly to the court of England, and unfold
His message ere he come, that a swift blessing
May soon return to this our suffering country
Under a hand accursed.

LORD   I'll send my prayers with him.   [Exeunt

D

(*stage direction*) Most editors identify the scene in a 'dark cave,' that is 'the pit of Acheron' mentioned in Act 3 Sc.5, l.15, a scene, however, probably not written by Shakespeare. But since the 'locks' open at the witch's command to admit Macbeth at his knocking (1.48) Shakespeare clearly has a building in mind.

1   *brinded cat*, i.e. Greymalkin (Act 1 Sc.1, l.8).   *brinded*, brindled, tabby.

2   *hedge-pig*, hedgehog.

3   *Harpier*. The familiar of the third witch, probably a corrupt form of 'harpy,' a monster with wings and claws and a woman's body. The harpies were ministers of revenge.

8   *Sweltered venom*, sweated poison.

12   *fenny*, from the marshes.

16   *fork*, forked tongue.   *blind-worm*, i.e. slow worm, formerly thought to be poisonous.

22   *dragon*. No more fabulous in Shakespeare's day than the rhinoceros. In 'the ancient Temples of the Heathen-Idolaters' the devil appeared 'in the ugly form and nature of the dragon.' (Topsell *History of Serpents*, 1608).

23   *mummy*, dried flesh. Mummified flesh was highly valued for its medicinal virtues. Wilson quotes from *Daemonologie* by James I, how the devil 'causeth them to joint dead corpses and to make powders thereof, mixing such other things there amongst, as he gives unto them.'   *gulf*, belly.

24   *ravined*. Gorged (with human prey) seems the best interpretation, but 'ravenous' and 'ravening' are possible.

25   *digged i' the dark*, i.e. to heighten the effect of the poison in the plant.

27   *yew*. Widely grown in graveyards, held to be poisonous in past ages, and a symbol of grief.

28   *Slivered*, sliced.   *in . . . eclipse*. An eclipse threatened disaster, and the supremacy of evil designs.

Act Four · Scene One

Thunder. Enter the three WITCHES

1 WITCH   Thrice the brinded cat hath mewed.

2 WITCH   Thrice and once the hedge-pig whined.

3 WITCH   Harpier cries! 'Tis time, 'Tis time!

1 WITCH   Round about the cauldron go,
In the poisoned entrails throw.   5
Toad, that under cold stone
Days and nights has thirty-one
Sweltered venom sleeping got,
Boil thou first i' the charmed pot.

ALL   Double, double toil and trouble,   10
Fire burn, and cauldron bubble.

2 WITCH   Fillet of a fenny snake,
In the cauldron boil and bake,
Eye of newt, and toe of frog,
Wool of bat, and tongue of dog,   15
Adder's fork, and blind-worm's sting,
Lizard's leg, and howlet's wing,
For a charm of powerful trouble,
Like a hell-broth boil and bubble.

ALL   Double, double toil and trouble,   20
Fire burn, and cauldron bubble.

3 WITCH   Scale of dragon, tooth of wolf,
Witches' mummy, maw and gulf
Of the ravined salt-sea shark,
Root of hemlock digged i' the dark,   25
Liver of blaspheming Jew,
Gall of goat, and slips of yew
Slivered in the moon's eclipse,

29   *Turk, Tartar's.* These people were renowned for savagery, and with the Jews (l.26), were anti-Christ.

30   *birth-strangled.* Hence unchristened.

32   *slab,* thick.

33   *chaudron,* guts.

38–43   *(stage direction) Enter Hecate . . . three witches.* Almost certainly this is an addition to the play, not intended by Shakespeare. It is safe to say that the extra witches and Hecate are introduced simply to perform the song, which appears also in Thomas Middleton's play *The Witch.* The passage is best ignored.

44   *the pricking . . . thumbs,* the pricking sensation in my thumbs.

46–7   *Open . . . knocks.* At the sound of distant knocking in the tiring house (backstage) the door leading to the main stage swings open on the witch's command.

48   *black,* evil.

50   *conjure,* adjure. Macbeth calls upon them, in the name of witchcraft ('that which you profess'), as if he had power of necromancy. His urgency soon devours him, and the turbulent language of his 'fit' gathers its own overwhelming momentum.

52–3   *Though . . . churches.* Witches were thought to raise storms at will. Shakespeare's emphasis of the conflict with churches is significant.

53   *yesty,* foaming.

54   *navigation,* shipping.

55   *bladed,* i.e. before the ear is formed.   *lodged,* laid flat.

57   *slope,* bend.

58–9   *though . . . together,* though the source of all future creation is annihilated in chaos. Cf. note on Act 1 Sc.3, l.58, and *King Lear,* Act 3 Sc.2, l.

        Strike flat the thick rotundity o' the world!
        Crack nature's moulds, all germens spill at once
        That makes ingrateful man!

     and *The Winter's Tale,* Act 4 Sc.4, l.490:

        Let nature crush the sides o' the earth together
        And mar the seeds within.

60   *sicken,* grows sick of destruction.

60–61   *Even . . . ask you.* In his invocation to the witches Macbeth lurches into a crescendo of destruction, till his final demand can only be spoken in a voice of desperate exhaustion. He is beside himself, possessed by his mission, and the witches' reaction acknowledges his total commitment to evil.

Nose of Turk, and Tartar's lips,
Finger of birth-strangled babe
Ditch-delivered by a drab,   30
Make the gruel thick and slab.
Add thereto a tiger's chaudron,
For the ingredients of our cauldron.

ALL   Double, double toil and trouble,   35
Fire burn, and cauldron bubble.

2 WITCH   Cool it with a baboon's blood,
Then the charm is firm and good.

Enter HECATE *and the other three* WITCHES

HECATE   O well done! I commend your pains,
And every one shall share i' the gains.   40
And now about the cauldron sing,
Like elves and fairies in a ring,
Enchanting all that you put in.

               [*music and a song,* 'Black spirits,' etc.]
                 [*Exit* HECATE *with the other three* WITCHES

2 WITCH   By the pricking of my thumbs,
Something wicked this way comes.   45
           Open, locks,
           Whoever knocks.

Enter MACBETH

MACBETH   How now, you secret, black, and midnight hags!
What is't you do?

ALL   A deed without a name.

MACBETH   I conjure you by that which you profess,   50
Howe'er you come to know it, answer me.
Though you untie the winds and let them fight
Against the churches, though the yesty waves
Confound and swallow navigation up,
Though bladed corn be lodged and trees blown down,   55
Though castles topple on their warders' heads,
Though palaces and pyramids do slope
Their heads to their foundations, though the treasure
Of nature's germens tumble all together,
Even till destruction sicken—answer me   60

63   *Call . . . see 'em.* His violence expresses his state of mind.
65   *farrow*, litter.
67   *high or low*, i.e. in rank.
68   *(stage direction) First Apparition*, etc. The witches' 'masters' were
      devils, and therefore able to 'foretell future events' and 'be
      seen when, and in what shape, and to whom they will'
      (Burton). The demons assume the shape of the apparitions,
      and speak with their own authority. Macbeth takes the
      'armed head' to represent Macduff. But in reality it foretells
      his own decapitation by Macduff. In all three apparitions
      Macbeth is deceived by the 'juggling fiends.'
72   *Enough.* 'He is in torment.' (Muir)
74   *harped*, guessed.
76   *(stage direction) a bloody child*, i.e. Macduff, 'from his mother's
      womb untimely ripped.'
84   *take . . . fate*, compel fate to underwrite its promise. Even when
      the promise seems complete, Macbeth mistrusts and again
      sets out to master fate.
85   *That . . . it lies*, so that I may deny that fear exists.
86   *in . . . thunder*, i.e. soundly. There is a hint at the notion that
      witches raised thunder.

To what I ask you.

1 WITCH   Speak.

2 WITCH   Demand.

3 WITCH   We'll answer.

1 WITCH Say if thou'dst rather hear it from our mouths,
Or from our masters?

MACBETH   Call 'em, let me see 'em.

1 WITCH Pour in sow's blood, that hath eaten
Her nine farrow; grease that's sweaten   65
From the murderer's gibbet throw
Into the flame.

ALL   Come high or low,
Thyself and office deftly show.

Thunder. FIRST APPARITION, *an armed head*

MACBETH Tell me, thou unknown power—

1 WITCH   He knows thy thought.
Hear his speech, but say thou nought.   70

1 APPARITION Macbeth, Macbeth, Macbeth! beware Macduff.
Beware the Thane of Fife. Dismiss me. Enough. *[Descends*

MACBETH Whate'er thou art, for thy good caution thanks.
Thou hast harped my fear aright. But one word more—

1 WITCH He will not be commanded. Here's another, 75
More potent than the first.

Thunder. SECOND APPARITION, *a bloody child*

2 APPARITION Macbeth, Macbeth, Macbeth!

MACBETH Had I three ears, I'd hear thee.

2 APPARITION Be bloody, bold and resolute. Laugh to scorn
The power of man, for none of woman born 80
Shall harm Macbeth.   *[Descends*

MACBETH Then live Macduff, what need I fear of thee?
But yet I'll make assurance double sure
And take a bond of fate. Thou shalt not live,
That I may tell pale-hearted fear it lies, 85
And sleep in spite of thunder.

86   *(stage direction) a child crowned*, i.e. Malcolm, who later gives the
       order to his soldiers to hew down branches as they approach
       Dunsinane.

88–9   *round And top*, supreme crown.

91   *chafes*, is angry.

95   *impress*, muster into an army.

96   *bodements*, prophecies.

97–100 *Rebellious . . . custom*. Macbeth, absorbed in the prophecies,
       identifies himself with the powers that are addressing him,
       and continuing their rhyme speaks his own prophecy. In the
       phrase 'Rebellious dead, rise never' he recollects Banquo's
       ghost and at the same time speaks out of the future, as if all
       his rebellious enemies have been dispatched. In his trance he
       speaks of himself as of a third person.

99   *lease of nature*, full term of life. Here (as often) Macbeth speaks
       in legal terms. His mind keeps recalling the question of law
       and trust.   *pay*, yield.

100   *mortal custom*, natural death.

101   *art*, particular skill.

106   *noise*, music. The music sounds while the cauldron sinks on
       the main trapdoor.

111   *(stage direction) eight kings*. The show (dumb-show) represents
       the eight kings of the Stuart line with Mary Queen of Scots,
       mother of James I, omitted. 'A glass' mirrors the future.

113   *hair*. The word could have the meaning 'aspect', 'outward
       characteristic' in Elizabethan English.

115   *Filthy*, repulsive.

116   *Start*, i.e. start from your sockets and see no more.

Thunder. THIRD APPARITION, *a child crowned, with a tree in his hand*

                    What is this,
That rises like the issue of a king,
And wears upon his baby brow the round
And top of sovereignty?

ALL   Listen, but speak not to it.

3 APPARITION   Be lion-mettled, proud and take no care   90
Who chafes, who frets, or where conspirers are.
Macbeth shall never vanquished be until
Great Birnam wood to high Dunsinane hill
Shall come against him.   [*Descends*

MACBETH   That will never be.
Who can impress the forest, bid the tree   95
Unfix his earth-bound root? Sweet bodements, good!
Rebellious dead, rise never till the wood
Of Birnam rise, and our high-placed Macbeth
Shall live the lease of nature, pay his breath
To time and mortal custom. Yet my heart   100
Throbs to know one thing: tell me, if your art
Can tell so much, shall Banquo's issue ever
Reign in this kingdom?

ALL   Seek to know no more.

MACBETH   I will be satisfied. Deny me this,
And an eternal curse fall on you. Let me know . . .   105
Why sinks that cauldron, and what noise is this? [*hautboys*]

1 WITCH   Show!

2 WITCH   Show!

3 WITCH   Show!

ALL   Show his eyes, and grieve his heart,   110
Come like shadows, so depart.

A show of eight kings, the last with a glass in his hand, BANQUO *following*

MACBETH   Thou art too like the spirit of Banquo. Down!
Thy crown does sear mine eyeballs, and thy hair,
Thou other gold-bound brow, is like the first . . .
A third is like the former . . . Filthy hags,   115
Why do you show me this? A fourth? Start, eyes!

117   *the crack of doom,* the trumpet blast or thunder-clap heralding
          Judgment Day.

119   *a glass,* i.e. a prospective glass, a crystal supposed to reveal the
          future.

121   *twofold balls,* two orbs.   *treble sceptres.* James I was crowned at
          Scone and at Westminster; one sceptre was used in Scotland,
          two in England.

123   *blood-boltered,* i.e. with his hair matted with blood.

125–32   *Ay sir . . . and vanish.* Almost without doubt not by Shakespeare,
          but an interpolation of disastrous effect to introduce the
          'dance.' Again, best ignored.

126   *thus amazedly,* in such bewilderment. They may well ask, as
          Macbeth knew the prophecy concerning Banquo from the
          outset. He acts against fate, and curses the prophecies when
          they do not match his wishes.

127   *sprites,* spirits.

129   *I'll . . . sound.* The music would sound from the musician's
          gallery high above the stage, so fulfilling the witch's injunc-
          tion.

130   *antic round,* fantastic dance.

131   *this great King.* Ostensibly Macbeth, but probably addressed by
          the interpolator to a King in the audience, probably James I.
          kindly, duly.

132   *Our . . . pay,* we showed him a respectful welcome. The
          speeches given to the witches in the interpolated passages
          are lady-like compared with the fury Shakespeare gives
          them. They no longer embody the forces of evil.

134   *aye,* always.

135   *without there,* from outside. Lennox has been standing guard
          offstage.

138   *Infected,* contaminated with the plague.

139   *damned . . . them.* He ironically damns himself, and this wish is
          fulfilled as each of his deeds to forestall the prophecies
          ironically further their fulfilment.

144   *anticipat'st,* forestall.

145–6   *The . . . with it,* the fleeting intention never gets fulfilled unless
          we act upon it as soon as we think of it.

147–8   *The very . . . hand* I shall at once turn wishes into deeds.

What, will the line stretch out to the crack of doom?
Another yet . . . A seventh? I'll see no more.
And yet the eighth appears, who bears a glass,
Which shows me many more, and some I see   120
That twofold balls and treble sceptres carry.
Horrible sight! . . . Now I see 'tis true,
For the blood-boltered Banquo smiles upon me,
And points at them for his. What, is this so?

1 WITCH   Ay sir, all this is so. But why   125
Stands Macbeth thus amazedly?
Come sisters, cheer we up his sprites,
And show the best of our delights.
I'll charm the air to give a sound,
While you perform your antic round,   130
That this great King may kindly say,
Our duties did his welcome pay. [*music. The* WITCHES *dance, and vanish*]

MACBETH   Where are they? Gone? Let this pernicious hour
Stand aye accursed in the calendar.
Come in, without there!

Enter LENNOX

LENNOX   What's your Grace's will?   135
MACBETH   Saw you the Weird Sisters?
LENNOX   No my lord.
MACBETH   Came they not by you?
LENNOX   No indeed my lord.
MACBETH   Infected by the air whereon they ride,
And damned all those that trust them. I did hear
The galloping of horse. Who was't came by?   140
LENNOX   'Tis two or three, my lord, that bring you word
Macduff is fled to England.
MACBETH   Fled to England?
LENNOX   Ay my good lord.
MACBETH   [*aside*] Time, thou anticipat'st my dread exploits.
The flighty purpose never is o'ertook   145
Unless the deed go with it. From this moment
The very firstlings of my heart shall be
The firstlings of my hand. And even now,

153   *trace . . . line*, are his closest relatives.
155   *But . . . sights!* Macbeth has finished with the witches and their
       apparitions, and they with him. He would also be finished
       with the visions that have plagued him. Evil as they were,
       the previous murders were motivated by expedience at least.
       No such justification is possible for Macbeth's present inten-
       tion. The powers of evil have accomplished their work in
       him. Macbeth is the embodiment of purposeless destruction,
       the utter antithesis to the concept of kingship and rule
       founded on divine reason. His condition is non-human; he
       murders instinctively, without conscience or concealment,
       and passes easily from a decision to murder to a talk with
       the 'gentlemen'. He is not seen again till Act 5 Sc.3.

Scene Two

1   *What . . . land?* The innocence that Lady Macduff represents is
       revealed in the question, and Ross's avoidance of an answer
       seems to underline it. Lady Macduff has nothing to do with
       political manoeuvring.
3–4   *When . . . traitors*, when we have not committed treason, we
       come under suspicion of treachery if we flee in fear/For
       Lady Macduff her husband is without guilt of any 'treachery'
       to Macbeth. However, she clearly thinks here and later
       that his flight has betrayed her and his family, and that un-
       warranted fear has led him to the betrayal.
7   *titles*, possessions.
9   *wants . . . touch*, lacks the instinctive love of a parent.
12   *All . . . the love.* He is possessed by fear, and is devoid of love.
       Critics have recognized a biblical echo in this line: 'There is
       no fear in love, but perfect love casteth out fear; for fear
       hath painfulness; and he that feareth is not perfect in love.'
       1 *John*, Ch.4 v.18.
13   *As little*, i.e. as little as the love—nothing.
14   *coz*, cousin. Used often as a term of endearment, without
       implying this relationship.
15   *school yourself*, have patience.
16–17 *best . . . season*, above all understands the convulsive age in
       which we are living/The word 'fits' recalls of course Mac-
       beth's state of mind, his compulsive killing, and is part of
       the imagery of sickness which Shakespeare now relates with
       increasing emphasis to Macbeth's Scotland.
19   *know ourselves*, i.e. to be traitors. Ross is saying that times are
       such that loyalties are confused, and that if Macduff has
       deserted his loved ones he has done so unwittingly.
19–22 *when . . . move*, when our fear gives rise to baseless rumours in
       which we trust, and insecurity is all around us/Ross breaks
       off abruptly. The image expresses the break-down of order.

To crown my thoughts with acts, be it thought and done.
The castle of Macduff I will surprise,   150
Seize upon Fife, give to the edge o' the sword
His wife, his babes, and all unfortunate souls
That trace him in his line. No boasting like a fool—
This deed I'll do before this purpose cool.
But no more sights! [*aloud*] Where are these gentlemen?   155
Come bring me where they are.   [*Exeunt*

Scene Two

Fife · Macduff's castle

Enter LADY MACDUFF · *her* SON · *and* ROSS

LADY MACDUFF   What had he done, to make him fly the land?
ROSS   You must have patience madam.
LADY MACDUFF   He had none.
  His flight was madness. When our actions do not,
  Our fears do make us traitors.
ROSS   You know not
  Whether it was his wisdom, or his fear.   5
LADY MACDUFF
  Wisdom! To leave his wife, to leave his babes,
  His mansion, and his titles in a place
  From whence himself does fly? He loves us not.
  He wants the natural touch. For the poor wren,
  The most diminutive of birds, will fight,   10
  Her young ones in her nest, against the owl.
  All is the fear, and nothing is the love;
  As little is the wisdom, where the flight
  So runs against all reason.
ROSS   My dearest coz,
  I pray you school yourself. But for your husband,   15
  He is noble, wise, judicious, and best knows
  The fits o' the season. I dare not speak much further,
  But cruel are the times, when we are traitors
  And do not know ourselves, when we hold rumour
  From what we fear, yet know not what we fear,   20

24-5   *Things . . . before.* The metaphor is taken by most critics to refer to the turning of the tide. This seems obtuse to me. It does not follow from the sea imagery of the previous lines, and a tide never ceases at its worst. Ross surely has in mind the commonplace notion of fortune's wheel, and is offering conventional solace. He can do little else.

25   *My pretty cousin.* Addressed to the son, or Lady Macduff's next line is very awkward. 'Pretty' could commonly mean 'gallant.'

29   *my disgrace,* i.e. by weeping.   *your discomfort,* depressing to you, discouraging.

30   *Sirrah.* The usual form of address to inferiors. Here Lady Macduff speaks curtly to check her grief.

34-5   *Poor . . . the gin?* The usual punctuation is a full stop, and Lady Macduff is taken to be saying that on such a diet her poor, half-starved son would not survive to be worth trapping. But this reduces the boy's reply to mere repetition. The line with its list of dangers makes tender mockery of the boy's courage, and 'poor' is an endearment. Her son's pun on the word gives his reply its sharpness, which is enhanced if the line is spoken enquiringly, matching her other questions in its weary resignation.

34   *lime,* birdlime.

35   *pitfall,* snare.   *gin,* trap.

36   *Poor . . . set for,* traps are not laid for scrawny little birds.

42   *wit,* intelligence.

45   *Ay . . . was.* A traitor to his family, that is. Her mood changes.

47   *one . . . lies,* i.e. an equivocator, one who 'lies like truth.'

49-50   *Everyone . . . hanged.* Critics usually recognize here a side glance at the trial and hanging of the Jesuit Garnet for his part in the Gunpowder Plot. Garnet used equivocation in his defence, and this intensified the argument about equivocation that had been current for some time. But the main dramatic point is Lady Macduff's gradually changing mood.

But float upon a wild and violent sea
Each way, and move—I take my leave of you—
Shall not be long but I'll be here again.
Things at the worst will cease or else climb upward
To what they were before . . . My pretty cousin,   25
Blessing upon you!

LADY MACDUFF
Fathered he is and yet he's fatherless.

ROSS I am so much a fool, should I stay longer,
It would be my disgrace and your discomfort.
I take my leave at once.   [*Exit*

LADY MACDUFF   Sirrah, your father's dead,   30
And what will you do now? How will you live?

SON As birds do mother.

LADY MACDUFF   What, with worms and flies?

SON With what I get I mean, and so do they.

LADY MACDUFF Poor bird, thou'dst never fear the net nor lime,
The pitfall nor the gin?

SON   Why should I mother?   35
Poor birds they are not set for.
My father is not dead, for all your saying.

LADY MACDUFF Yes, he is dead. How wilt thou do for a father?

SON Nay, how will you do for a husband?

LADY MACDUFF Why I can buy me twenty at any market.   40

SON Then you'll buy 'em to sell again.

LADY MACDUFF Thou speak'st with all thy wit,
And yet i' faith, with wit enough for thee.

SON Was my father a traitor, mother?

LADY MACDUFF Ay, that he was.   45

SON What is a traitor?

LADY MACDUFF Why one that swears and lies.

SON And be all traitors that do so?

LADY MACDUFF Everyone that does so is a traitor, and must be
hanged.   50

SON And must they all be hanged that swear and lie?

LADY MACDUFF Every one.

55–6 *Then . . . them.* The eye of innocence sees the truth, applicable both to Shakespeare's London and Macbeth's Scotland. The conversation intensifies the pathos, and Macbeth's assassins are about to silence this awareness.

56 *enow,* enough.

61 *Poor . . . talk'st.* Lady Macduff listens with affection. The boy is typical of a cultured infant of good family. The Renaissance child was carefully tutored to a precociousness which we might find tiresome, but which was then unreservedly fostered and admired. In this scene Shakespeare makes notable dramatic use of this cultivated forwardness in contemporary childhood.

63 *in your . . . perfect,* I well know you as a lady of high estate.

64 *doubt,* fear.   *nearly,* closely.

65 *homely,* simple.

66 *little ones.* The familiar biblical echo (*Matthew,* Ch. 18 v. 6) must be intended: 'But who shall offend one of these little ones which believe in me, it were better for him that a millstone were hanged about his neck, and that he were drowned in the depth of the sea.' Indeed the Elizabethan imagination would immediately associate Macbeth's third murder with the Slaughter of the Innocents, so familiar to them in Christian teaching.

67 *savage,* uncivilised, rude.

68 *fell,* savage.

70 *(stage direction) Exit.* The 'homely man's advice' reminds us that all men are not creatures of Macbeth. It is important that he is not a nobleman, and that he calls himself 'homely' rather than humble. The intimate family atmosphere is more carefully evoked here than in either of the other murders, and it is this homely order at the very basis of society that Macbeth's destruction is now reaching. And the dual abandonment (by Ross and the Messenger) heightens the pathos, and underlines the defenceless innocence that Macbeth is now annihilating.

71–2 *I remember . . . world.* The recollection seems to set Lady Macduff's habitual thought already beyond 'this earthly world.'

75 *womanly.* An interesting choice of adjective. She represents feminine simplicity, and we may recollect by contrast Lady Macbeth's invocation in Act1 Sc.5, ll.32–52. It is apparently 'manly' to do harm in Macbeth's kingdom.

76 *faces.* The word could mean 'masks,' and probably does here.

80 *shag-haired.* Wilson draws attention to the fact that a ruffian was especially distinguished 'as a swaggering bully . . . by wearing the hair long.'

81 *Young . . . treachery,* spawned in treachery.

SON   Who must hang them?

LADY MACDUFF   Why, the honest men.

SON   Then the liars and swearers are fools, for there are liars and   55
swearers enow to beat the honest men and hang up them.

LADY MACDUFF   Now God help thee, poor monkey. But how wilt
thou do for a father?

SON   If he were dead, you'd weep for him. If you would not, it were
a good sign that I should quickly have a new father.   60

LADY MACDUFF   Poor prattler, how thou talk'st!

Enter a MESSENGER

MESSENGER   Bless you fair dame. I am not to you known,
Though in your state of honour I am perfect.
I doubt some danger does approach you nearly.
If you will take a homely man's advice,   65
Be not found here. Hence with your little ones.
To fright you thus, methinks I am too savage;
To do worse to you were fell cruelty,
Which is too nigh your person. Heaven preserve you,
I dare abide no longer.   [*Exit*

LADY MACDUFF   Whither should I fly?   70
I have done no harm. But I remember now
I am in this earthly world, where to do harm
Is often laudable, to do good sometime
Accounted dangerous folly. Why then, alas,
Do I put up that womanly defence,   75
To say I have done no harm?

Enter MURDERERS

What are these faces?

1 MURDERER   Where is your husband?

LADY MACDUFF   I hope in no place so unsanctified
Where such as thou mayst find him.

1 MURDERER   He's a traitor.

SON   Thou liest thou shag-haired villain!

1 MURDERER   What, you egg! [*stabs him*]   80
Young fry of treachery!

82   *(stage direction) dies*. There is no dialogue for the removal of the
body. He probably dies moving to the inner stage.

(stage direction) Exit. By varying the thoughts and moods of
Lady Macduff and the boy, Shakespeare gives the scene implications far beyond its brief length. They bring within their
compass so many aspects of family life. There is the instinctive loyalty at the end when mother and son both rally to
Macduff's defence. After the earlier conversation this is
supremely convincing.

Scene Three

1–2   *Let . . . empty*. Malcolm begins the testing of Macduff with a
conventional poetic phrase inviting him to lament the
situation.

3   *mortal*, deadly.   *good*. Not a word that one readily associates
with the valour of which Macduff is speaking. But it suits the
main point in the scene, and words sometimes seem to come
in like this, almost from the back of Shakespeare's mind.

4   *Bestride*, stand astride guarding.   *downfall*, i.e. downfallen.
birthdom, native land.

6   *that*, so that.

8   *Like . . . dolour*, a similar sorrowful cry. 'Syllable' was used for
words of one syllable.

10   *to friend*, my ally.

12   *tyrant*. As well as meaning 'cruel despot,' the word could also
mean 'usurper,' as in *Henry the Sixth, Part 3*, Act 3 Sc.3:

> To prove him tyrant, this reason may suffice,
> That Henry liveth still; but were he dead,
> Yet here Prince Edward stands, King Henry's son.

Malcolm, as Shakespeare's audience would instinctively
understand, was objecting to Macbeth as oppressor and
usurper, two concepts commonly set together by writers.
whose sole name, whose name once mentioned.

13   *honest*, honourable, virtuous.

14–15   *but something . . . me*, but you may merit a reward at his hands
by betraying me/The Folio has 'discerne' for 'deserve,' giving
the meaning 'you may tell his nature from his treatment of
me.'

15   *and wisdom*, and it is politic.

17   *an angry god*. The phrase compares Macbeth with a heathen
god, contrasting with the saintly alliance supporting Malcolm.

18   *treacherous*. The word keeps recurring, charged with different
implications.

19–20   *recoil . . . charge*, yield to a royal command.

21   *transpose*, alter.

22   *still*, always.   *the brightest*, i.e. Lucifer, Satan.

23–4   *Though . . . so*, though evil men put on an appearance of virtue, true worth looks no less virtuous for that.

24–5   *I . . . doubts*. Macduff hopes for an expedition against Macbeth,
and Malcolm suspects him for leaving his family.

SON   He has killed me mother,
  Run away I pray you. [*dies*]
    [*Exit* LADY MACDUFF, *crying 'Murder!' and pursued by the* MURDERERS

Scene Three

England · The King's palace

Enter MALCOLM *and* MACDUFF

MALCOLM   Let us seek out some desolate shade, and there
  Weep our sad bosoms empty.
MACDUFF   Let us rather
  Hold fast the mortal sword, and like good men,
  Bestride our downfall birthdom. Each new morn
  New widows howl, new orphans cry, new sorrows   5
  Strike heaven on the face, that it resounds
  As if it felt with Scotland, and yelled out
  Like syllable of dolour.
MALCOLM   What I believe, I'll wail,
  What know, believe. And what I can redress,
  As I shall find the time to friend, I will.   10
  What you have spoke, it may be so perchance.
  This tyrant whose sole name blisters our tongues
  Was once thought honest. You have loved him well—
  He hath not touched you yet. I am young, but something
  You may deserve of him through me, and wisdom   15
  To offer up a weak, poor, innocent lamb
  To appease an angry god.
MACDUFF   I am not treacherous.
MALCOLM   But Macbeth is.
  A good and virtuous nature may recoil
  In an imperial charge. But I shall crave your pardon.   20
  That which you are, my thoughts cannot transpose.
  Angels are bright still, though the brightest fell.
  Though all things foul would wear the brows of grace,
  Yet grace must still look so.
MACDUFF   I have lost my hopes.
MALCOLM   Perchance even there where I did find my doubts.   25

26   *rawness*, defenceless state.
27   *motives*, i.e. of affection.
29–30 *Let . . . safeties*, realize that my mistrust is not intended to
       denigrate you, but to safeguard myself.
29   *jealousies*, mistrust, suspicion.
33   *goodness*, i.e. Malcolm.   *wrongs*, ill-gotten possessions.
34   *The title . . . affeered*, your right to the crown is confirmed/
       'Affeered' (a legal term) is an emendation generally accepted
       by editors for the Folio 'affear'd.' The passage could mean
       'the rightful holder of the title is afraid,' or there could be
       a quibble.
37   *to boot*, as well.
38   *I . . . you*, it is not only utter distrust that makes me speak as
       I do/Malcolm is leading into the exposition of his own
       (pretended) defects, which he would not inflict on Scotland.
41   *withal*, at the same time.
42   *right*, rightful claim.
43   *gracious England*, i.e. Edward the Confessor.
46   *wear . . . sword*, hoist it on the point of my sword.
48   *sundry*, various.   *than ever*, i.e. than ever before.
49   *By*, on account of.   *succeed*, succeed to the throne.
       What should he be? Who can that be?
51   *particulars*, intimate details.   *grafted*, implanted.
52   *opened*, i.e. as buds.
55   *confineless harms*, unbounded vices.
58   *luxurious, avaricious.* 'Luxurious' means 'lustful.' Bradley sug-
       gested that these two terms 'surprise us. Who would have
       expected avarice or lechery in Macbeth?' It is a good ques-
       tion. However Malcolm goes on to attribute these two vices
       particularly to himself, and having these vices plus the
       others named which apply so readily to Macbeth, Malcolm
       attempts to show himself 'a devil more damned in evils, to
       top Macbeth.' Moreover, there is the technical difficulty for
       Shakespeare of over-reaching in a few lines of description
       the specific evils already so overwhelmingly identified in
       Macbeth. The way out is to concentrate on lust and greed,
       and these were in any case commonly attributed to tyrants
59   *Sudden*, violent.   *smacking*, with a flavour.

Why in that rawness left you wife and child,
Those precious motives, those strong knots of love,
Without leave-taking? . . . I pray you,
Let not my jealousies be your dishonours,
But mine own safeties. You may be rightly just,   30
Whatever I shall think.

MACDUFF   Bleed, bleed, poor country!
Great tyranny, lay thou thy basis sure,
For goodness dare not check thee. Wear thou thy wrongs,
The title is affeered. Fare thee well lord,
I would not be the villain that thou think'st   35
For the whole space that's in the tyrant's grasp
And the rich East to boot.

MALCOLM   Be not offended.
I speak not as in absolute fear of you.
I think our country sinks beneath the yoke.
It weeps, it bleeds, and each new day a gash   40
Is added to her wounds. I think withal,
There would be hands uplifted in my right,
And here from gracious England have I offer
Of goodly thousands. But for all this,
When I shall tread upon the tyrant's head   45
Or wear it on my sword, yet my poor country
Shall have more vices than it had before,
More suffer, and more sundry ways than ever,
By him that shall succeed.

MACDUFF   What should he be?

MALCOLM   It is myself I mean, in whom I know   50
All the particulars of vice so grafted,
That when they shall be opened black Macbeth
Will seem as pure as snow and the poor state
Esteem him as a lamb, being compared
With my confineless harms.

MACDUFF   Not in the legions   55
Of horrid hell can come a devil more damned
In evils, to top Macbeth.

MALCOLM   I grant him bloody,
Luxurious, avaricious, false, deceitful,
Sudden, malicious, smacking of every sin

63   *cistern,* a pond of standing water. The metaphor follows naturally from the word 'bottom' (1.60), and is quickly turned and developed in the next few lines, all in a way typical of Shakespeare.

64   *continent impediments,* restraints of chastity, with an allusion to the bounds within which a 'cistern' is 'contained.'

65   *will,* unbridled wishes.

66–7   *Boundless . . . tyranny.* The seventeenth century often recognized two forces, the will and reason, to be in conflict in man's nature. Reason, the God-given quality distinguishing man from brute, and (as Milton said) making him 'talk with angels,' should govern, and the will should not be allowed to usurp this control to tyrannize the 'little kingdom' of man's being.

68   *The untimely . . . throne,* the cause of many happy reigns coming to untimely ends.

71   *Convey,* secretly possess.

72   *cold,* chaste.   *the time,* the age we live in, people today.

73   *dames,* ladies of rank.

75–6   *As will . . . inclined,* as will offer themselves to one of your eminence, finding you disposed to receive them.

76   *it,* i.e. greatness.

77   *ill-composed affection,* unbalanced nature.

78   *staunchless,* insatiable.

79   *cut off,* kill.

80   *his,* that man's.

82–3   *that . . . unjust,* so that I would fabricate unjustifiable disputes.

86   *summer-seeming.* Lust passes like the heat of summer, while avarice persists into the winter of age.

87   *The sword . . . kings,* the death of our kings who have met a violent end.

88   *foisons,* abundance.   *to fill . . . will.* The image of ll.62–5 is again caught up. We see that avarice, like any other intemperance, arises from the ungoverned will, and conflicts with reason.

89   *mere own,* own possessions.   *portable,* bearable.

90   *With . . . weighed,* considered alongside your other kingly virtues.

91   *king-becoming graces,* virtues that become a king. A major point in the scene is to offset the true graces of kingship against Macbeth and against the false description Malcolm gives of himself.

92   *temperance,* self-control.   *stableness,* constancy.

93   *Bounty,* generosity.

94   *Devotion,* reverence.

95   *relish,* trace.

That has a name. But there's no bottom, none,   60
In my voluptuousness. Your wives your daughters,
Your matrons and your maids, could not fill up
The cistern of my lust, and my desire
All continent impediments would o'erbear
That did oppose my will. Better Macbeth   65
Than such an one to reign.

MACDUFF   Boundless intemperance
In nature is a tyranny. It hath been
The untimely emptying of the happy throne,
And fall of many kings. But fear not yet
To take upon you what is yours. You may   70
Convey your pleasures in a spacious plenty
And yet seem cold, the time you may so hoodwink.
We have willing dames enough. There cannot be
That vulture in you to devour so many
As will to greatness dedicate themselves,   75
Finding it so inclined.

MALCOLM   With this there grows
In my most ill-composed affection such
A staunchless avarice, that were I King,
I should cut off the nobles for their lands,
Desire his jewels and this other's house,   80
And my more-having would be as a sauce
To make me hunger more, that I should forge
Quarrels unjust against the good and loyal,
Destroying them for wealth.

MACDUFF   This avarice
Sticks deeper, grows with more pernicious root   85
Than summer-seeming lust, and it hath been
The sword of our slain kings. Yet do not fear.
Scotland hath foisons to fill up your will
Of your mere own. All these are portable,
With other graces weighed.   90

MALCOLM But I have none. The king-becoming graces,
As justice, verity, temperance, stableness,
Bounty, perseverance, mercy, lowliness,
Devotion, patience, courage, fortitude—
I have no relish of them, but abound   95

96   *division*, variation. In music 'division' meant the playing of a melody with florid variations and extravagant phrases. *several*, separate.

97–100   *had I . . . earth.* Personal sins, unrelated to Macbeth, have been discounted. Suddenly the style changes, and it is as if Macbeth is speaking. At the same time, it is a powerful echo of what Macbeth has in fact done, and the destruction of 'all unity on earth' is a central theme. And it is at this point that Macduff's lament for Scotland overwhelms him. Moreover it is this, the direct self-identification of Malcolm with Macbeth in purpose, style, imagery and over-wrought tone, that finally drives Macduff to acknowledge Malcolm's unfitness for the throne. Shakespeare indirectly achieves much more in these four lines.

98   *milk of concord*, see note on Act 1 Sc.5,ll.15-16.

99   *confound*, overthrow.

104   *untitled*, usurping.

106   *truest issue.* Once again Shakespeare emphasizes Malcolm's right, by contrast with Macbeth's 'untitled' state.

107–8   *By . . . breed*, stands accused of charges authorized by himself, and defames his own royal house.

108–11   *Thy . . . lived.* Holinshed gives no suggestion of their saintliness. Shakespeare writes in the piety Macbeth has destroyed.

111   *Died . . . lived*, prepared herself for death each day in prayer.

112   *thou . . . thyself*, with which you accuse yourself.

113   *Hath*, have.

116   *scruples*, uneasy suspicions.

118   *trains*, devices.   *win*, lure.

119   *modest wisdom*, commonsense.   *plucks me*, restrains me.

122   *to thy direction*, under your guidance.

123   *Unspeak . . . detraction*, retract the slanders I have spoken against myself.   *abjure*, deny on oath.

124   *taints and blames*, depravity and disrepute.

125   *For*, as.

125–6   *I am . . . forsworn*, I have never had a mistress, and have never broken my pledged word.

131–2   *What . . . command.* Righteousness has been explicitly identified in Malcolm, in a passage that some critics feel is contrived. As Malcolm puts himself under Macduff's command, the latter becomes Macbeth's chief adversary, fulfilling the prophecy.

In the division of each several crime,
Acting it many ways. Nay, had I power, I should
Pour the sweet milk of concord into hell,
Uproar the universal peace, confound
All unity on earth.

MACDUFF   O Scotland, Scotland!   100

MALCOLM   If such a one be fit to govern, speak.
I am as I have spoken.

MACDUFF   Fit to govern?
No, not to live. O nation miserable,
With an untitled tyrant bloody-sceptred,
When shalt thou see thy wholesome days again,   105
Since that the truest issue of thy throne
By his own interdiction stands accused,
And does blaspheme his breed? Thy royal father
Was a most sainted king. The queen that bore thee,
Oftener upon her knees than on her feet,   110
Died every day she lived. Fare thee well,
These evils thou repeat'st upon thyself
Hath banished me from Scotland. O my breast,
Thy hope ends here.

MALCOLM   Macduff, this noble passion,
Child of integrity, hath from my soul   115
Wiped the black scruples, reconciled my thoughts
To thy good truth and honour. Devilish Macbeth
By many of these trains hath sought to win me
Into his power, and modest wisdom plucks me
From over-credulous haste. But God above   120
Deal between thee and me! For even now
I put myself to thy direction and
Unspeak mine own detraction—here abjure
The taints and blames I laid upon myself
For strangers to my nature. I am yet   125
Unknown to woman, never was forsworn,
Scarcely have coveted what was mine own,
At no time broke my faith, would not betray
The devil to his fellow and delight
No less in truth than life. My first false speaking   130
Was this upon myself. What I am truly,

135   *at a point,* fully equipped.

136-7   *the chance . . . quarrel,* may the chance that right will prevail be as great as our cause is just.

No matter how tyrannical Macbeth's rule, he is still the anointed King, and in Stuart eyes any rebellion was indefensible, even on behalf of a rightful claimant to the throne. Therefore at the crucial point in the play, when rebellion is discussed and raised, Shakespeare cannot simply give a favourable account of a foreign levy fostering an insurrection. He has to justify it, and does so by simplifying the issue to a conflict of good versus evil. Malcolm's 'admissions' and the retraction enhance the simplifying effect and dismiss other considerations, and sanctity becomes Malcolm's ally against the devil in Scotland. Critics have called the speeches here boring and stilted. But it seems to me that the rather heavy lack of subtlety is part of the effect, disarming questions by giving the issues formality—making them 'obvious.' Shakespeare was writing on dangerous political ground, and the rather artificial façade, and the conventional ordinariness to which the conflict is *temporarily* confined, were safer than any philosophical subtlety would have been. And the relaxation is a dramatic necessity.

142   *stay,* await.   *convinces,* defeats.

143   *great . . . art,* utmost endeavours of medical skill.

144   *sanctity . . . hand.* The healing power is directly identified as sanctity. So saintliness, royalty and healing are identified against the evil, tyranny and sickness of Macbeth.

145   *presently,* immediately.   *amend,* recover.

146   *the Evil,* the king's evil, scrofula.

149   *solicits,* entreats. Contrast Macbeth's 'supernatural soliciting.'

150   *visited,* afflicted.

152   *mere,* utter.

153   *golden stamp,* a gold coin, called an 'angel', stamped with the archangel Michael and a dragon.

155-6   *To . . . benediction.* Edward the Confessor, as Holinshed reported, was thought 'to have had the gift of healing infirmities and diseases' and to have left the power to heal scrofula with his touch 'as it were a portion of inheritance unto his successors, the kings of this realm.' King James 'touched for the scrofula' on the anniversary of his accession, and valued the practice as demonstrating his true lineage.

156   *virtue,* divine faculty.

157   *heavenly . . . prophecy.* Contrast the devilish prophecies of the weird sisters.

159   *speak . . . grace,* proclaim his infinite virtue/The whole passage (ll.140–59) may have been taken by James I as an oblique compliment to himself. Dramatically it associates Malcolm indisputably with sanctity and the powers of good, contrasts directly with all Macbeth represents, and lends supreme authority to the forces of rebellion. And if James I's vanity did acknowledge a compliment, it meant that he identified himself with Malcolm's cause, and Shakespeare had justified it completely.

Is thine, and my poor country's, to command,
Whither indeed, before thy here-approach,
Old Siward with ten thousand warlike men
Already at a point was setting forth.   135
Now we'll together, and the chance of goodness
Be like our warranted quarrel . . . Why are you silent?

MACDUFF   Such welcome and unwelcome things at once
'Tis hard to reconcile.

Enter a DOCTOR

MALCOLM   Well, more anon.
Comes the King forth, I pray you?   140

DOCTOR   Ay sir, there are a crew of wretched souls
That stay his cure. Their malady convinces
The great assay of art, but at his touch,
Such sanctity hath heaven given his hand,
They presently amend.

MALCOLM   I thank you doctor.   [*Exit* DOCTOR 145

MACDUFF   What's the disease he means?

MALCOLM   'Tis called the Evil—
A most miraculous work in this good King,
Which often since my here-remain in England
I have seen him do. How he solicits heaven,
Himself best knows. But strangely visited people,   150
All swoln and ulcerous, pitiful to the eye,
The mere despair of surgery, he cures,
Hanging a golden stamp about their necks,
Put on with holy prayers; and 'tis spoken,
To the succeeding royalty he leaves   155
The healing benediction. With this strange virtue,
He hath a heavenly gift of prophecy,
And sundry blessings hang about his throne,
That speak him full of grace.

Enter ROSS

MACDUFF   See who comes here.

MALCOLM   My countryman. But yet I know him not.   160

MACDUFF   My ever-gentle cousin, welcome hither.

162–3   *betimes . . . strangers,* take away at once that which parts us—
Macbeth.

166–7   *where . . . smile,* where no one except the utterly insensitive is
ever seen to smile.

169   *Are made, not marked,* being commonplace, go unremarked.

170   *modern ecstasy,* paltry tantrum.

173   *or ere,* before.   *relation,* narrative.

174   *nice,* precise.

175   *hiss the speaker,* i.e. for bringing news already stale.

176   *teems,* breeds.

177   *well.* Cf *Antony and Cleopatra,* Act 2 Sc.5: 'we use To say the dead
are well.'

179   *The . . . peace.* Ross equivocates, which heightens the suspense
and builds up Macduff's reaction.

181–2   *When . . . borne.* Ross refers to the news of the murder of
Macduff's family, but again shies away.

183   *out,* i.e. against Macbeth.

184   *Which . . . witnessed,* which was confirmed to my satisfaction.

185   *power afoot,* forces on the march.

186   *Now . . . help,* now is the moment to intervene.

188   *doff,* throw off.

MALCOLM   I know him now. Good God, betimes remove
　The means that makes us strangers.

ROSS   Sir, amen.

MACDUFF   Stands Scotland where it did?

ROSS   Alas poor country,
　Almost afraid to know itself. It cannot   165
　Be called our mother, but our grave, where nothing
　But who knows nothing is once seen to smile,
　Where sighs and groans and shrieks that rend the air
　Are made, not marked; where violent sorrow seems
　A modern ecstasy. The dead man's knell   170
　Is there scarce asked for who, and good men's lives
　Expire before the flowers in their caps
　Dying or ere they sicken.

MACDUFF   O relation
　Too nice and yet too true!

MALCOLM   What's the newest grief?

ROSS   That of an hour's age doth hiss the speaker.   175
　Each minute teems a new one.

MACDUFF   How does my wife?

ROSS   Why, well.

MACDUFF   And all my children?

ROSS   Well too.

MACDUFF   The tyrant has not battered at their peace?

ROSS   No. They were well at peace, when I did leave 'em.

MACDUFF   Be not a niggard of your speech. How goes't?   180

ROSS   When I came hither to transport the tidings
　Which I have heavily borne, there ran a rumour
　Of many worthy fellows that were out,
　Which was to my belief witnessed the rather,
　For that I saw the tyrant's power afoot.   185
　Now is the time of help. Your eye in Scotland
　Would create soldiers, make our women fight
　To doff their dire distresses.

MALCOLM   Be't their comfort
　We are coming thither. Gracious England hath
　Lent us good Siward and ten thousand men—   190

192   *gives out,* proclaims.
194   *would be,* ought to be.   *desert,* vacant.
195   *latch,* catch.
196   *The general cause,* the general ill state of the country.
        cause, illness, malady.   *fee-grief,* private sorrow.
202   *possess,* occupy.
205–7   *To relate . . . you,* if I were to describe the way they were killed,
        the shock would add your death to theirs, who were slaught-
        ered like innocent deer.
206   *quarry,* game slaughtered in the chase.
209–10 *The grief . . . break.* In urging Macduff to give vent to his grief
        Malcolm repeats a commonplace of Jacobean medicine. The
        suppression of grief was dangerous, cf. *Hamlet,* Act 1 Sc.2,l.159:
            But break, my heart, for I must hold my tongue
        where the same proverbial thought has such a different ring
        from Malcolm's phrasing. Here the rhyme expresses the
        triteness of the advice and the shallowness of words, which
        Macduff either does not hear or ignores. Malcolm's reaction
        to the news, here and a little later, emphasizes the devas-
        tating effect on Macduff.
210   *o'er-fraught,* over-burdened.
212   *must be,* had to be.
214–5   *Let's . . . grief.* The mortal sorrow ('deadly grief') refers prim-
        arily to the news Macduff has heard, and then to the state
        of Scotland. For revenge as a relief to sorrow, see note on
        l.229.
216   *He . . . children.* As all critics point out, 'he' may refer to
        Macbeth, either (1) because he has no children upon whom
        Macduff might be revenged, or (2) because his being child-
        less enabled Macbeth to entertain the deed. Or (3) 'he' may refer
        to Malcolm, who would not have made the suggestion of
        ll.214–5 if he had children. (1) seems to me a misjudgment
        of the frame of mind Shakespeare is conveying; (2) seems
        almost pointlessly weak; (3) is surely right? Malcolm has at
        last broken Macduff's mortally dangerous preoccupation
        ('deadly grief'), and draws this desolating reaction. Macduff's
        thoughts turn for the first time to Macbeth (and then only
        momentarily) in the exclamation of the next line.

An older and a better soldier none
That Christendom gives out.

Ross   Would I could answer
This comfort with the like. But I have words
That would be howled out in the desert air
Where hearing should not latch them.

MACDUFF   What concern they?   195
The general cause? Or is it a fee-grief
Due to some single breast?

Ross   No mind that's honest
But in it shares some woe, though the main part
Pertains to you alone.

MACDUFF   If it be mine,
Keep it not from me, quickly let me have it.   200

Ross   Let not your ears despise my tongue for ever,
Which shall possess them with the heaviest sound
That ever yet they heard.

MACDUFF   Humh! I guess at it.

Ross   Your castle is surprised, your wife and babes
Savagely slaughtered. To relate the manner,   205
Were on the quarry of these murdered deer
To add the death of you.

MALCOLM   Merciful heaven!
What man, ne'er pull your hat upon your brows,
Give sorrow words. The grief that does not speak
Whispers the o'er-fraught heart and bids it break.   210

MACDUFF   My children too?

Ross   Wife, children, servants, all
That could be found.

MACDUFF   And I must be from thence!
My wife killed too?

Ross   I have said.

MALCOLM   Be comforted.
Let's make us medicines of our great revenge
To cure this deadly grief.   215

MACDUFF   He has no children . . . All my pretty ones?
Did you say all? . . . O hell-kite! . . . All?

218   *dam,* mother.
219   *At . . . swoop,* i.e. of the 'hell-kite.' Shakespeare's vivid phrase
        has become colloquial.
220   *Dispute,* stand up to.
221–3   *But . . . to me.* This seems to confirm the reading of l.216.
225   *Naught,* sinful.
226   *demerits,* transgressions.
227   *Heaven . . . now.* Despite Malcolm's conventional advice,
        Macduff's first coherent reaction is not towards revenge. It
        is a confession and a submission to divine will, ending in a
        prayer. Macbeth's chief adversary is thus associated with the
        sanctity surrounding Malcolm's cause.
229   *Convert,* change.   *Blunt . . . enrage it.* It was thought grief
        'strikes the heart, makes it tremble and pine away.' while
        anger overheats it. Therefore anger alleviated the physical
        effects of grief. Malcolm is still using terms of medicine, and
        thinking in part of Macduff's physical state. Recognition of
        this, that it was thought necessary to relieve the impact of
        grief, brings understanding to Malcolm's reactions in this
        episode. And most effective is the resolute way Macduff
        quietly ignores the commonplace sound advice.
231–5   *But gentle . . . too.* Macduff becomes heaven's advocate against
        the 'fiend', and an instrument of justice, rather than a rebel
        feverishly 'enraged' like Macbeth.
232   *intermission,* delay.   *Front to front,* face to face.
236   *power,* army.
237   *Our . . . leave,* all we have left to do is take leave of the King.
238   *the Powers,* i.e. the order of angels particularly responsible for
        countering the advance of Satan.
239   *Put . . . instruments,* arm themselves.   *cheer,* encouragement.

What, all my pretty chickens and their dam
At one fell swoop?

MALCOLM Dispute it like a man.

MACDUFF   I shall do so;   220
But I must also feel it as a man.
I cannot but remember such things were
That were most precious to me. Did heaven look on
And would not take their part? Sinful Macduff,
They were all struck for thee. Naught that I am,   225
Not for their own demerits, but for mine
Fell slaughter on their souls. Heaven rest them now.

MALCOLM Be this the whetstone of your sword, let grief
Convert to anger. Blunt not the heart, enrage it.

MACDUFF O I could play the woman with mine eyes   230
And braggart with my tongue. But gentle heavens,
Cut short all intermission. Front to front
Bring thou this fiend of Scotland and myself—
Within my sword's length set him. If he 'scape,
Heaven forgive him too.

MALCOLM   This tune goes manly.   235
Come, go we to the King. Our power is ready,
Our lack is nothing but our leave. Macbeth
Is ripe for shaking, and the Powers above
Put on their instruments. Receive what cheer you may—
The night is long that never finds the day.   [*Exeunt* 240

1   *watched,* sat up.
3   *into the field,* i.e. against the Scots rebels 'that were out.'
4   *nightgown,* dressing-gown.
5   *closet,* chest for valuables.   *fold it.* So that she conveniently knew where the fold would come when she sealed it, and the writing did not run across the fold.
8   *A great . . . nature,* a violent derangement in her constitution.
     at once, at the same time.   *benefit,* gift.
9   *do . . . watching,* act as if she were awake.
     slumbery agitation, activity in sleep.
10   *actual performances,* deliberate acts.
12   *after her,* as her actual words.
13   *meet,* fitting.
15   *(stage direction) a taper,* a candle.
16   *This . . . guise,* this is the usual way.
17   *close,* hidden.
22   *are.* Many editors amend this Folio reading to 'is.' But 'sense' may be looked upon as plural—'faculties.'

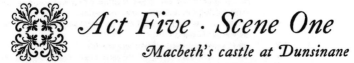

Act Five · Scene One

Macbeth's castle at Dunsinane

Enter a DOCTOR OF PHYSIC *and a* WAITING GENTLEWOMAN

DOCTOR I have two nights watched with you, but can perceive no truth in your report. When was it she last walked?

GENTLEWOMAN Since his Majesty went into the field, I have seen her rise from her bed, throw her nightgown upon her, unlock her closet, take forth paper, fold it, write upon't, read it, afterwards 5 seal it, and again return to bed; yet all this while in a most fast sleep.

DOCTOR A great perturbation in nature, to receive at once the bene-fit of sleep, and do the effects of watching. In this slumbery agit-ation, besides her walking and other actual performances, what at 10 any time have you heard her say?

GENTLEWOMAN That sir, which I will not report after her.

DOCTOR You may to me, and 'tis most meet you should.

GENTLEWOMAN Neither to you nor anyone, having no witness to confirm my speech. 15

Enter LADY MACBETH *with a taper*

Lo you, here she comes. This is her very guise, and upon my life fast asleep. Observe her; stand close.

DOCTOR How came she by that light?

GENTLEWOMAN Why it stood by her. She has light by her contin-ually, 'tis her command. 20

DOCTOR You see her eyes are open.

GENTLEWOMAN Ay but their sense are shut.

DOCTOR What is it she does now? Look how she rubs her hands.

GENTLEWOMAN It is an accustomed action with her, to seem thus washing her hands. I have known her continue in this a quarter 25 of an hour.

27   *a spot.* The blood on her hands is the obsession upon which
        Lady Macbeth's reason founders. It is with Macbeth's men-
        tion of the 'sorry sight' of his blood-stained hands immedi-
        ately after the first murder (Act2Sc.2, l.20) that she begins
        the long suppression of her feelings to strengthen her hus-
        band. And her hands were blood-stained on her terrifying
        return to the murdered Duncan who had resembled her
        father 'as he slept.'

29   *satisfy my remembrance,* refresh my memory.

30–31   *One . . . do't.* Either Lady Macbeth hears (or imagines she
        hears) a clock strike, or more likely it is the recollection of
        the bell she struck at Act2 Sc.1, l.61.

31   *Fie,* for shame!

33   *accompt,* account.

33–4   *Yet . . . him.* Yet another reference which in its horror makes
        her 'perturbation in nature' true to seventeenth-century
        medicine. Burton told how 'some terrible object heard or
        seen . . . strikes such a deep impression, that the parties can
        never be recovered, causing more grievous and fiercer
        melancholy . . . than any inward cause.'

35   *mark,* notice.

38   *starting,* i.e. 'these flaws and starts,' Act3 Sc.4, l.62.

39   *Go to.* An expression of reproach.   *You.* Taken usually to
        refer to Lady Macbeth, not to the Gentlewoman. If so it is
        the only time the Doctor addresses himself to Lady Macbeth.
        The Gentlewoman's next remark suits either interpretation.

41   *has known,* has experienced.

42–3   *Here's . . . hand.* The evocative nature of smells is well known.
        The idea of Lady Macbeth perfuming her hands to sweeten
        away the smell of blood is more appalling in its pervasive
        continuity than even the unending washing.

44   *The heart . . . charged* A clinical observation, see note on
        Act5 Sc.3, ll.44–5.

46   *dignity,* high estate.

49   *This . . . practice,* this disorder is beyond my skill.

52–4   *Wash . . . on's grave.* Times are out of sequence, and as in dreams
        events run together; but through the confusion Lady
        Macbeth's imagination recollects the strain of reconciling
        and strengthening her husband, and bearing the weight of
        his 'fits'. She has kept her self-control, and she has broken
        inwardly. The recollections of this scene confirm the tragic
        pity of her total, though misguided, devotion. Nothing in
        Shakespeare is facile, and this 'fiend-like queen' has an
        unwavering, even selfless fidelity.

57   *give me your hand.* The basic human sympathy, the tenderness
        towards her husband, survives even the desolation of their
        crimes. This is part of the meaning of the play, and makes
        it tragic rather than melodramatic. After this the next sen-
        tence becomes a complete confession of guilt and acknow-
        ledges the failure of evil. It suggests that even the terrible
        deeds and the satanic domination have not dispossessed her
        humanity entirely.

61   *Foul whisperings,* rumours of evil deeds.

LADY MACBETH   Yet here's a spot.

DOCTOR   Hark! she speaks. I will set down what comes from her, to satisfy my remembrance the more strongly.

LADY MACBETH   Out damned spot, out I say! One ... two. Why then   30
'tis time to do't. Hell is murky. Fie my lord, fie! A soldier, and afeard? What need we fear who knows it, when none can call our power to accompt? Yet who would have thought the old man to have had so much blood in him?

DOCTOR   Do you mark that?   35

LADY MACBETH   The Thane of Fife had a wife—where is she now? What, will these hands ne'er be clean? . . . No more o' that my lord, no more o' that. You mar all with this starting.

DOCTOR   Go to, go to! You have known what you should not.

GENTLEWOMAN   She has spoke what she should not, I am sure of that.   40
Heaven knows what she has known.

LADY MACBETH   Here's the smell of the blood still. All the perfumes of Arabia will not sweeten this little hand. Oh, oh, oh!

DOCTOR   What a sigh is there! The heart is sorely charged.

GENTLEWOMAN   I would not have such a heart in my bosom for the   45
dignity of the whole body.

DOCTOR   Well, well, well.

GENTLEWOMAN   Pray God it be, sir.

DOCTOR   This disease is beyond my practice. Yet I have known those which have walked in their sleep who have died holily in their   50
beds.

LADY MACBETH   Wash your hands, put on your nightgown, look not so pale. I tell you yet again Banquo's buried—he cannot come out on's grave.

DOCTOR   Even so?   55

LADY MACBETH   To bed, to bed. There's knocking at the gate.
Come, come, come, come, give me your hand. What's done cannot be undone. To bed, to bed, to bed.   [Exit

DOCTOR   Will she go now to bed?

GENTLEWOMAN   Directly.   60

DOCTOR   Foul whisperings are abroad. Unnatural deeds
Do breed unnatural troubles. Infected minds

66   *annoyance,* injury. Melancholy, 'the Devil's bath,' was thought
      to be a special consequence of demonic possession, and
      tended 'the whole system towards black bile,' giving rise to
      terrifying dreams, despair and suicidal thoughts.

67   *still . . . upon her,* watch her continually and carefully.

68   *mated,* bewildered.   *amazed,* perplexed.

Scene Two   3   *Revenges . . . them,* desire for revenge enflames their spirits.
      It is the same idea as Malcolm's in Act4Sc.3, l.229, and is con-
      tinued in the next three lines. Shakespeare's knowledge of
      medicine was acute, and where we see only a figure of speech
      he was usually speaking factually in accordance with Eliza-
      bethan medical teaching. This is especially so in *Macbeth,*
      where disease is so frequently referred to, and the play's full
      impact depends to some extent upon recognizing the direct
      accuracy of Shakespeare's observations.

3–5   *for their . . . man,* for their grievous ills would rouse the dead
      to answer the battle cry with their blood/The paradox that
      a grievous illness ('dear cause') could rouse the dead is based
      on the pun on 'cause meaning also 'complaint' 'indictment'.

6   *well,* probably.

8   *file,* list.

10   *unrough,* beardless.

11   *Protest . . . manhood,* give evidence of their manhood for the
      first time.

15–16 *He . . . rule,* he cannot bring under control the disorder that
      rages within and around him/'His distempered cause' means
      'his illness,' and the line implies both Macbeth and Scotland
      were irrevocably diseased. The idea is continued here
      through the familiar clothing imagery, and prepares for the
      almost manic fury of Macbeth in the final scenes.

18   *minutely,* every minute.   *upbraid,* reproach.
      his faith-breach, his own treachery.

19   *in command,* under duress.

To their deaf pillows will discharge their secrets.
More needs she the divine than the physician.
God, God forgive us all. Look after her,   65
Remove from her the means of all annoyance,
And still keep eyes upon her. So, good night.
My mind she has mated and amazed my sight.
I think, but dare not speak.

GENTLEWOMAN   Good night, good doctor.   [*Exeunt*

Scene Two

Near Dunsinane

Drum and colours. Enter MENTEITH · CAITHNESS · ANGUS · LENNOX ·
and Soldiers

MENTEITH   The English power is near, led on by Malcolm,
His uncle Siward and the good Macduff.
Revenges burn in them—for their dear causes
Would to the bleeding and the grim alarm
Excite the mortified man.

ANGUS   Near Birnam wood   5
Shall we well meet them. That way are they coming.

CAITHNESS   Who knows if Donalbain be with his brother?

LENNOX   For certain sir, he is not. I have a file
Of all the gentry. There is Siward's son,
And many unrough youths that even now   10
Protest their first of manhood.

MENTEITH   What does the tyrant?

CAITHNESS   Great Dunsinane he strongly fortifies.
Some say he's mad; others, that lesser hate him,
Do call it valiant fury. But for certain,
He cannot buckle his distempered cause   15
Within the belt of rule.

ANGUS   Now does he feel
His secret murders sticking on his hands,
Now minutely revolts upbraid his faith-breach.
Those he commands move only in command,
Nothing in love. Now does he feel his title   20

23   *pestered senses*, plagued nerves.   *recoil*, give way, break. Menteith takes up Caithness's point in ll.14–16.

27   *the medicine*, i.e. Malcolm.   *weal*, commonwealth.

28–9 *pour . . . us*, let us shed our blood to the last drop to cure our
       land of its ills.

28   *purge*, the practice of bleeding to alleviate a sickness by drawing from the veins the excess humours.

30   *dew the sovereign flower*, nurture the flower of kings.   *dew*,
       bedew. Dew was originally thought to fall gently from
       heaven, and to be effective in bringing flowers to bloom.
       sovereign. Applied to medicine it meant 'supremely excellent.'

Scene Three 1   *them*, his thanes.

3   *taint*, be infected with.

4–5   *The spirits . . . thus*, The apparitions that know all things to
       come on earth have prophesied thus to me.

7   *have power upon thee*. The phrase implies spiritual domination,
       spell-binding.

8   *epicures*, self-indulgent weaklings. The phrase is contemptuous, and based on a misunderstanding of the teaching of
       Epicurus, the Greek philosopher.

9–10 *The mind . . . fear*. The rhyme mocks the boast as Macbeth
       makes it. His assertiveness expresses his insecurity, which is
       confirmed by his brutal anger in the next line.   *sway by*, govern myself with.

11   *loon*, a worthless rogue, a fool. While the main point about
       'cream-faced' here, and 'whey-face' in l.17, is the paleness,
       there is also the association of milk with contemptible mildness, as elsewhere in the play.

Hang loose about him, like a giant's robe
Upon a dwarfish thief.

MENTEITH   Who then shall blame
His pestered senses to recoil and start,
When all that is within him does condemn
Itself for being there?

CAITHNESS   Well, march we on,   25
To give obedience where 'tis truly owed.
Meet we the medicine of the sickly weal,
And with him pour we, in our country's purge,
Each drop of us.

LENNOX   Or so much as it needs
To dew the sovereign flower and drown the weeds.   30
Make we our march towards Birnam.   [*Exeunt marching*

Scene Three

Macbeth's castle

Enter MACBETH · DOCTOR · *and Attendants*

MACBETH   Bring me no more reports, let them fly all!
Till Birnam wood remove to Dunsinane
I cannot taint with fear. What's the boy Malcolm—
Was he not born of woman? The spirits that know
All mortal consequence have pronounced me thus: 5
'Fear not Macbeth, no man that's born of woman
Shall e'er have power upon thee' . . . Then fly false thanes
And mingle with the English epicures.
The mind I sway by and the heart I bear
Shall never sag with doubt, nor shake with fear.   10

Enter a SERVANT

The devil damn thee black thou cream-faced loon!
Where got'st thou that goose look?

SERVANT   There is ten thousand—

MACBETH   Geese, villain?

SERVANT   Soldiers, sir.

MACBETH   Go prick thy face and over-red thy fear,

15 *lily-livered,* cowardly. *patch,* fool. The liver was thought to be the seat of passion and courage. Cf .*The Merchant of Venice,* Act3 Sc.2,ll.83–6: 'How many cowards . . . Who, inward searched, have livers white as milk.'

17 *Are . . . fear,* give rise to fear in others.

20 *push,* critical engagement.

21 *cheer,* hearten—with the 'sick at heart' in l.19 in mind. 'Cheer' and 'chair' (enthrone) were close in pronunciation in Shakespeare's day, and the quibble leads on to 'disseat.'

22 *My way,* course of life. Johnson, and other eighteenth-century editors, wished to alter 'way' to 'May', for the sake of the uniformity they admired in imagery. The line as it stands is typically Shakespearean.

23 *sear,* withered.

24–6 *And that . . . have.* The movement of the lines is reflective and pitiful. The abstract qualities of honour, love and obedience seem to be summarised in 'troops of friends,' making Macbeth's consciousness of his loss the more desolating. Shakespeare writes from a sympathetic identity even with Macbeth. It is a good example of what Keats called Shakespeare's 'negative capability.'

27 *mouth-honour,* lip service. *breath,* words spoken.

28 *poor heart,* simple man. *fain,* gladly.

35 *moe,* more. *skirr,* scour.

37 *How . . . doctor?* In his frantic preoccupation Macbeth ignores the physician till now. Or possibly the doctor does not enter till this point.

38 *thick-coming fancies,* a host of fantastic illusions.

40 *minister to,* administer a remedy to. *diseased.* Here probably 'tormented' (a common meaning), rather than the modern sense as at l.51.

41 *a rooted sorrow.* 'Sorrow . . . is a cause of madness, a cause of many other incurable diseases . . . and if it take root once, it ends in despair.'(Burton) Among the other terrifying recollections we tend to neglect the hint that 'sorrow' was rooted in her memory.

42 *Raze . . . brain,* erase the distresses engraved upon the brain.

43 *oblivious antidote,* medicine to induce forgetfulness. 'Troubles of the brain' were thought to have a direct effect upon the heart. Hence, by obliterating memories, the doctor could cure the physical ailment.

44–5 *stuffed,* heavy laden. *perilous stuff . . . heart.* 'The fierceness and madness of grief . . . gathering of much melancholy blood about the heart, which collection extinguisheth the good spirits; and the black blood drawn from the spleen and diffused under the ribs on the left side, make those perilous . . . convulsions, which happen to them that are troubled with sorrow.' (Burton)

Thou lily-livered boy. What soldiers, patch?   15
Death of thy soul, those linen cheeks of thine
Are counsellors to fear. What soldiers, whey-face?

SERVANT The English force, so please you.

MACBETH Take thy face hence.   [*Exit* SERVANT
                         Seyton! . . . I am sick at heart,
When I behold—Seyton, I say! . . . This push   20
Will cheer me ever or disseat me now.
I have lived long enough. My way of life
Is fallen into the sear, the yellow leaf,
And that which should accompany old age,
As honour, love, obedience, troops of friends,   25
I must not look to have. But in their stead
Curses, not loud but deep, mouth-honour, breath
Which the poor heart would fain deny and dare not.
Seyton!

Enter SEYTON

SEYTON What's your gracious pleasure?

MACBETH   What news more?   30

SEYTON All is confirmed my lord, which was reported.

MACBETH I'll fight till from my bones my flesh be hacked.
Give me my armour.

SEYTON   'Tis not needed yet.

MACBETH I'll put it on.
Send out moe horses, skirr the country round.   35
Hang those that talk of fear. Give me mine armour . . .
How does your patient, doctor?

DOCTOR   Not so sick my lord,
As she is troubled with thick-coming fancies
That keep her from her rest.

MACBETH   Cure her of that.
Canst thou not minister to a mind diseased,   40
Pluck from the memory a rooted sorrow,
Raze out the written troubles of the brain,
And with some sweet oblivious antidote
Cleanse the stuffed bosom of that perilous stuff
Which weighs upon the heart?

45-6   *Therein . . . himself.* By using the word 'himself' the Doctor
avoids a personal slight on Lady Macbeth, and offers a general
observation that engages Macbeth himself. The central
theme in the play is the interacting destruction, physical,
spiritual and mental, caused by submission to evil. The Doctor is saying that he can deal with physical ills, but not with
the soul, will and reason. He is not denying a link between
these and physical health. Indeed this link (commonplace
medical teaching) was essential to Shakespeare's purpose.

48   *staff.* A staff was carried by the commanding officer.

50-51   *cast The water,* diagnose an illness from an examination of the
urine. The 'correspondence' between the human body and
a commonwealth was constantly drawn in medical and
philosophical treatises. This well-worn convention was
useful to Shakespeare whose dual theme is the parallel
effect of evil on Macbeth's 'state of man' and the commonwealth of Scotland.

58   *it,* i.e. some part of his armour.

59   *bane,* murder. The word is forced into the line to make the
rhyming jingle sound hollow, like Macbeth's courage that
it bolsters up.

Scene Four   2   *chambers . . . safe,* i.e. that men will be able to sleep without
fear of intruders/The line recollects the murders of Duncan
and of Macduff's family, and again firmly associates the
invading Malcolm with order.

6   *discovery,* reconnaissance.

8   *We . . . but,* all reports confirm that.   *confident,* presumptuous, over-weening.

DOCTOR　　　　　　　　　　　　Therein the patient　　　　　　45
　　Must minister to himself.

MACBETH　Throw physic to the dogs, I'll none of it.
　　Come, put mine armour on. Give me my staff.
　　Seyton, send out—Doctor, the thanes fly from me . . .
　　Come sir, dispatch . . . If thou couldst, doctor, cast　　50
　　The water of my land, find her disease
　　And purge it to a sound and pristine health,
　　I would applaud thee to the very echo
　　That should applaud again . . . Pull't off I say . . .
　　What rhubarb, senna, or what purgative drug　　　55
　　Would scour these English hence? Hear'st thou of them?

DOCTOR　Ay my good lord—your royal preparation
　　Makes us hear something.

MACBETH　　　　　　　　　　Bring it after me.
　　I will not be afraid of death and bane,
　　Till Birnam forest come to Dunsinane.　　　　　　[Exit　60

DOCTOR　Were I from Dunsinane away, and clear,
　　Profit again should hardly draw me here.　　　　　[Exeunt

Scene Four

Birnam wood

Drum and colours · Enter MALCOLM · SIWARD *and* YOUNG SIWARD · MACDUFF ·
MENTEITH · CAITHNESS · ANGUS · LENNOX · ROSS · *and* SOLDIERS *marching*

MALCOLM　Cousins, I hope the days are near at hand
　　That chambers will be safe.

MENTEITH　　　　　　　　　　We doubt it nothing.

SIWARD　What wood is this before us?

MENTEITH　　　　　　　　　　The wood of Birnam.

MALCOLM　Let every soldier hew him down a bough
　　And bear't before him. Thereby shall we shadow　　5
　　The numbers of our host, and make discovery
　　Err in report of us.

SOLDIER　　　　　　　It shall be done.

SIWARD　We learn no other but the confident tyrant

9 *Keeps*, fortifies himself. *endure*, tolerate.

11 *advantage . . . gone*, a chance to get away.

12 *more and less*, noble and common people.
  given . . . revolt, revolted against him.

14–16 *Let . . . soldiership*, let us await the outcome of the battle before we pass judgment, and get down to the business of fighting.

18 *What . . . owe*, what we have won and lost.

19–20 *Thoughts . . . arbitrate*, wishful thinking only raises false hopes; only giving battle will settle the issue/Siward only repeats at length and in rhyme the warning tersely given to Malcolm by Macduff.

21 *war*. Besides its normal meaning, the word could mean 'an army in battle array.'

Scene Five

1 *outward walls*, outer ramparts.

4 *ague*, fever.

5 *Were . . . forced*, if they had not been reinforced.

6 *dareful*, defiantly.

7 *home*, to the end.

8 *the cry*. Not of lamentation, but horror.

10 *senses*, nerves. *cooled*, gone cold.

11 *fell of hair*. Usually paraphrased as 'scalp.' But primarily it means 'an animal hide with its hair,' and by giving self-expression to Macbeth's subconscious identification with a beast, Shakespeare makes him deny his own humanity. This is the most important 'meaning' in the phrase.

12 *dismal treatise*, sinister report.

14–15 *Direness . . . me*, horror with which my murderous thoughts are intimate can never make me start/By 'hard use' Macbeth has now overcome his 'initiate fear,' and with it lost his 'human kindness.'

    Keeps still in Dunsinane, and will endure
    Our setting down before't

MALCOLM   'Tis his main hope.   10
    For where there is advantage to be gone,
    Both more and less have given him the revolt,
    And none serve with him but constrained things
    Whose hearts are absent too.

MACDUFF   Let our just censures
    Attend the true event, and put we on   15
    Industrious soldiership.

SIWARD   The time approaches
    That will with due decision make us know
    What we shall say we have, and what we owe.
    Thoughts speculative their unsure hopes relate,
    But certain issue strokes must arbitrate;   20
    Towards which advance the war.   *[Exeunt, marching*

Scene Five

Macbeth's castle

Drum and colours. Enter MACBETH · SEYTON · *and Soldiers*

MACBETH   Hang out our banners on the outward walls,
    The cry is still 'They come'. Our castle's strength
    Will laugh a siege to scorn. Here let them lie
    Till famine and the ague eat them up.
    Were they not forced with those that should be ours,   5
    We might have met them dareful, beard to beard,
    And beat them backward home. [*a cry within*]
                      What is that noise?

SEYTON   It is the cry of women, my good lord.   *[Exit*

MACBETH   I have almost forgot the taste of fears.
    The time has been, my senses would have cooled   10
    To hear a night-shriek, and my fell of hair
    Would at a dismal treatise rouse and stir
    As life were in't. I have supped full with horrors.
    Direness, familiar to my slaughterous thoughts,
    Cannot once start me.

17   *She . . . hereafter.* Either 'she would have died sooner or later,'
      or 'she should have died at a later, less awkward time.' The
      ambiguity may be intentional, and the chief point is Mac-
      beth's heartless lack of interest in Lady Macbeth's fate.

18   *time,* proper time. Macbeth seems stunned at the untimely
      injustice (to him) of Lady Macbeth's death, and his complaint
      at the ill-timing is a reflection of the self-dramatization in
      him that we saw as early as Duncan's murder. This thought
      at this moment sets him beyond feeling, and measures the
      extent to which their experience has destroyed the relation-
      ship between Macbeth and his wife.   *word,* announcement.
      But in its ordinary sense it also refers to the word 'dead,' and
      extends this into a future of tomorrows.

20   *Creeps . . . day,* one day follows another in a stealthy, paltry
      succession/His wife's death is one in a tedious sequence—
      'this petty pace.'

21   *To . . . time,* to the last letter in the annals of time.

22–3 *And all . . . death.* The apparently insignificant word 'and' is
      important, confirming that death has been at the back of
      his mind during the previous three lines, when he was
      speaking of the future. The observation is terrifying in its
      callousness, when we recall that the 'fool' of the present
      moment is his wife.

23   *brief candle.* The transition from 'lighted fools' to the idea of
      the candle here suggests that Macbeth's murders by candle-
      light are possessing his mind, and directing the expressions
      he chooses subconsciously to voice his despair. So Shake-
      speare writes at more than one level, and the drama gains
      depth. Shakespeare more than once compared death to the
      snuffing out of a candle; and the triviality of this action leads
      to the next idea.

24   *walking shadow.* In candlelight we see our walking shadows
      (Duncan is recalled), and 'shadow' also meant something
      unreal, a phantom. Actors were at best 'but shadows.'
      poor, pitiable.

27   *sound and fury,* frenzied noise.

28   *Signifying nothing.* Lady Macbeth might never have lived, and
      his despair is complete. Despair was regarded by doctors as
      particular evidence of the devil's domination.

31   *should,* am bound to.

40   *cling,* shrivel up.

42   *I pall in resolution,* my assurance is failing.

43   *doubt the equivocation,* suspect the two-edged promises.

46   *out!* The news and its implication of false prophecy under-
      mines his reason, and he recklessly abandons his impregnable
      position in the castle. Macbeth's reaction here is convincingly
      motivated, and the news that the prophecies appear to be
      equivocal ironically drives Macbeth to a gesture that enables
      the prophecies to be fulfilled. It is as if his own destruction is
      controlling him.

Re-enter SEYTON

                              Wherefore was that cry?   15
SEYTON   The Queen, my lord, is dead.
MACBETH   She should have died hereafter.
   There would have been a time for such a word.
   Tomorrow, and tomorrow, and tomorrow
   Creeps in this petty pace from day to day,   20
   To the last syllable of recorded time,
   And all our yesterdays have lighted fools
   The way to dusty death. Out, out, brief candle!
   Life's but a walking shadow, a poor player
   That struts and frets his hour upon the stage   25
   And then is heard no more. It is a tale
   Told by an idiot, full of sound and fury,
   Signifying nothing.

Enter a MESSENGER

   Thou comest to use thy tongue—thy story quickly.
MESSENGER   Gracious my lord,   30
   I should report that which I say I saw,
   But know not how to do't.
MACBETH   Well, say sir.
MESSENGER   As I did stand my watch upon the hill,
   I looked toward Birnam, and anon methought
   The wood began to move.
MACBETH   Liar and slave!   35
MESSENGER   Let me endure your wrath if't be not so.
   Within this three mile may you see it coming.
   I say, a moving grove.
MACBETH   If thou speak'st false,
   Upon the next tree shalt thou hang alive
   Till famine cling thee. If thy speech be sooth   40
   I care not if thou dost for me as much . . .
   I pall in resolution, and begin
   To doubt the equivocation of the fiend
   That lies like truth: 'Fear not, till Birnam wood
   Do come to Dunsinane'. And now a wood   45
   Comes toward Dunsinane . . . Arm, arm, and out!

*Notes &
Commentary*

47	*avouches*, claims to be true.
50	*estate*, order, structure. *world*, universe.
	undone, disrupted.
52	*harness*, armour.

Scene Six

2	*And show . . . are*, show yourselves to be soldiers.
4	*first battle*, main army.
6	*order*, plan of campaign.
7–8	*Do . . . fight*, if only we can meet with the usurper's forces tonight, let us be beaten if we cannot put up a fight.
10	*harbingers*, heralds.

Scene Seven

	(stage direction) Enter Macbeth. Now that the fighting has begun, Macbeth never appears on stage with the few allies said to be left to him. He is alone, a cornered animal, his conduct desperate, the negation of control and reason. On the other hand, there is confidence and assured conversation on Malcolm's side; it is the power of law against brute inhumanity. At the same time, his isolation enhances Macbeth's stature and significance.
1–2	*They . . . course.* Bear-baiting was a common entertainment in Elizabethan times. The bear was chained to a stake and set upon by mastiffs, the bout being technically termed a 'course.'
2	*What's he*, what kind of man is he?

If this which he avouches does appear,
There is nor flying hence, nor tarrying here.
I 'gin to be aweary of the sun
And wish the estate o' the world were now undone.   50
Ring the alarum bell! Blow wind, come wrack!
At least we'll die with harness on our back.   [*Exeunt*

Scene Six

Before the castle

Drum and colours. Enter MALCOLM · SIWARD · MACDUFF · *and their army, with boughs*

MALCOLM   Now near enough. Your leafy screens throw down,
And show like those you are. You, worthy uncle,
Shall with my cousin, your right noble son,
Lead our first battle. Worthy Macduff and we
Shall take upon's what else remains to do,   5
According to our order.

SIWARD   Fare you well.
Do we but find the tyrant's power tonight,
Let us be beaten if we cannot fight.

MACDUFF   Make all our trumpets speak, give them all breath,
Those clamorous harbingers of blood and death.   [*Exeunt. Alarums* 10

Scene Seven

Before the castle

Alarums. Enter MACBETH

MACBETH   They have tied me to a stake. I cannot fly,
But bear-like I must fight the course . . . What's he
That was not born of woman? Such a one
Am I to fear, or none.

Enter YOUNG SIWARD

YOUNG SIWARD   What is thy name?

7, 8 *hell, devil.* Macbeth is again associated with hell and the devil as the final climax approaches.

10 *abhorred,* abominable.

10–11 *with my . . . speak'st.* Young Siward uses the language of the challenge and trial by combat.

11 *(stage direction) Young Siward is slain.* Macbeth's next remark shows that young Siward is killed on stage. Yet if the body is visible to Macduff who enters next, it is odd that he does not remark on it. And certainly it cannot be visible to old Siward at l.24. The body may be 'brought off the field' (difficult in the time allowed), or he dies in the inner stage and the traverse is drawn, or he falls into the yard alley, as Banquo doubtless did.

11–13 *Thou . . . born.* The casually easy slaughter of the boy Siward feeds Macbeth's confidence in this assurance, making his meeting with Macduff the more tense, and finally the more devastating. Also Shakespeare reminds us again of the equivocations.

16 *still,* for ever.

17 *kerns,* Irish foot soldiers.

18 *staves,* spears. *Either thou,* i.e. either you face me.

20 *undeeded,* unused.

22 *bruited,* reported. The noises are off stage.

24 *gently rendered,* meekly surrendered.

27 *The day . . . yours,* you have almost carried the day.

29 *strike beside us.* Probably it means 'fight by our side' though it has been taken to mean 'deliberately miss us by letting their blows fall beside us.'

MACBETH   Thou'lt be afraid to hear it.   5
YOUNG SIWARD   No, though thou call'st thyself a hotter name
   Than any is in hell.
MACBETH   My name's Macbeth.
YOUNG SIWARD   The devil himself could not pronounce a title
   More hateful to mine ear.
MACBETH   No, nor more fearful.
YOUNG SIWARD   Thou liest, abhorred tyrant, with my sword   10
   I'll prove the lie thou speak'st. [*They fight, and* YOUNG SIWARD *is slain*]
MACBETH   Thou wast born of woman.
   But swords I smile at, weapons laugh to scorn,
   Brandished by man that's of a woman born.   [*Exit*

Alarums. Enter MACDUFF

MACDUFF   That way the noise is. Tyrant, show thy face.
   If thou be'st slain, and with no stroke of mine,   15
   My wife and children's ghosts will haunt me still.
   I cannot strike at wretched kerns whose arms
   Are hired to bear their staves. Either thou, Macbeth,
   Or else my sword with an unbattered edge
   I sheathe again undeeded . . . There thou shouldst be.   20
   By this great clatter, one of greatest note
   Seems bruited. Let me find him, fortune,
   And more I beg not.   [*Exit. Alarums*

Enter MALCOLM *and* OLD SIWARD

SIWARD   This way my lord, the castle's gently rendered
   The tyrant's people on both sides do fight.   25
   The noble thanes do bravely in the war.
   The day almost itself professes yours,
   And little is to do.
MALCOLM   We have met with foes
   That strike beside us.
SIWARD   Enter sir, the castle.   [*Exeunt. Alarums*

1   *play . . . fool*, i.e. kill myself. Suicide was considered by the
       Romans to be an honourable alternative to surrender.
2   *lives*, i.e. other men living.
5–6   *my soul . . . already*. Chambers saw this as 'the only real touch
       of remorse in Macbeth.' It seems to me that he is thinking
       of himself, and there is an arrogance in the words that is
       extended in his next speech.
5   *charged*, burdened.
8   *Than . . . out*, than words can express.
       Thou . . . labour, you waste your energy.
9   *intrenchant*, invulnerable.
10   *impress*, mark, wound.
11   *crests*, helmets, and hence warriors.
12   *a charmed life*, a life protected by supernatural powers.
13   *Despair*, i.e. despair of.
14   *angel*, i.e. evil angel, demon.   *still*, always.
16   *Untimely ripped*. Macduff explains that he was not born nat-
       urally, but by Caesarean section. The line allows for a pause
       before Macbeth finds words.
18   *better . . . of man*, i.e. his spirit, as against 'the dregs of life,'
       his body. Cf. *Sonnet* 74: 'My spirit is thine, the better part
       of me.'
19   *juggling*, dissembling.
20   *palter . . . sense*, cheat us with equivocations.
21–2   *That . . . hope*, who keep us listening to fair promises, and deny
       us the fulfilment of our expectations/Banquo's warning in
       Act1 Sc.3, ll.123–6 is recognized as true.
24   *show . . . time*, the popular spectacle of the age.
25   *monsters*, freaks.
26   *painted . . . pole*, i.e. painted on a cloth or board fastened to
       a pole, to advertise the side-show.

Scene Eight

The battlefield

Enter MACBETH

MACBETH   Why should I play the Roman fool, and die
On mine own sword? Whiles I see lives, the gashes
Do better upon them.

Enter MACDUFF

MACDUFF   Turn, hell-hound, turn!

MACBETH   Of all men else I have avoided thee.
But get thee back—my soul is too much charged   5
With blood of thine already.

MACDUFF   I have no words.
My voice is in my sword, thou bloodier villain
Than terms can give thee out! [*They fight. Alarums*]

MACBETH   Thou losest labour.
As easy mayst thou the intrenchant air
With thy keen sword impress, as make me bleed.   10
Let fall thy blade on vulnerable crests—
I bear a charmed life, which must not yield
To one of woman born.

MACDUFF   Despair thy charm
And let the angel whom thou still hast served
Tell thee, Macduff was from his mother's womb   15
Untimely ripped.

MACBETH   Accursed be that tongue that tells me so,
For it hath cowed my better part of man.
And be these juggling fiends no more believed
That palter with us in a double sense,   20
That keep the word of promise to our ear
And break it to our hope . . . I'll not fight with thee.

MACDUFF   Then yield thee coward,
And live to be the show and gaze o' the time.
We'll have thee, as our rarer monsters are,   25

31   *And thou opposed*, and you my opponent.

32   *try the last.* Either 'test the last prophecy,' or 'fight to the end.'

34   *(stage direction) Exeunt . . . slain.* This is in the Folio, and indicates a prolonged struggle. The alarums mark its continuation off stage, where Macbeth may be killed. If they re-enter fighting, Macbeth could be driven into the inner stage, where the traverse could be drawn to hide his body.

Scene Nine

    (stage direction) Retreat. Flourish. The 'retreat' was sounded to call off a pursuit, the 'flourish' heralded a ceremonial entry.

1   *we miss*, who are missing.

2   *go off*, die.   *by . . . see*, judging by those I see here already.

7–8   *The . . . fought*, and his exploits had no sooner proved him to be a man, in the position he fought for without flinching.

12   *hurts*, wounds.   *before*, i.e. on the front of his body, indicating he died facing his foe.

16   *his . . . knolled*, the bell has been tolled for his death. Siward means that no further ceremony is needed.

Painted upon a pole, and underwrit,
'Here may you see the tyrant.'
MACBETH   I will not yield
To kiss the ground before young Malcolm's feet,
And to be baited with the rabble's curse.
Though Birnam Wood be come to Dunsinane,   30
And thou opposed, being of no woman born,
Yet I will try the last. Before my body
I throw my warlike shield. Lay on Macduff.
And damned be him that first cries 'Hold, enough!'
                [Exeunt fighting. Alarums. Enter fighting and MACBETH *slain*

Scene Nine

In the castle

Retreat. Flourish. Enter, with drum and colours, MALCOLM · OLD SIWARD · ROSS ·
    Thanes and Soldiers

MALCOLM   I would the friends we miss were safe arrived.

SIWARD   Some must go off, and yet by these I see,
    So great a day as this is cheaply bought.

MALCOLM   Macduff is missing, and your noble son.

ROSS   Your son my lord, has paid a soldier's debt.   5
    He only lived but till he was a man,
    The which no sooner had his prowess confirmed
    In the unshrinking station where he fought,
    But like a man he died.

SIWARD   Then he is dead?

ROSS   Ay, and brought off the field. Your cause of sorrow   10
    Must not be measured by his worth, for then
    It hath no end.

SIWARD   Had he his hurts before?

ROSS   Ay, on the front.

SIWARD   Why then, God's soldier be he.
    Had I as many sons as I have hairs,
    I would not wish them to a fairer death.   15
    And so, his knell is knolled.

18   *parted well*, died bravely.   *paid his score*, did his duty.
19   *newer comfort*, fresh and favourable news.
20   *stands*, i.e. on a pole. Traitors' heads were commonly exhibited on poles, especially at the Southwark end of London Bridge.
21   *the time*. Not only 'the present age,' but 'mankind.'   *free*, liberated. It carries also an implication of redemption from evil. This is the effect now that 'the usurper' is replaced by the rightful monarch.
22   *compassed . . . pearl*, surrounded by the nobility of Scotland. 'Pearl' was used figuratively for something supremely precious or noble.
23–4   *That . . . mine*, who echo my greeting in their hearts, and whom I now ask to join with me in proclaiming aloud.
27   *Before . . . loves*, before I reckon and repay the loyalty each of you has shown/The contractual element in the relationship between monarch and his aristocracy was natural and quite seemly.
31   *Which . . . time*, which has to be establshed anew at the start of this new era.
34   *Producing forth*, hunting out.   *cruel ministers*, vicious agents.
35   *dead butcher, fiend-like queen*. Malcolm's view, and the slanted opinion necessary at the re-establishment of order. The epithets significantly reverse the status of Macbeth and Lady Macbeth, making him the rough agent of her evil designs. And the death of Macbeth is butchery—a physical immediacy that is avoided in his queen's remoter end.
36   *self and*, her own.
38   *That . . . us*, that demands our attention.
38–9   *by . . . place*. The restoration of true government is complete, its projects graced with divine approval and conforming to the limits of order.
39   *in measure*, with a sense of proportion.

MALCOLM   He's worth more sorrow,
　And that I'll spend for him.
SIWARD   He's worth no more.
　They say he parted well, and paid his score.
　And so God be with him. Here comes newer comfort.

Enter MACDUFF, *with* MACBETH's *head*

MACDUFF Hail King, for so thou art. Behold where stands   20
　The usurper's cursed head. The time is free.
　I see thee compassed with thy kingdom's pearl,
　That speak my salutation in their minds,
　Whose voices I desire aloud with mine—
　Hail, King of Scotland!
ALL   Hail, King of Scotland! [*flourish*]   25
MALCOLM We shall not spend a large expense of time,
　Before we reckon with your several loves,
　And make us even with you. My thanes and kinsmen,
　Henceforth be earls, the first that ever Scotland
　In such an honour named. What's more to do,   30
　Which would be planted newly with the time—
　As calling home our exiled friends abroad,
　That fled the snares of watchful tyranny,
　Producing forth the cruel ministers
　Of this dead butcher and his fiend-like queen,   35
　Who as 'tis thought, by self and violent hands
　Took off her life—this, and what needful else
　That calls upon us, by the grace of Grace,
　We will perform in measure, time and place.
　So thanks to all at once, and to each one,   40
　Whom we invite to see us crowned at Scone.   [*Flourish. Exeunt*

THREE

When we get back to the flat, and after we've eaten, Billy insists spies always keep notes about their investigations. I say I think that's a great idea. Billy says he is pleased about that because he can't write them, what with him being only seven and not so good at spelling.

So these are my notes about what happened on our first SNOOP secret mission to 22 Cavalier Approach, Honeydown Hills. I present them without comment:

SNOOP
secret mission number one

FACT NUMBER ONE: The woman's voice we heard earlier wasn't Pearl, as I suspected. Billy said he knew it wasn't her all along (he made me add this bit to the notes).

We heard the woman say she was going to paint the walls in Pigeon Grey. Billy whispered to me that this might be a clue. I said I had no idea how that was a clue to why Pearl wasn't there. Billy said he had no idea either, but it sounded like something a spy would say.

FACT NUMBER TWO: There was a man with her. We heard the name Harry. We didn't think it was a red herring — he really was called Harry, because she kept saying it over and over. Harry grunted a lot. At first, Billy thought he might be a gorilla. (He wasn't.)

FACT NUMBER THREE: They were on the move downstairs and so we needed a good hiding place. There were three options:

a) the bathroom, but if we locked the door they might think we were intruders and ring the police.

b) we could sneak out our bedroom window and shimmy down a pipe. I looked out to see how far down the garden was. No way, too dangerous, I decided. (I saw something else though. Pearl's portrait was lying in the garden with a huge hole punched right through her face. It made my stomach feel bubbly.)

c) the airing cupboard.

Billy suggested another option: how about we closed our eyes and then no one would see us? Well, it was a suggestion, but I went with my own choice and so c) it was.

At this stage, once we'd got in the airing cupboard, Billy said the people downstairs were robbers in our house.

I said they were not, because robbers do not usually talk about painting the walls.

Billy said they might be robbers who cleaned up after themselves by painting the walls with a pigeon.

I ignored him. What else could I do?

Billy said spies in SNOOP did not ignore each other. I said they did if one spy had jelly for brains. Billy nudged me in the guts.

Note: it hurt. I squealed.

Billy said it was his invisible elbow that attacked me.

I said there was no such thing as an invisible elbow.

Billy said it was as real as his invisible tackle earlier.

I said he was not very funny.

Billy said I was not very funny either.

FACT NUMBER FOUR: As we argued, someone discovered our hiding place. Still, spies can control any situation they're presented with, so we pretended it was perfectly normal for one boy in a balaclava and another dressed as a sheep to be in an airing cupboard. At this point, Billy says he told the woman he was a spy with SNOOP. He has asked me to write that down although no one could hear him say it through the balaclava so I can't present this as fact as there were no witnesses.

Description of woman: Brown hair scraped back in a ponytail, neck scarf that looked like a midnight sky, pregnant (or has swallowed a bowling ball).

Description of man, Harry: Not an actual ape, although definitely from the same family, judging by the amount of hair poking out of the neck of his shirt.

Quick rundown of what happened next:

Billy said we lived there.

Woman said we didn't. Woman said the people who lived there had done a flit because the estate agent they visited this morning told them so. He also said he'd like someone to move in straight away and the previous tenants left behind their old furniture. Woman said she liked it here very much and it would be perfect when they had the baby and she'd tell the estate agent so when she contacted him later.

Billy, who wasn't in the slightest bit interested, asked where Pearl was, because she had been living here with us for the past two years and now she'd disappeared. Billy said Pearl used to love us to the moon and back and that was a lot of love. He couldn't remember how many kilometres worth. But I could, 768,800.

The woman asked if Pearl was our mother.

Billy said she was our number two mummy.

The man said maybe he should ring our number one mummy and sort this mess out.

I was so angry I told him that could be tricky unless he had a hotline to God. The man said I was very lippy indeed. After that I wanted to say he had more cheek than a hamster but instead I said thank you very much, then decided this was the time to do a ewe-turn. (Actually I meant U-turn, but when writing these notes I realized ewe-turn was funnier so went with that.)

Anyway, I turned around and told Billy to run.

Billy did nothing. So I shouted "RUN!" at the top of my lungs. Billy still didn't move, but I started running anyway and dragged him behind me by the top of his balaclava, which incidentally came off and gave away his identity. Billy has since said it doesn't matter because he pulled a funny face at the time and that meant no one could recognize him in future.

The woman yelled, "Leave your key on the way out. I don't want to find you popping up in the toilet next time." I thought that only happened with rats. I didn't tell her that though, because I was too busy trying to run away as if I was a sheep escaping a sheepdog.

I threw the key into the air; it arced like a tiny silver rainbow and then fell to the floor with a tinkle like a heart shattering.

As we ran down the road, Billy huffed, "When we find Pearl, I'm going to ask her."

"Ask her what?" I puffed back.

"Ask her why everyone leaves us in the end." Billy put his balaclava back on and that was that.

This is the end of my notes on the first SNOOP secret mission to 22 Cavalier Approach, Honeydown Hills.

No doubt about it, our first SNOOP secret mission was a failure. Billy said it was because Pearl had probably run off to the circus: SMART BILLY'S, apparently. I said I thought he'd got the name the wrong way round. No, Billy told me, he'd made up the circus name himself after someone he knew very well and it was definitely Smart Billy. Well, I didn't think he knew anyone smart by the name of Billy but I didn't like to say so. Instead, I told Billy there was no way Pearl could be at a circus and he said she might be because he once heard her say she had to walk a tightrope. I said that it was just a turn of phrase, but Billy wasn't listening because he was too busy getting out his animals and pretending they were in Smart Billy's circus. Billy made the hippo a trapeze artist and the plastic dinosaur the clown. To be honest, if I came face-to-face with a dinosaur I'm not sure I'd be laughing.

I decide that we might have failed at our first attempt to bring Pearl back but we're going to keep trying because Billy's not the same without Pearl. Last night, before bed, he drew Pearl inside a heart and asked me if she still loved him. I said she did and nothing would change that and it didn't matter if we failed the first time round because we could always try again. I'm not going to fail on my plan to say goodbye to Mum either. Not having said goodbye to her is like a tiny splinter under my skin. Sometimes I don't notice it and other times I feel it's there and I know I have to deal with it or it'll stay there for ever.

I'm sitting in Mum's favourite armchair now and it feels warm, safe and comforting, and I'm writing THE GOODBYE LIST. It is a list of ways to say goodbye to Mum and I'm going to make it really special. I have decided I will come up with ten ways to say goodbye and I'll try each and every one of them and I'll know when I hit on the right one because I'll have that fizzy feeling in my tummy as if I've been eating mega sour sweets.

THE GOODBYE LIST

1. Write a poem called "Goodbye"
2. Write the word out in sparklers
3. Create a little shrine

4. Draw a picture
5. Send a balloon into the sky
6. Name a star
7. Design my own tattoo
8. Plant a seed
9. Just say goodbye
10. Can't think of a number ten so will say nothing here until I have an idea

The rest of the half-term holiday I get busy trying out THE GOODBYE LIST. For starters I try number three and build a shrine to Mum using Billy's building bricks. Only by the time I go to the toilet and come back, Billy has already pulled it apart and says I'm not allowed to play with his toys. I say I wasn't and Billy says it's nothing to be embarrassed about because Dad never is when he plays with that remote control helicopter he keeps under his bed. Thing is, I don't bother trying to build another shrine to Mum, because somehow a few plastic bricks don't seem to be good enough. Nope, a shrine is definitely not how I want to say goodbye to my mum.

Next, I try writing a poem.

Goodbye, didn't the time fly?
You had to go, I don't know why.
I still think of you and sigh.
This is my poem to say goodbye.

In the end that doesn't feel right either and it makes me sad. So sad that Dad comes into the bedroom and says I shouldn't be moping about. I say I like moping about and Dad says there is plenty of time for that when I'm a teenager.

"Dad?" My voice goes so high only dogs can hear it. "Do you think I could have some sparklers?" Number two on THE GOODBYE LIST, here I come. But then there I go, because Dad replies, "Remember, remember, it's nowhere near the fifth of November."

Then he says, "Becket?" and his voice goes even higher than mine. "Sit down. I have something to tell you."

I have a feeling I'm not going to like this.

I am right.

"I know this will be a little shock but now the half-term break is almost over and we're settled into this new flat, I've arranged for you both to go to a new school. It's called Bleeding Heart and it's closer to this flat than your old school. You can walk home together

44

now." Dad reaches out and tries to take my hand, only I pull away.

Little shock? No, a little shock is when you touch a door handle and you get a tiny jolt of static. This is a huge shock, nearly enough to blow me right off my feet and give me crazy hair, like when you rub your head with a balloon. Well, I don't mind saying that my jaw is on the floor, along with my stomach. After I've recovered, I tell Dad I won't be going to a new school. Isn't it bad enough that we're in a new flat?

Dad, his voice as soft as butter, says, "You will." Then he adds that he's heard it's very nice there. Who has he heard that from? I ask him. Dad says the head. At this point, I'm so angry I have to check my own pulse.

"Look, Dad!" I wail. "The stress is sending my heart rate sky-high." Dad says I have the heart of an ox and I say I don't actually. I have the heart of a ten-year-old human and right now it's about to explode into one million pieces. I add, "What about my mates at my old school? Will I see them again?"

Dad says I'll make new friends.

What kind of living hell is this? I haven't said goodbye to Mum, I haven't said goodbye to Pearl and now I haven't said goodbye to my mates either.

45

Later on Billy has a nightmare and nudges me awake at five forty-three in the morning. I crawl out of bed, saying I can tell him a story to make him fall asleep again. It's just what Mum used to do for me. Billy says he'd like that and we both sit in Mum's armchair, curled up like two little prawn crackers.

At first I don't have a clue what sort of story to tell, but that's when I have an idea.

"Let me tell you a story," I say, "of two boys – two brothers – who were making a journey, a journey in an armchair." I look down. "An armchair just like this. Let me tell you how they survived the most terrible storm and how the armchair made sure they travelled safely to their destination."

Billy swallows and looks up at me. "Okay."

"A long time ago, two boys set off on a journey, along with many others. They weren't sure what the land they were going to was like, but they knew they could no longer stay on the land they had lived on for many years, because it was disappearing. So they had to move forward to survive. They bundled up all their belongings, which wasn't much, just what they were wearing and an old armchair. They climbed on board the armchair and pushed it off into the ocean. Others did the same, with their own vessels. It was sunny for the longest time and

46

after a while the two boys could see the new land in the distance. Everything was going exactly as they'd hoped. They were going to make it."

"I like this story," says Billy. "The armchair was safe."

"It was," I reply, "for a while. But when they were halfway across the ocean, the air changed and the clouds got heavy and dark. There was a storm coming." Billy cuddles closer to me. "The rain came first and it felt like lots of tiny swords because it was so sharp. Then there was thunder, loud like thousands of party poppers going off all at once. And the lightning lit up the land in front of them and it seemed further away than they'd first thought. One of the brothers wanted to turn back, but the land behind them had disappeared for good."

"I don't like the storm in this story," whispers Billy, slumping down in the armchair.

"All they could do was hope the storm would pass. Only it didn't pass as quickly as they thought it would. They clung onto the chair, afraid of what would happen to them. They waved at others who were making the journey too, but they were invisible to those around them, because everyone else had troubles of their own riding out the storm."

Billy's face slackens and he bends forward. "They were invisible?"

"Well, not actually invisible," I reply. "But others didn't notice them even though they were crying out for help. Perhaps they couldn't hear because the wind was so loud. Again the boys called out. They called to the sky, the air and the sea."

Shaking his head, Billy responds, "Did anyone hear?"

"Oh, yes. Someone heard."

"Godzilla," says Billy, perking up. "I mean, the Loch Ness Monster."

"Neither," I reply. "They couldn't see who it was but they heard a voice, carried on the wind, saying: *I am the whisper in the wind, the rustle of the leaves, the shiver of winter and the warm breath of summer, I am the cloud galleon that sails the sky and the moon that skips across the surface of the water.*" I put on a whole new voice for this bit, imagining myself winning an Oscar for storytelling.

"Ooh," says Billy. I smile, thinking he's impressed with my storytelling. Perhaps I'm as good at it as Mum was. Billy's eyes droop. "I don't like that silly whispering wind stuff though," he murmurs. Billy puts his thumb into his mouth and begins to drift back to sleep.

"I promise to tell you who the voice belongs to another night," I whisper, as Billy lets out a tiny sigh. "I promise you this story will have a happy-ever-after."

FOUR

The half-term break is over and we have not found Pearl and I have not discovered how to say goodbye to Mum no matter how much I want to. Saying goodbye to someone you wish you could stay with every minute is the hardest thing ever. I've thought about it so much my head feels muffled and that is no good because today is my first day at Bleeding Heart School *and* my eleventh birthday and Dad is shouting at me to hurry up and open my cards.

I trudge into the kitchen, where Billy is waving five cards in my face. The first one is from Dad. It has a picture of a man playing golf on a hilly green. I do not like golf. It says: *Happy 40th. You're not quite over the hill yet.* Dad shrugs and says he was in a hurry, sorry.

Card two is from Ibiza Nana. Dad says he gave her our new address straight away because she didn't want to miss my special day. The card she's sent has a blue bear on the front. She still thinks I'm about two.

The third card is from Billy. He lets me open that one myself. There's a brown smudge on the front. When he sees my horrified face he says it's nothing yucky, just a squashed worm.

Card four is from Cat Woman. She has written that a little bird told her it was my birthday. That little bird must have been a bald headed eagle because Dad admits it was him who mentioned it when he popped down to Crops and Bobbers when we were out playing invisible football.

Card five has to be from Pearl. Tearing the envelope apart, I stare at the contents. The message says: COME VISIT BIFFO'S WAREHOUSE. It's just one of those stupid flyers that companies send out.

I'm not going to cry. I'm not. I don't. I want to though. I want to cry because today is my birthday and it's supposed to be brilliant and already it isn't.

When Dad sees I'm disappointed he claps his hands together and says it is presents next. He sets them on the table. I'm guessing I haven't got the life-size plastic skeleton I wanted, unless Dad has wrapped the skeleton bone by bone. Present one is a hardback notebook. Billy is totally disgusted with this, by the way, which serves him right for opening my birthday gifts in the first place.

"For your medical notes," says Dad, slurping tea from his Top Dad mug. I try to nod my head, only it's hard with the weight of disappointment on my shoulders.

Present two: a second-hand medical book about healing herbs. Someone has written notes in the margin. When I mention that I'd rather have a new one, Dad says money is a bit tight and new things don't grow on trees. But that's a lie because new leaves grow on trees every spring – that's all I'm saying.

Present three: Ibiza Nana has sent me a knitted cardigan. There is a place for cardigans, and also musical Christmas jumpers, scarves and mittens that would fit a long-fingered gorilla, and it is under the bed. Clearly the idea of buying something suitable for an eleven-year-old has passed Ibiza Nana by, like computers, non-alcoholic drinks, mobile phones and tablets (unless they're in small pots with the days of the week on them).

Present four: Billy gives me a collection of dead flies

in a matchbox. He's always rescuing bugs and making sure they're okay. Not these flies. They are less than okay. They are dead. Billy points inside the box and says fly number one, the one without wings, is Mr Walk. I nod. Fly two, without wings or legs: Mr Roll Around. I say it's the best present I've ever had. Billy says he could get me some more bugs. I say I'm not sure my heart can take the excitement.

As we're about to leave for school, Dad pulls me to one side. "There's a present five," he whispers, his voice wheezy with excitement. "I didn't give it to you at the table. This is the present you've been waiting for, son."

Hallelujah! The life-size skeleton is hidden in a cupboard. I knew it was. Dad will whip it out at any moment and I'll declare it to be called Mr Bones. All those other presents I've just opened were tasters, because the main present is yet to come. I'll act surprised. Of course I will.

Unfortunately, I don't have to *act* surprised at all. I *am* surprised, as Dad hands me a bit of paper folded into a weird shape and says, "This is it."

Dad says he's pleased that I'm so stunned. To be honest, he was a bit surprised by it all too. Turns out, Dad was moving around a few of the boxes we brought with us and he found this on the floor and thought of me.

Let's get this straight, Dad found a bit of paper on the floor and thought: *Hey, my son would LOVE this for his birthday instead of the skeleton he asked for.*

"I think it's funny how it turned up on your birthday. It reminded me of something from the past." Dad pauses, his eyes unfocused. Then he closes them gently and whispers, "Once, a long time ago, your mum and I went on a date. It was to this great burger bar called Two's Company in Honeydown Hills. It's not there any more."

Oh.

Dad opens his eyes again and sighs. "Your mum had fries and I had a triple burger with fried onions – soft as a slipper they were – and there was an egg on top." Dad pauses and smacks his lips together, remembering it fondly. A second later he shakes his head. "But I'm not talking about the food. At the end of the meal your mum folded up the napkin into a little star. Your mum was so good at making things. She gave me the folded star and a kiss that night."

"But this isn't a star, it looks like a bird," I reply, staring at it and thinking Dad's definitely not getting a kiss from me. "You said Mum made stars so where did the bird come from?"

"I don't know. I just found it lying in the corner of the

living room, like I said. I didn't notice it at first and then when I was moving things around I spotted it. It reminded me of that date with your mother. Truth is, I lost your Mum's star," says Dad, rubbing the koi carp tattoo on his arm absent-mindedly. "If only I knew then how precious that star was…" The words float away like a helium balloon let go by a child.

I stare at the tiny bird in my palm before shoving it in my blazer pocket and whispering, "Today is rubbish and a stupid paper bird that the previous flat owner probably left behind when they moved isn't going to make it any better."

Nothing is.

Dad deposits Billy and me in the reception area at Bleeding Heart School. The secretary, who introduces herself as Mrs Parsnips, gives Dad a wodge of paper to fill in and then takes him away somewhere. As Dad disappears, Billy tugs on my blazer and whispers that Pearl should have been here to drop us off at school. He asks if she ever sent a text back and I say she hasn't yet but she still might.

"But what if she forgets who we are?" says Billy, shuffling from one foot to the other.

"She won't," I reply.

"Granddad Albert did before he died," says Billy. "Every time we visited him he didn't know who we were. Ibiza Nana had to say I was Billy over and over."

"He wasn't well," I explain.

Then Dad returns and grabs Billy and me into the biggest hug ever, nearly crushing our bones to dust. He only stops to let another boy rush through. With a final cheery wave goodbye, Dad's off; we watch as he climbs into The Codfather van and zooms away as fast as his flat tyre will carry him. The one-eyed cod disappears over the horizon.

As the secretary excuses herself to take a phone call, Billy's eyes brim with water. "I wanted Pearl to be here more than anything," he wails. "I wanted one of Pearl's special hugs and now I can't have one."

Desperately I try to hush Billy, telling him Pearl's probably having a great time at the circus, um, flipping around on a soft mat and laughing at the Tyrannosaurus rex. Billy wipes his eyes and tells me he doesn't think she's at the circus any more. She's been kidnapped by aliens instead. He saw a strange light in the sky recently. It might have been a spaceship.

"Or could it have been an aeroplane?"

But Billy isn't listening to me because he's too busy

saying he's scared that Pearl's gone for ever, just like Mum.

"Mum didn't go on a spaceship though," I mutter. "You know that."

The secretary finishes her call. She directs me to my new class and then takes Billy off to his. As they walk into the distance, I hear Billy say, "Thank you, Mrs Parsnips."

"It's Parsons," she replies and laughs.

"Go in, they don't bite."

I'm peering in through the small porthole to my classroom when this voice booms behind me. Quivering, I open the door and venture my foot in. All eyes swivel towards me like a whole room of zombies sensing fresh meat. Well, if that's the case, they do bite. Repeatedly.

"Go on, inside a bit more. You won't learn anything in the corridor."

No, but I'll still be alive.

Once I'm in the classroom properly, the voice from behind says, "I'm Mr Beagle and, class, this is Becket Rumsey, he will be joining us here. Becket, there is a place at the back, please take a pew and then I'll take the register."

A few minutes later I'm in my seat, playing around with my new pencil case as Mr Beagle calls out the names. As he reaches D on the register I take out a pen and write GOODBYE across my knuckles, remembering number seven on my list (design my own tattoo). Perhaps this is the way to say goodbye to Mum. I give the two Os eyes. Next, I draw a few teardrops. They look like squashed flies. Then I realize I've been drawing with permanent pen and so I start licking my hand like a thirsty dog. Mr Beagle has moved onto M.

"Oi, licky lips," whispers a girl with cornrows sitting at the desk next to me. I put my tongue away. "Want a bracelet? I've made it especially for you. Honestly, it's for you." She fires a rubber bracelet with a tiny butterfly charm on it across to me and it lands right in front of my pencil case.

I shrug. How could she have made it for me when this is the first time she's ever clapped eyes on me? "I don't wear bracelets," I mumble back.

The girl says that I'll want to wear this one. "Put it on."

Thinking it would be rude not to, particularly as this is my first day, I shove the bracelet on my wrist and stare at it.

"Looks good," she mutters. She's either short-sighted

or lying. "I'm Nevaeh, by the way, and that bracelet is your lucky charm." She glances towards Mr Beagle, who is now onto P. "By the way, it's bad luck to take it off," hisses Nevaeh. "You must wear it until it falls off by itself and when that happens something amazing will occur. I got the idea from this story I read where the lady wore a green string on her wrist and it was supposed to protect her from danger. She couldn't take it off until it fell off."

I only manage to squeak, "Did it fall off?"

"Yes, after she broke her wrist."

"So, it didn't protect her from danger then?"

Great, that's all I need. Day one and I'm stuck with a rubber butterfly bracelet that I can't take off thanks to a crazy girl. What I need to do now is keep right away from her.

It turns out there are a few other people at Bleeding Heart that I reckon I need to avoid. The first is the boy who sits in the row in front of me, with hands like ham slices and a face like a bulldog chewing a wasp. He answered to the name Robert Absolom on the register. I went to the toilet halfway through morning class, and when I walked back in, he looked at me like I was something yucky. I tried to smile but he pointed at my shoe and then I realized I'd got some toilet roll attached to it instead of attached to the toilet bowl. Mr Beagle got very excited when he saw it and told us how the average person goes to the toilet about 2,500 times a year. A boy in the front row said he goes at least double that and everyone laughed.

"Thank you, Donté Moffatt," said Mr Beagle, before adding, "World Toilet Day is November 19th and recycled toilet paper does not mean using old toilet paper."

The third person I think I need to avoid is the girl with the plait so big Tarzan phoned and asked if he could have his jungle rope back. At morning break she sidled up to me, said her name was Mimi and welcomed me to the class, saying everyone thinks I'm ace but it's only because I'm new. Once I'm old no one will care any more. In fact, she already doesn't care. She's too busy doing ballet, chess, French and kung fu to have time to be interested in me. Then she glared at me and skipped away.

An hour later, I've decided I do not like anyone in this class. I will ask Dad when I get home if I can come and work with him on the fish delivery rounds. He'll only have to change the words on the van slightly: THE CODFATHER AND THE CODSON.

As I'm working out what I can say to Dad to convince him, Mr Beagle says it's time to finish a project they were doing before half-term. "We were looking at important items from our past, but we didn't get the chance to look at *your* important items before half-term, so I asked you to bring them in today. Becket, you can just talk about anything important from your childhood. You don't need the item. Perhaps you can start, in fact?"

I'm so shocked, my intestines feel like they've just fallen out of my pants. Gutted! At least I know exactly what my important item would be: my mum's armchair. But I can imagine it now: I say my important item is my mum's armchair and then the teacher asks me why (because teachers are like robots programmed to ask questions). Then I have to lie, because I don't want to tell everyone it's where I feel safe, it's where Mum told me stories and I curled up beside her and felt happy. I don't want to tell everyone it's important because I still have the armchair but I don't have Mum. Anyway, Robert Absolom will sneer at whatever I say, Mimi will probably strangle me with her plait and Nevaeh will try to force me into wearing more jewellery.

My fingers are so shaky I would totally ace it at playing the maracas in music class. Only we're not in music class so I have to shove them into my blazer pockets so no one notices. And that's when it happens. I feel something: the tiny paper bird that Dad found on the floor. I pull it from my pocket and put it on the desk. Perhaps I can make up some story about that. There is an air-suck of appreciation from Mr Beagle as he spots the bird, and I'm guessing he's so impressed that I've magically brought something in without even knowing about the project that he has vacuumed all the air from the room. He says this is brilliant, I am brilliant and I can feel Mimi bristle in front of me. Nevaeh points to the bracelet and mouths, "It's amazing," only it's nothing to do with the stupid bracelet because it hasn't fallen off yet, it's still stuck on my wrist.

And then Mr Beagle writes two words on the whiteboard:

A LEGEND

FiVE

Wow! Mr Beagle has recognized what I knew already. I am a legend! To think I was having a bad birthday. Now, I'm a legend in my own lifetime. Ace is what it is. Oh yes, ham-hand boy Robert is looking round at me and I'm looking right back – not so yucky now, eh? Nevaeh is still pointing at the bracelet and Mimi is stewing in her own anger, because obviously I am a legend and it's not just because I'm new.

Mr Beagle raises his hand and wiggles his fingers, which is quite a feat considering he's got digits the size of pork sausages. "This little origami crane that Becket has brought in is incredibly special. And I can tell you that, folded within its wings, there is the most amazing legend of all. Pin back your ears."

You can't do that, unless you have a pinnaplasty (which is on page 255 of my copy of *Marvin's Medical Manual*). Only, I sort of do it anyway, because I'm desperate to hear the legend of my little paper bird. Even if it means it's not me that's the legend after all.

Mr Beagle clears his throat. "Once upon a time, in a land of cherry blossom, samurai warriors, great mysteries, magic and myths, there was a legend that many had heard of." Mr Beagle sails between the desks with my paper crane in his palm.

"My dad says myths are female moths," says Donté Moffatt. Mr Beagle stops abruptly and says female moths are called female moths and being quiet is called saying nothing in case the teacher gives you extra work.

"Now, where was I before I was interrupted?" asks Mr Beagle, as if he hadn't only told us one solitary sentence. He begins sailing between the desks again. "Ah, yes, the legend of one thousand origami cranes is where I was. It says that if a person manages to fold one thousand origami cranes, like this one" – Mr Beagle holds it aloft like it's the world's biggest diamond – "then they shall be granted one magical wish. The crane is a mystical creature that is said to live for a thousand years, which is why you need a thousand paper cranes for a wish – one for every year of the crane's life."

Donté Moffatt hoists up his hand and says, "Spiderman down my nan's bingo hall looks about a thousand years old."

Mr Beagle says it's lovely to hear a story where an elderly gentleman has been named after a superhero like Spiderman; that even when you're old, you can still be brave and active.

"Oh, *he* calls himself Spiderman, not anyone else," replies Donté, adding, "He says it's because he's like a spider. Once he's in the bath he finds it really hard to get out again."

Mr Beagle clears his throat again and makes a halt sign with his hand, which is clearly the signal for Donté Moffatt to zip his lip. "Time and time again, people would try to achieve one magical wish," Mr Beagle continues. "Some did, while others failed. As the years passed, the legend of the paper crane grew. Paper cranes were given as wedding gifts in the hope that the couple would have one thousand years of happiness. They were also given to new babies to bless the baby with a lucky life.

"That is the legend of the paper crane and as soon as I saw Becket's item I remembered having read about it.

Why is it important to you, Becket?"

"My dad gave it to me," I reply, slightly gobsmacked.

"Well, that's lovely," says Mr Beagle, walking towards the bookshelf. He runs his finger along the book spines before finding a book and pulling it out.

I am like a mint sweet in cola I'm fizzing with so much happiness. The legend of the paper crane is the best birthday present ever! It hands down beats the story I read about how the obese William the Conqueror exploded at his own funeral and all the monks in the abbey were covered in his rotten guts, *and* the one about how Romans gargled with urine to keep their breath fresh. I look around and a few people look like they've got a hula-hoop jammed in their mouths. Mimi is one of them.

"I can tell you're all stunned," says Mr Beagle proudly, sailing back down the classroom aisle, his tie fluttering behind him like a flag. "Thank you for allowing us to see this wonderful item, Becket." Mr Beagle delivers the crane back into one of my palms and the book he picked from the shelf into the other. He says it's about origami and it might be of interest to me and I can return it when I've finished reading it.

Everyone gives me a little round of applause. It's as though I'm a hero, even though I've done precisely zero.

As Mr Beagle goes on talking, I take a sneaky look at the crane. Oh, how wrong I was to think it wasn't anything important. I can see now that this paper crane is the *best*. By association, I am now bathing in the golden bath water of brilliance. I am surrounded by the foam of fabulousness. I am soaking in the soap bubbles of smarts. My paper crane, the one that I thought was just folded paper, is actually quite incredible, because Mr Beagle says so.

My paper crane can give me a wish.

What could be a better birthday present than that?

THE ORIGAMI BOOK FOR BEGINNERS:
NEVER TOO MUCH PAPERWORK!

1. Start with a square piece of paper. (Heck yes, I can do this. I'm feeling confident.)
2. Fold the top corner to the bottom corner. (This is a piece of cake. Call me Becket Origami Rumsey Esq. Although I won't answer to my initials.)
3. Crease the paper and open it up once more and then fold it down again but sideways. (I just read that a few times to get the hang of it. Maybe I'll just read it again.)

4. You should have lovely creases now. Bring the top three corners to the bottom corner. Now flatten the piece of paper. (Flattening I can do, it's folding I'm getting a bit confused about. My creases are increasingly rubbish.)

5. Fold the top to the centre and unfold and then fold everything down and unfold. (I am folding. I am unfolding. I am folding. I am foaming. At the mouth.)

6. Open your top flap. (What top flap? I have no flap. I am flap-less. Would a cat flap count? Would it be easier to scale Everest with a toothpick than it is to make an origami crane? The answer is: yes, I think it would.)

7. Bring the flap down and press the sides at the same time. (No, wait. I've got something here. It's a paper fortune teller. I'll just twist it between my fingers a few times and open it up. I half expect someone to have written YOU'RE STUPID on the inside.)

8. Turn the model over and repeat on the other side and fold the upper flaps to the centre and repeat on the other side and then fold up the two parts that look like legs and crease and unfold and then reverse and fold the legs along the

creases and then inside reverse and fold one side. You now have a head. (I have a head. I had to cut the shape with scissors though.)

9. Fold the wings and your crane is complete. (I have a bird that looks like a triangle with a trimmed head and a cat flap for a bum.)

I dedicate my entire evening to making paper cranes according to the instructions in the book Mr Beagle gave me earlier. My first attempt is so bad I should set up a blog in my ICT class called Crane Wrecks. In the end, I tore the first bird up. My second attempt isn't dreadful. My third looks like it belongs to the bird family. I'm saying dodo. My fourth is the best.

Oh yes, it seems I am well on the way to getting my wish. And since I haven't found Pearl and I haven't worked out how to say goodbye to Mum, that's what I'm going to use my wish for. Okay, so I know it's sort of two wishes, but I don't like to follow rules.

The next day, when Billy and I are walking to school, I tell him my birthday was better than I thought. There is a spring in my step. I wave to Cat Woman, who we see through the glass at Crops and Bobbers. I say hello to the pavement, the clouds, the hedge, a stray dog peeing up a lamp post. Although I soon stop saying "Hello" and start saying "Scoot" when the dog attempts to pee on my school shoes as I pass. When Billy asks what made it so good, I tell him "A piece of paper" and I'm not lying. Perplexed, Billy says he has loads of paper but it never makes him feel so excited. I say he hasn't got the right piece of paper. So, I explain about the paper crane and how the teacher gave me a book on origami and now I'm making more cranes to get a wish. Billy says he'd like a wish of his own. I already know what Billy would wish for so I tell him we'll find Pearl, I promise. Billy smiles and I smile back, throwing my arm around his shoulder. Today is a good day.

I'm still grinning when I get to school. Even maths can't swipe the smile off my face.

"You're very happy with yourself," says Nevaeh, as I cross the school playground at morning break. "I saw you grinning to yourself in class. You were even happy when Mr Beagle gave us that maths test. Is it the bracelet? Oh, I know it must be. Has something amazing happened already?"

I shake my head. "It's not the bracelet," I say. Nevaeh looks like I've just stamped on her foot wearing some very large clown shoes. "Um...okay, it is the bracelet.

It must be doing something, because I'm so happy." I cross my fingers, because everyone knows if you cross your fingers you can say anything you like.

"See! I knew it would." Nevaeh's face glows like I've just shoved a buttercup under her chin. "That's brilliant." She tugs up my sleeve to check on the bracelet and then looks disappointed. "You're just saying all that, Becket. The bracelet can't have worked because it hasn't snapped off yet, which means you're telling me fibs." Nevaeh leans against the wall, her brows knitted together like one long slug.

"No way." I cross my fingers again.

"The bracelet doesn't lie. If you're still wearing it then nothing amazing has happened and you're just saying it has to get rid of me. Well, you can't get rid of the bracelet and you can't get rid of me."

"Why do you think these bracelets make things happen?" I ask.

"It's not the bracelet so much," explains Nevaeh. "It's the butterfly really. Anyway, I know you need something good in your life. You just have to believe."

Goggle-eyed, I stare down at the rubber bracelet and the tiny blue butterfly that is dangling off it. Sure, I've seen butterflies before, but I've never thought they were all that special. I mean, they start off as ugly caterpillars.

What's great about butterflies? I ask her.

"Butterflies are our loved ones," Nevaeh tells me, "coming back to bring us love and luck."

My heart stutters. I just about manage to squeeze out the words that I don't need a loved one coming back to make me feel happy. I'm lying though because I'd give anything to have my mum come back. I'd give anything to tell her I love her one more time. I'd give anything for a hug, a smile, a kiss.

"Oh yes you do," replies Nevaeh, as if she can read my mind.

SIX

When I get home from school I bring out the paper cranes. I'm going to keep making them until my wish comes true. Forget what Nevaeh says about the bracelet. Bracelets don't work. "The paper cranes are better," I whisper. If there was a fight between a butterfly and a crane, the crane would win wings down.

That's when I get to thinking. I've already made four cranes, even if the last one was the only one that was any good and, by rights, that means some of my wish should come true, even if it's just a tiny part. I check my phone to see if Pearl has texted us yet.

Nope.

Okay, maybe I haven't made enough cranes yet.

I make twenty more.

Still no text from Pearl.

I make twenty more.

There is a sea of paper on the bedroom floor.

I decide to give Pearl a little nudge, because the cranes are giving me courage. I send her an emoji story.

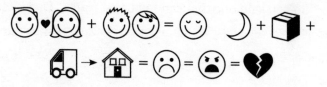

Nothing.

But I'm not giving up on the cranes yet.

And I'm not giving up on Pearl yet either.

My heart feels like a brick under an elephant when I go into the kitchen for dinner. Dad asks why the long face and Billy says it's because I'm a little horse, which is not even funny. Dad says he ordered the food from Mr Wong's and helps himself to a dumpling. We're living on takeaways at the moment. Don't get me wrong, I like takeaway, but not every day. Dad says it's because he can't work the oven.

"Want some?" asks Dad, swallowing down another

dumpling. I can see it pass his Adam's apple. He wipes the grease from his fingers on his koi carp so that its scales glisten, then he asks what sort of day we've both had.

"I got a gold star today," says Billy proudly. "The teacher asked me if my daddy won two thousand pounds on the lottery and gave me half, what would I have?"

"So you said one thousand pounds, right?" Dad picks up some seaweed with a pair of wooden chopsticks and drops it into his mouth. Dark green strands dangle from his lips like coloured streamers on St Patrick's Day. Slowly he slurps them all in and chews until his teeth are full of green flecks.

"I said I'd have a heart attack," answers Billy.

Dad coughs and punches himself in the chest. Then, just as I'm considering the Heimlich manoeuvre, he smiles and says that Billy did well to get a star for that and he's glad Billy's settling in.

"Then, on the way home from school, I had a good look in the mud and that was even more exciting than the gold star," Billy goes on. I just nod because Billy is always poking about in the mud and I'm so used to it now that I hardly even notice he does it any more. "Plus I've got a huge secret that I can't tell anyone." He stops playing with a spare pair of wooden chopsticks long enough to give me a big wink.

Billy repeats that he has a secret and winks at me again. He presses so hard on the chopsticks that one snaps. Not liking where Billy is taking this conversation and because I know that winking is a SNOOP secret mission sign, I swing my foot out and Dad suddenly howls like a werewolf. When Dad asks me what that was for, I tell him I was just checking his patellar reflex – at his age you've got to keep an eye on these things.

"Aren't you interested in my secret?" Clearly Billy isn't giving up, even though I'm ignoring him so much he could be wearing a cloak of invisibility.

You see, Billy's big secret can only be one thing if it's linked to SNOOP. My stomach spins like a paper windmill when I think about how he's going to tell Dad that we went to give Pearl a letter at our old house and now we're sending her emojis. Dad will flip like a tiddlywinks counter if he hears that. I also ask myself why Billy is bringing this up now but then I give up asking myself such difficult questions because why Billy does anything is still a complete mystery to me.

To stop Billy saying anything else, I tell Dad I need a drink of water and when he asks why I can't get it myself I say it's because I'm a little hoarse. Billy cracks up at that, repeating "A little horse" over and over.

With Dad heading to the sink, I whisper to Billy that he's not allowed to tell Dad about anything we've done with SNOOP or we'll be in big trouble. And by big, I mean Big-Ben-as-a-pocket-watch size big.

"Okay," hisses Billy. "I won't say a word." He touches his nose to show it's our secret.

"Remember, we'll never find Pearl if you mention any of this to Dad. He won't want us to be spies. He doesn't seem to want us to find Pearl. Do you understand? You can't tell him the secret." I emphasize the words to make sure Billy is getting me.

I hear the gush of water from the tap as Dad fills my glass.

"But that wasn't the secret I was talking about anyway," whispers Billy.

"What was with the eye winking then?" I stare at Billy. "It's our SNOOP sign."

"Oh," hisses Billy. "I forgot about that. I just had something in my eye. Probably a bit of mud because I found a snail earlier when we were walking back from school and called him Brian and put him straight in my pocket." Billy starts humming to himself. "Then I gave him a new home."

"What's so secret about that?" I ask.

"The new home is in your bed."

77

I am so annoyed about not only not getting a text back from Pearl, but also finding a slimy maze in my bed, that I ask Dad if I can go out for a walk after dinner. Billy says he wants to come with me but Dad says he needs a bath; he can't go to school smelly. Billy says I do and then he huffs and puffs about having to stay at home more than the wolf in *The Three Little Pigs*.

When I get outside, and far enough away from our flat not to be spotted, I pull the stupid snail I've retrieved from my bed out of my pocket and fire it into someone's garden, saying, "Sorry, mate, but I don't share my bed with snails." That's when I realize there is someone in that same garden and I've just lobbed a snail missile at his head.

Quickly, I duck down behind a hedge as the person rubs the back of his head, half glances around and then turns again to continue digging this hole. My SNOOP instincts kick right in and I think there has been a crime committed and this boy is about to bury something. Or someone.

I imagine what would happen if, as a SNOOP spy, I ring the police and say:

Me: I need to speak to an officer about a crime taking place on Chantry Row, Eden Estate, Eden.

Police: I see. Can you explain what sort of crime it is? We can be with you in minutes.

Me: Someone is digging a hole. This proves something.

Police: Yes, it proves they are digging a hole.

Me: What if they are about to bury a body?

Police: How big is the hole, sir?

Me: Not very big.

Police: It's not a body then. Can you please identify what they place in the hole?

Me: Oh, it's a plant.

Police: (hangs up)

It's true – I see the boy place nothing more exciting than a plant in the ground before arranging soil over the base. Then he steps back to admire his work. That's when I see them properly: his hands, his big ham hands. Realizing who the boy is, I gallop away as fast as my legs will carry me. (At this stage, I'm wishing I *am* a little horse.)

When I get home, Billy is waiting for me, his hair dripping onto a towel round his shoulders. Judging by his scrunched-up face, he's not happy. He pulls me into the bedroom and says that Brian has gone now too, just like Pearl. He drags my duvet off the bed and waves it under my nose. "Look, I put him in your bed and now he's gone," he cries. "This is another mystery for SNOOP to investigate. Perhaps he's hiding somewhere in the bedroom." And he insists I help him look for the snail.

We don't find Brian, which doesn't surprise me because I already know exactly where Brian is. I don't tell Billy that Brian is probably very happily lolling in the newly dug earth in Robert Absolom's garden. Instead I lie and say that we should regroup again tomorrow in daylight. I mean, we wouldn't want to stand on Brian if he's on the floor. Shocked, Billy agrees.

When Billy finishes drying his hair with the towel, he asks me again if Pearl has been in touch. Two seconds later, after I've checked my phone, I shake my head.

"Maybe she's busy," I tell Billy.

"Too busy for us," whispers Billy. "How can our almost mum be too busy for her children?"

I don't know the answer.

SEVEN

After Billy goes to sleep, I get out some pieces of paper and attempt to make at least ten more paper cranes. I don't mind saying that it feels like Pearl has dropped off the face of the earth. Billy's right, it is a mystery. And why was her portrait in the garden at our old house? Why was there a hole punched through it? Who would do something so horrible? That's another mystery I can't figure out.

I make one crane after the other, pleased that I'm getting good at it. Buoyed up by my new-found folding skills, I think I'll attempt another goodbye to Mum, seeing as I can't really text Pearl again so soon after sending the last one. So I pad over to the window and pull back the curtains. The moon is like a giant wheel of cheese in the sky and the stars glitter and blink at me, tucked into their navy blanket.

"Mum," I whisper, trying not to disturb Billy. I turn back and look at him and he snuffles softly like a piglet. "Number six on THE GOODBYE LIST is to say goodbye to you by naming a star." I turn back to the window. "I hope this is the right way to do it. None of the other ways felt big enough. I asked Dad for some seeds last night – that was number eight on the list – and he asked if I meant bird seeds and I said plant seeds and he said actually it didn't matter because he had neither." My toes grip the carpet. Mum is so important that I worry no goodbye will ever be worthy. Inhaling, I ask, "Is naming a star enough?" I stare out towards heaven and the moonbeams wash my face in silver. One star is brighter than all the others and I press my fingertip to the glass. It leaves a tiny planet of heat. "I am calling this star 'Mum'," I whisper. "Goodbye, Mum." My eyes prickle as I realize that the star is still bright and it's going to be there for ever and Mum isn't and it feels all wrong.

At five forty-three in the morning Billy wakes me from a dream, saying he's had another nightmare. I take him to Mum's chair again and say I'll tell him more of the story about how two brothers sailed the ocean in an armchair.

I tell him how the other people in their vessels could not hear the mysterious voice the boys had heard. They were adults and maybe they didn't believe in magic the way the two boys did. "The boys believed that if they called for help it would come," I say. "And even though they could not see the person who spoke to them, they knew that that person was all around, because the voice seemed to be in the sea, the sky and the earth. One of the boys even wondered if the voice was inside himself."

"Inside himself?" Billy murmurs. "What...?" But before he can finish the question, he yawns the biggest yawn. His eyes are drooping too. So I tell him to go back to bed, because the story can wait.

In morning lessons, I am secretly drawing a picture called GOODBYE MUM (number four on THE GOODBYE LIST) when Mr Beagle shouts that he's got an exciting project for the class and can we please keep our eyelids wide open? He turns to face the interactive whiteboard, but then adds, "Becket, I'm talking to you. Please stop drawing pictures under the desk and pay attention." What is it with teachers? Do they go to teachers' school to learn how to have eyes in the back of their head?

I quickly scrunch up the drawing and hide it in my rucksack. It was no masterpiece anyway. I wanted to draw me and Mum together. I had this big speech bubble saying goodbye and Mum was looking at me. Only I couldn't really remember what Mum looked like, so I had to guess, and I think I guessed wrong because Mum sort of looked like Queen Kong. So there was no way this was the correct goodbye either.

"Right, we're going to be working on this," continues Mr Beagle. He brings up some pictures on the interactive whiteboard of a group of smiling children drawing pictures in their classroom. Then there's another shot of them choosing plants and digging in muddy patches, and finally there's one of them standing triumphantly in front of a small garden patch.

Apparently, we're going to be doing exactly the same thing. This will be a chance to take something unloved and turn it into something very special that will flourish and grow under our care. Mr Beagle says this is a project that will work on many levels – and then he forgets to tell us what these levels are, other than planting stuff in a rough patch of ground at the back of the playground, near the old white wall. But according to Mr Beagle, when the garden is complete we're going to invite our parents along to view our labours and marvel open-mouthed at the beauty we've created. At least that's the plan.

"This is a living project and something you can sink your teeth into."

"The only thing I'd like to sink my teeth into is a burger," whispers Donté Moffatt.

I lean over and say I know a good burger van called Burger, She Wrote. Dad bought our dinner from it last week.

"What's more, we're going to The Garden of Eden garden centre on Friday for our Year Six trip," says Mr Beagle. "There we will be looking at, writing about, and sketching the plants that we'd like to include in our garden. Now, I don't want you all to get overexcited, but part of this project is a competition. You will each come up with a design for the final garden and I will pick the best one for us to use when we start planting on the rough patch of ground." Mr Beagle stops, looks around at the bored faces and says, "There will be a prize."

The class nearly takes the roof off.

"It's a winner's certificate."

The roof is firmly back on.

Mr Beagle says it's called Project Observation Of Plants.

Donté Moffatt says that's POOP and Mr Beagle says it isn't, thank you very much, and if Donté says that word one more time he'll be writing lines about POOP (which doesn't sound all that great, if you ask me).

Mimi says, "I'm not working on anything POOP. I have high standards even if you lot don't. One day I'm going to say—"

"That you've worked on POOP!" shrieks Donté Moffatt. Mr Beagle utters the word "Lines" and Donté Moffatt pretends he's quieter than a graveyard.

Mimi narrows her eyes. "One day I'm going to say I was in a class of idiots but I got through it." She turns around and looks in my direction.

Confused, I turn around to see if she's looking at someone behind me and then I realize I'm in the last row.

Mr Beagle says, "Simmer down," like he's talking to a load of overexcited kettles, not kids. "Project Observation Of Plants is exactly that. I want you all to observe the plants and how they grow. This will be so exciting." I think Mr Beagle's idea of exciting and mine are pretty different. "Anyway, I want you to start by writing down things or people that could inspire you in this project. Does your grandmother remind you of roses because she wears rose perfume? Stick that on the list. You could plant a rose garden."

"Or does your dad smell of manure?" Donté Moffatt laughs at his own joke. "You could plant a garden of—" And then Mr Beagle is rushing towards Donté, blustering about how he needs to pipe down or he'll be in trouble.

"Hey," I mumble, leaning forward and tugging on Robert's blazer in front of me. "You'd be good at planting a garden." He turns around and glares at me. When I try to say that he'd be good with soil and stuff he asks me why and his eyes narrow. Right now, saying I hit him on the head with a snail cannonball last night doesn't seem like the brightest idea in the world.

"Er…because you've got big hands," I mutter, wishing the ground would open and swallow me up. Unfortunately, the ground doesn't and Robert thumps the desk and tells me I know nothing about plants and what they mean to him.

I didn't say I did.

"A POOP garden," laughs Billy as we walk towards Dad's van after school. Dad told us this morning he'd pick us up but didn't say why. "I don't think I want one of those POOP gardens at school. Smelly! Although..." Billy thinks about it for a second and grins. "Would you get lots of bugs in it? I like bugs. Even bugs in POOP."

I flip my school bag over my shoulder. "I suppose," I say. "We're going to plant a whole garden patch and then our parents can come and see what we've grown."

Billy's eyes flick to the pavement. The smile drops from his face. "But we haven't found Pearl so that means our parents can't come and everyone will know we don't have a mummy if it's only Daddy that comes."

I tell him we'll find Pearl before that, I promise. But if I'm going to keep that promise we're going to have to ramp SNOOP up a notch. In fact, we're both going to have to go all out to make contact with Pearl in time to come to the unveiling of POOP. Billy isn't listening though, because he's ducked down and is rummaging through a patch of mud. When I tell him he hasn't got time for that because Dad's here, Billy bobs back up with a snail in his hand, shouting that it's Brian.

"It's not Brian and we don't need any more snails bringing home," I mumble, thinking how I've only just managed to get the slime off my duvet.

"It *is* Brian," says Billy, popping him in his blazer pocket. "I'd recognize that face anywhere."

Dad is waiting for us, the engine idling. "Here, chocolate bars," says Dad, throwing them at us as we climb in and do up our seat belts. "We're going on a little shopping trip."

"For what?" I get my chops around the chocolate, spraying shrapnel all over the seat.

"Decorating our lad pad, my son, decorating our lad pad." Dad puts his foot down. "We're going to make the flat shinier than a goldfish in a golden wrapper." Then he looks down at my wrist and says, "Ooh, what's that on your wrist? I haven't noticed it before." Sometimes I think Dad wouldn't even notice if a zombie introduced himself and said, "Pleased to eat you."

"Oh yeah." I give the bracelet a twang, hoping it might break and fall off. "A girl in my class gave it to me on the first day of school. I can't take it off." Dad asks me why and I mumble something about it being stuck, and then I change the subject and say we're going on a school trip on Friday that Mr Beagle told us all about today. Dad asks me where: an indoor skiing centre, an adventure playground, a mountain biking course?

"The local garden centre," I reply, trying to sound enthusiastic. "We have to observe the plants, make notes on them and then design our own garden. There's a class competition and the winner will have their garden design used on an old patch of ground. Parents are going to be invited to come and view it." I pause and swallow down a chunk of chocolate before adding, "Do you think Pearl would come if I invited her?" I let the words sort of dangle in the air like Dad's pine-tree air freshener.

Dad doesn't look at me; instead he keeps his eyes on the road and gives a little cough before saying she's probably very busy. My fellow SNOOP spy elbows me to pursue my line of questioning. So that's what I do.

"I still think Pearl would love to see the POOP garden," I reply carefully. "Maybe I could I ring her myself because I've got her phone number..."

The Codfather van suddenly feels like it is sucked dry of air and I want to gasp a little, or clutch my throat dramatically. Surely what I said wasn't that bad? Only it feels like it was; like I just said the worst thing in the world.

"No, you're not ringing Pearl," snorts Dad. "I've already told you this. She's too busy for POOP or anything else and we're busy too, getting on with our lives."

That's it. There's no way I can ask any more

questions because a furry little creature feels like it has curled up in my windpipe, making it impossible to do anything but grunt. Beside me, Billy turns away and looks out the window of the van. This is bad because I can't see his eyes. If they're watering, I don't know. All I can do is look straight ahead and try not to cry myself. What's more, the stupid seat belt is cutting off the circulation to my belly – or maybe it's just that every time Pearl's mentioned and Dad gets frostier than a snowman in the Arctic, it makes my tummy ache.

Eventually we reach Eden's shopping mall.

"Now, boys, this is going to be a lovely afternoon because..." Dad pauses before continuing, "it's our lad pad we're shopping for. A place where we can eat takeaways, watch whatever TV we like and don't have to worry about eating healthy food, or tripping over silly tubes of paint. And there isn't someone using my razor."

But I liked eating healthy food and the time I stood on Pearl's tube of brown paint and it squirted on the carpet was hilarious because I told Dad Billy had diarrhoea. I liked all those things and I liked having Pearl there and so did Billy.

With that, Dad zooms straight into a department store, picking up bits for the flat and then setting them back if he's not sure. He picks up a cushion with a scorpion printed on it and Billy says he doesn't want to park his bum on that. Annoyed, Dad sets it back, and chooses a pair of plain beige cushions and a throw the colour of porridge, saying it's a perfect match for our living room. Yes, it looks like sick. Next, he picks a silver photo frame, a glass vase, towels, a canvas that says "Life doesn't get better than this", toilet brush, flannels and a few strings of fairy lights. In the corner, tucked away, I spy cushions with blue swallows on them and I ask Dad if we can get one of those.

He nods.

It reminds me of Mum's wallpaper in our old house at Honeydown Hills. It makes me feel happy. I will put it in Mum's armchair.

Then Dad is off to the section full of artificial flowers. There are splashy poppies and sweet peas that look like they're wearing frilly bonnets, a rainbow of roses and lilies. Lifting a handful of lilies, Dad says we must get some because they were Mum's favourite flower. It's the first I've heard of it and I stare at the long white silky trumpets in Dad's hand and think how they'll never die.

When Dad goes off to pay for his items, Billy pulls me by the elbow over to the light section. Underneath lights like blown bubbles and dangling swan feathers, he says, "I could draw a missing person poster for Pearl. You said we needed to ramp up SNOOP."

Oh no. I shake my head. Portraits aren't Billy's strong point. Last time he drew me, I looked like a monster with two heads – both ugly. When Billy sees me shaking my head, he says we could phone the police instead. That's the only other thing left to do.

"And say what?" Exasperated, I roll my eyes.

"Pearl's on a spaceship and we need her back?"

"Great idea," I mutter, as Dad returns, overloaded with bags.

As we trot out of the shopping mall I see a man in the car park holding loads of helium balloons. I remember number five on THE GOODBYE LIST: a balloon. Dad thinks I'm being daft when I insist I need the horse balloon more than I've ever needed anything before. He thinks I'm a bit old for balloons, so I tell him no one is too old for balloons or why would grown men book those adventure hot-air balloon trips? Dad says I have a point.

So I am the proud owner of a horse balloon. Mum was never interested in horses but then again she was never interested in giraffes either and that was the only other type of animal helium balloon they had. Billy opted for the *Happy Birthday Princess* balloon and when Dad said no one had a birthday, Billy said Dad could call it an early birthday present for him (as in, eight months early). Anyway, Billy said he *was* a princess, so that counted.

As we walk towards The Codfather van, I let the ribbon loosen around my fingers. Gently it unravels as I whisper, "Goodbye, Mum," and then I let the horse go. There, I've done it. I've said another goodbye. Maybe this is the one that will feel right. Only the horse doesn't gallop away on the wind far enough, because Billy grabs the ribbon at the speed of light and says he'll keep the balloon if I don't want it.

The whole way back to the flat I am squashed in the passenger seat not only by Billy's pink birthday balloon but by the back end of my own horse.

EIGHT

Dad has a bright idea as we ascend the steps towards our flat. He's going to knock on Cat Woman's door and when she answers he's going to ask her if she'd like to come to our surprise flat-decorating party. The surprise obviously being that Cat isn't expecting to be put to work as our interior designer this evening.

When Cat answers the door and Dad explains we've been shopping and we'd love her help, she doesn't seem to mind. In fact, her face lights up like an arcade game and she says she enjoyed chatting to Dad the last time and she'd love to give us a hand.

"Only one?" says Dad and laughs. "I think you'll

require both, because the flat needs some serious attention."

Cat laughs too.

Five minutes later Cat turns up in our flat with her hair in a messy bun secured with a comb. Within half an hour she has positioned the beige cushions on a diagonal on the old sofa, propped the canvas on the mantelpiece, hung the fairy lights over the window, put the silver photo frame on a shelf and told us to find a photo for it and put the fake lilies in the vase and placed them on the table.

As Cat steps back and admires the flowers, I say, "They're my mum's favourites."

"She's dead though," pipes up Billy. I blink.

Cat doesn't say anything. Instead she pulls up her sleeve and shows me a tiny lily tattoo on her wrist. "Look," she whispers. "Lilies are my mum's favourite flower too."

Just as I'm about to ask more questions about the tattoo, Dad appears with a toilet brush, waving it in the air and asking what he's supposed to do with it. Cat grins and says it's up to him but she usually shoves it down the toilet with a bit of bleach. Dad laughs and soon, with a bit more work, the flat is looking more cheerful than it did when we moved in. To be fair, I think it's because Cat's here and she's made Dad put on the radio at full blast and now she's singing at the top of her voice. It sort of feels as though the sun has just come out from behind a cloud.

Even Billy is happily wandering around, wearing the muddy-coloured throw and pretending he's invisible. Every so often Cat tickles him through the fabric and I can hear Billy snort and laugh before running away again.

As a reward for everyone, Dad says he'll order in a pizza (our favourite) and asks what we'd like. Billy and I choose cheese and tomato, Dad wants spicy pepperoni and Cat says she doesn't mind and will eat anything. So Dad orders half and half. Cat ends up giving Billy her last slice of pizza and when she says she'd better get home Billy doesn't want her to go and gives her the biggest hug. Cat hugs him straight back, only it's longer and tighter.

It gives me a warm feeling in my tummy.

Mind you, that could have been the pizza.

When Cat's gone, I sit on the sofa and stare at the lilies for the longest time. Reaching out and rubbing the soft petals between my fingers, I think about how there's so much about Mum that I don't know. But instead of feeling sad about it, I feel just that little bit better because when I find out new stuff about Mum it makes her feel alive to me again, like she's all around me and it wasn't the end. Tonight, I mentioned Mum and it didn't feel strange talking about her.

Billy joins me on the sofa and says, "Do you think we'll ever see Pearl again?" He adds how he really liked having Cat around earlier but she's not Pearl. Pearl is just that bit more special.

Billy's right, because Dad always told us pearls are special. He said they're one-of-a-kind, beautiful, and if you find one it's magical and you'll want to hold onto it for ever. Once he told us how real pearls are made. The magic starts when a tiny speck of grit gets under the skin of an oyster. To protect itself, the oyster covers the object in the same stuff that makes up its shell, eventually forming a pearl. In all his time in the fish factory and on the fish delivery rounds, Dad said he had never found a real pearl. But in real life he *had* found one, because Pearl was every bit as beautiful and special as a proper pearl.

But Dad didn't hold onto his Pearl for ever, like he said. He let her go. And I still don't understand why.

At school today something weird happens at morning break, something that helps SNOOP big time. Just as I'd almost given up on finding Pearl, I discover exactly where she is – and it's all thanks to Mimi Dixon.

It starts off with Mimi beckoning me over in the playground. She's drinking a carton of orange juice, and as I walk towards her, she crushes it with one hand and fires it into the bin. When I reach her, she sucks in her cheeks.

"What's with the face?" I ask.

Mimi stares at me and says she is practising for when she's on *America's Next Top Model.* I say she doesn't live in America and she says they've had a UK invasion before. (I realize that none of this explains how she helped me find out Pearl's whereabouts. But what she utters next does.)

"You're not even here," says Mimi, relaxing her pout. She folds her arms and leans back against the wall.

"How come I'm talking to you then?" I reply, getting a bit tired of Mimi's attitude.

Mimi ignores me and says, "You're just a figment of my imagination." She pushes herself off the wall and reaches into her blazer pocket, pulling out a watermelon lipgloss that she slicks over her lips.

"Your imagination is ace." Yes, I'm quite good at giving attitude back.

Mimi puts the lipgloss away and spits, "Actually, my imagination *is* ace. I'm good at everything. I do loads of after-school clubs and have medals for my kung fu. And..." Mimi waves her arms. "I'm top of the class here too and no new person coming in is going to take that away from me – especially one who's not even really here." This girl is clearly crackers. I begin to walk away. "You can't walk away from me because you're not even supposed to be here!"

Sweet Baby Cheeses! What is wrong with her?

"I know you're being homeschooled, and if you're being homeschooled you're not supposed to be here." When I turn, Mimi pulls a face at me. If Ibiza Nana was here she'd warn Mimi that her face will stick like that if the wind changes. What's more, with a face like that she's never going to win a model competition, in America or anywhere else. "It must be true because it was your mum that said you're being homeschooled. And that means you should be at home, not here, and I'm going to tell on you."

Um...nope, my mum did not say that.

Turns out, Mimi's cousin, Chloe-Jasmine, met my mum and had a little chat with her.

Hold your horses, as Ibiza Nana would say (not that she has ever held horses, because Ibiza Nana did not like horses after an unfortunate incident with one that mistook her finger for a carrot). "I think your cousin is mistaken," I say.

Mimi's voice is smug when she says, "Chloe-Jasmine goes to your old school and I was at her house and I happened to mention there was a new boy in my class called Becket Rumsey and she said she knew all about you. Chloe-Jasmine said you'd left your school in a mega-hurry and never came back after half-term and everyone was talking about you. Then one day Chloe-Jasmine bumped into your mum, who was putting up these posters in Honeydown Hills for her new painting classes..."

"I don't think so," I whisper, remembering that there was a girl called Chloe in the year below me. My friend, Spud, used to say she had teeth like a hippopotamus, which sort of figures, because Mimi's teeth are a bit like that too.

"Yes, it was your mum." Mimi nods so much it's a wonder her head doesn't fall off. "Chloe-Jasmine had seen her at the school gates before when she was picking you up from school and everyone knew she was an artist. Chloe-Jasmine got talking to her about art because her dad likes drawing. Anyway, your mum said she was doing life classes in Honeydown Hills and Eden if her dad wanted to attend. When Chloe-Jasmine told her mum, her mum said no way was her dad painting naked ladies. Anyway, Chloe-Jasmine got talking about you and asked where you were and your mum said you were being homeschooled. Yet here you are."

I insist it's all a mix-up but I feel my eyes prickle with unformed tears and it isn't because Chloe-Jasmine mistook Pearl for my mum, but because Pearl has been pretending she's still part of our lives when we haven't spoken to her in over a week. What's more, Pearl hasn't answered our texts either. Why is Pearl lying about me? A real mum would never do that.

"I see you're still wearing the butterfly bracelet," whispers Nevaeh, writing down that the coloured part of the eye is the pupil in our science test.

"I," I mutter, pointing.

"I...what?" Nevaeh hisses back.

"I-ris, not the pupil." I write down my answer as Mr Beagle asks the next question. He glances at his watch and says we don't have long before lunch and can we please speed up a little bit.

"I saw you talking to Mimi in the playground," whispers Nevaeh. She writes that the long pipe that shifts food from the back of your throat to your stomach is called *drain*. "You looked sad."

"Oesophagus," I murmur. "Not drainpipe. Even if I was, it has nothing to do with the bracelet so what do you care?"

I think again about how Pearl has been lying about me. Nevaeh's right. I *am* sad about it – after I spoke to Mimi, I spent ages sitting on my own on the gravel pathway, picking at a tuft of grass.

Nevaeh writes down oesophagus – well, I think that's what she writes but she can't spell it properly. It looks like O-Soft-A-Gus. "I do care. I don't give butterfly bracelets to everyone, you know. They're only for people that need something special in their life. Then, when that special thing happens, you don't need the bracelet and..."

Yeah, yeah, yeah. I've heard all this malarkey before. I scribble down *cerebrum* for the name of the biggest part of the brain. "I don't want to rain on your chips," I whisper, "but butterflies aren't dead people saying hi. They're just butterflies and they don't talk. They're everywhere too. I don't care about butterflies or caterpillars or spiders. You need to talk to my brother,

103

Billy. He loves stuff like that. He's got a snail." I sigh. "Dead people can't come back, no matter how much you wish they could."

"I don't think that's true." Nevaeh writes the word *butterfly* on her science test paper, which is stupid because *butterfly* isn't the answer to *What is the human body's biggest organ?* "My sister did."

Just as my mouth drops open, Mr Beagle says, "What do you find inside your skull?" As I'm about to write down *brain*, Mr Beagle hollers, "A load of hot air, that's what. Whoever is chit-chatting with their overused jawbone, can they please be quiet? This is an important test and I want to see who knows their answers, not who knows their neighbour's answers."

Mimi glances over at me and grins. Seriously, she's really got it in for me. Firstly telling me that I'm not all that great just because I'm new, then telling me that I'm being homeschooled, and now this – smiling when I get told off.

When the bell goes, Mr Beagle says we're to leave the test papers on the table and scram. I scram as fast as I can because I want to talk to Nevaeh about her sister.

Nevaeh is nowhere to be seen at lunch, but Robert Absolom is sitting on the wall drawing on a piece of paper. I am about to walk past him but then something makes me stop and sit down. Robert eases away from me like I've got a particularly contagious disease and then puts his hand over the piece of paper so I can't see what he's drawing.

I introduce myself properly and put my hand out, because that's what Dad does when he's meeting someone, although they usually frown because he's covered in fish guts. Robert leaves my hand hanging and says everyone calls him Knuckles.

"Okay, Knuckles, I'm not being nosey," I say, even though I am being extremely nosey and want to see what he's doodling. "Um...I only wanted to say that I didn't mean to upset you the other day. It's just that I thought you might be interested in plants, but maybe you're not."

"Actually, I am interested," Knuckles says through gritted teeth. He folds up the piece of paper and shoves it into his pocket. "But it's not what you think."

I don't know what I'm thinking, to be fair.

"I'm doing it for my dad." Knuckles's eyes drop and he knots his fingers together in his lap. He tells me that his dad taught him everything he knew about plants. He was brilliant at making small seeds grow into great big trees. Without warning, Knuckles does a sigh so long

I half expect a man with a stopwatch from Guinness World Records to jump out of a hedge. "Anyway, that's all over now." His jaw tightens.

"Why?"

"Because my dad's gone and that's it. You wouldn't understand." Knuckles rises from the wall, stuffs his hands into his trouser pockets and stalks away from me without looking back.

Oh, I understand all right.

NINE

SNOOP
secret mission number two

Billy says I must write this all down before I forget it and definitely before I eat my dinner. Although I don't think I will ever forget what just happened to us less than twenty-five minutes ago. These are the notes from the mission we undertook earlier.

AFTER SCHOOL: I told Billy I knew where Pearl was, or more that I had a sort of hunch thanks to what Mimi told me at school earlier. Billy asked what a hunch was. I said it didn't matter, but we needed to find a local paper to see the ads.

THE RECYCLING BINS AT 4.01 P.M.: I found a copy of the local newspaper, the Eden Echo. On page 13, underneath an ad for Charlie Chicken's Takeaway, there was an ad for Pearl's Painting Classes. The mobile number was correct. We had found her. Billy said: "THIS IS THE BEST DAY EVER."

There were three venues to choose from: the Scouts' Hall in Honeydown Hills (Sundays), Civic Centre in Tower Point (Mondays and Tuesdays) and Saint Bartholomew's Church Hall in Eden (Wednesdays and Thursdays).

AT 4.08 P.M.: I looked up Saint Bartholomew's on Google Maps. It was only a short walk from our flat.

AT 4.25 P.M.: We mentioned the church to Dad. Dad had never heard of it. Dad asked why we were religious all of a sudden. Then he said we could try the bread wafers but not the wine. We deduced from this that Dad knew nothing about Pearl's Painting Classes.

PLAN TO GET OUT OF THE HOUSE TO VISIT
SAINT BARTHOLOMEW'S: We came up with nothing
for ages. Then at 4.45 p.m. Billy said something so
utterly stupid it was utterly genius. Dad actually lost
the power of speech for a moment when he heard it,
which was a bonus. Billy said we were going to walk
his pet snail, Brian. When Dad finally regained the
use of his voice he began to protest, but Billy said
he'd left behind all his other friends when we moved
and Brian was all he'd got. Dad gave up and said he'd
get chips for dinner.

Billy said: "Can Brian have a battered sausage?"
Dad said he could.

OUTSIDE THE FLAT: Billy insisted on actually
taking Brian for a walk. For the record, after five
minutes I made the sound of a ringing phone and
said, "Hello, Hollywood? My brother, Billy, has a story
that you could make into an action movie. It's about
a snail. All the action takes place five hours after
you've left the cinema." Then I told Billy I wasn't
waiting around for Brian any longer. Billy pulled a
face and told Brian to cover his ears so he couldn't
hear what his horrible brother was saying. Whether
Brian did, I'm not sure. I didn't know where his ears

were – or his hands for that matter.

AT 5.13 P.M.: We found Saint Bartholomew's and Billy stared at a small poster outside that said Pearl's Painting Classes (starting at 4.30 p.m.). All welcome.
    We entered the premises.

DESCRIPTION OF THE PREMISES: The hallway was narrow and had a large noticeboard with lots of leaflets for flower arranging and toddler groups pinned to it. There was a small woven cross high on the white wall and a basket of pink carnations. (Billy poked around in these for ages.) Off the hallway there were six wooden doors; the first led to the kitchen and the second had a sign saying it was a toilet, but it seemed to be locked because I tried the handle. The third room was a small office, with no one in there. I could hear a radio playing somewhere behind one of the other doors.

The toilet door suddenly opened before we could investigate. Billy grabbed my arm. I think he was scared. He says he wasn't but I am reporting it anyway. A man wearing a loose dressing gown walked out. Colour: beige (the dressing gown, not the man). The front of it fell open as he was trying to tie the

cord around the waist. He was naked underneath.
I think he gave us a smile, although my eyes were
somewhere else so I can't be sure. He opened one
of the other doors and disappeared through it.

Billy said: "Brian doesn't want a battered sausage
any more." Then he said the man must be very cold.

I could neither confirm nor deny this.

AT 5.17 P.M.: I peered through the glass window into
the room where the man had gone. Billy stood on my
toes to get a better look too. The room had five easels
holding canvases.

In my line of vision: Pearl (talking to a group of
people).

We had found her. We were in Pearl's world again.
MISSION: complete.

Billy made a little squeak of joy. I made a little
squeak too, because it felt like Billy was breaking my
metatarsals (foot bones).

Billy said it was Pearl.

For the record, I already knew that.

Naked Man was lying on a sofa like one of those
fancy Sphynx cats with lots of hairless wrinkles. (It
made my stomach curl like a fortune-telling fish from
a Christmas cracker.) Pearl walked over to Naked

Man and positioned him differently to the way he had been sitting before (which was quite tricky because there was an awful lot of bare flesh to avoid). Next, she touched his cheek with her finger and laughed before going back behind the easels.

I asked Billy if he wanted to go in and talk to Pearl.

Billy said no.

I said this was our chance to say "hello" or "goodbye" or anything.

Billy said no.

I said do you want to go home?

Billy said yes.

ON THE WAY HOME: Billy suddenly shouted that he'd forgotten Brian. I asked where Brian had gone and Billy said he'd left him in the flower basket in the church hall. So I said Billy was to channel Brian and not to move a centimetre, and I'd run back and rescue Brian. For the record, I said I would be two minutes.

FINAL NOTE ON SECRET MISSION NUMBER TWO: Everything worked out okay with Brian.

SECRET FINAL NOTE ON SECRET MISSION NUMBER TWO: I told Billy that was the end of my notes about what happened earlier. I said there wasn't much else to report.

I lied.

WHAT REALLY HAPPENED AFTERWARDS: When I reached the church hall to rescue Brian, everyone was coming out so I waited. Then Pearl and Naked Man came out…together. I hardly recognized him with his clothes on. When they glanced my way I had to throw myself into someone's garden. I got a hedgie (my underpants caught on the hedge and they were pulled up to my armpits). I landed beside a gnome with a fishing rod.

Every few seconds I checked what Pearl and Naked Man were doing.

They were talking.

My mobile went off.

Now they were not talking, they were looking.

In my direction.

Quickly I turned my phone off, slipped it into the gnome's hand and crawled commando-style along the garden until I was hidden behind a bin.

"Come here," Pearl called to Naked Man. I watched

as she leaned over the hedge and stared at the gnome. "That gnome has a phone. Who would do something as crazy as that?" she said.

I was trying not to breathe but then I did it anyway because I like breathing.

"Maybe he's got it so he can phone gnome," Naked Man replied. He opened his mouth wide as he laughed. I think I counted about six fillings. Anyway, having seen him naked, he's not got much to laugh about.

Pearl said she could swear the gnome got a phone call. Naked Man tugged Pearl's coat. It was the pink coat Dad bought her from a boutique in the precinct near our old house. Naked Man said he wanted to go back to Pearl's for some Quality Street.

I wanted to go back to Pearl's for some Quality Street. Then I realized he hadn't said Quality Street at all, he'd said quality time. Then I realized I didn't know where Pearl's place was and quality time was in no way as good as having a chocolate Green Triangle.

Naked Man kissed Pearl, a smacker right on the lips. It is not right to kiss people you work with like that. Okay, on the cheeks, yes. Maybe even both cheeks if you're French or you can't decide which cheek you want to go with.

I deduced there and then that Pearl and Naked Man are a couple and she couldn't have moved on from Dad faster if she was on a moving travelator.

Pearl and Naked Man jumped in a car and zoomed away. Fiat Panda (white, splattered with seagull droppings).

I prised my mobile from the cold hard hands of the gnome, climbed back over the hedge, entered the church premises and rummaged through the carnations.

Brian was gone.

The slippery little slimeball had seen his chance and raced off as fast as his rubbery suckers would carry him. I always knew Brian was putting on that "slow" thing. I was cursing (under my breath – I was in a church hall, after all).

I was scared to tell Billy that Brian number two was lost.

"I found Brian," Billy said to me when I reached him.

I said Billy hadn't even put Brian in the basket, had he? Billy said he had but guess what? I didn't want to guess. Billy then said he was just sitting on the wall waiting for me, when he turned around and looked in the mud and saw Brian. "He must've followed me," said Billy.

"Must've followed you," I grunted, slapping my forehead so hard I nearly knocked myself out. Note to myself: I must not slap myself again. It hurts.

Billy carried Brian number three carefully in his hand as we walked home. He said, "I didn't like the rudey-nudey man whose clothes fell off."

"I know," I said.

"I didn't much like his—"

"YES," I said.

Then Billy said all this: "You don't think Pearl was his girlfriend, do you? Because sometimes boyfriends and girlfriends take off their clothes and then they make funny laughing noises and then the lady lays an egg and becomes a mummy."

Where did he get that information? I asked Billy.

"A boy in my class told me that's what happens when you're a grown-up and he heard the funny noises once. But I said I make funny noises all the time." Billy clicked his tongue and made a little piglike snort and then growled at me. As I was about to tell him it's okay to do animal impressions because I was pretty good at being a sloth, he tugged on my coat sleeve, forcing me to stop. "Why is it so hard to keep a mummy after she's laid the egg?"

"I don't know. Maybe we're just not the same as other people."

"People who have mummys?" Billy stopped and stared up at me, looking lost. "I want to be normal like them, Becket."

"You are normal, Billy. Not everyone has a mummy, you know."

"But everyone would like one," replied Billy.

TEN

There's no way Pearl is coming back to us if she has Naked Man. This has thrown SNOOP into a mess. I stare up at a stain on our bedroom ceiling. It is shaped like the world, if the UK was missing. Oh, and the United States and Australia. Basically it's nothing like the world.

Closing my eyes, I tell myself that from this point on I'm only making paper cranes to get my wish to say goodbye to Mum, because there's no point in wishing to find Pearl because we've already done that. I haven't told Billy Naked Man is Pearl's boyfriend, although it seems like he already guessed. He didn't eat his chips when we got back and Brian didn't eat the battered sausage. I ate everything instead and now my belly aches BIG time. I curl up into a tiny ball, clutching my stomach. This isn't how it was supposed to go. By now we were supposed to have Pearl back, ready to visit the POOP garden as soon as it's done. Now, everything in my entire life is POOP and it's nothing to do with Project Observations Of Plants.

At five forty-three the next morning, Billy appears in front of me like a ghost. He tugs my duvet and says he's had another nightmare. Climbing out of bed, I take him to Mum's armchair and adjust the swallow cushion so Billy can lie back on it. "Sit here," I whisper and I bring my duvet over and sit down and wrap it around us two. We're like a big caterpillar. "The armchair is safe." And I continue the story I was telling Billy about the two boys on an armchair of their own.

"The storm did not stop," I say, "and the armchair was tossed about so violently that one of the boys began to slip. His brother tried to hold onto him but his clothes were so wet that he lost his grip. He couldn't save the boy from falling into the water. The boy left on the armchair screamed that his brother had fallen and then he jumped in after him and the armchair was left bobbing on the surface with no passengers. But no matter how it rained and how much it rocked from side to side, the armchair did not sink. It stayed right there on the ocean surface, waiting for the boys to come back. As if it knew that, before too long, they would."

When Billy falls asleep I think about how we're the two boys in the story. I think about how we're all at sea and how our past is disappearing. But most of all I think about how I'm afraid of the future.

It makes my stomach ache all over again.

That morning before we go to school, I remind Dad it's our Year Six school trip to The Garden of Eden garden centre today. Dad looks at me and says he had forgotten. "I told you about it when we went shopping," I offer, shovelling chocolate cereal into my mouth. Dad blows on his mug of tea before taking a slurp and says it's okay and what do I need? "Three pounds," I reply quickly. "We're allowed to buy a pencil."

Dad suddenly grunts and sets his mug down, then flops his hands onto the table. "Three pounds for a pencil?" Then he says it again, even though I heard him quite clearly the first time. "In my day you could have bought a packet of pencils, felt tips, a sharpener and a big eraser for that and still had enough left over for a sherbet dip."

In his day he could probably have bought all those things and a Mercedes car and still had enough left over to buy a speedboat. When I tell him so, Dad snorts and says there's three pounds in his wallet and he'll have less of the cheek. The wallet's in his jeans pocket in his bedroom.

To be precise: it's in his jeans pocket lying on the floor in his bedroom. As I'm about to reach down and seize the wallet, I notice the photo frame we bought in the shopping mall. Dad has placed a photo of Mum inside it and left it on his bedside table. My fingers reach forward and as I pick up the frame it's as though someone is plucking on my heart strings. With the photo frame in my hand I sit, cross-legged, on the bed. Mum is standing in front of an ocean and looks so close I could almost reach into the photo and touch her. I try, but my fingers are stopped by the cold glass.

"I wish more than anything you were here with me now, Mum." I feel silly talking to myself. Peering closer, I see she is holding an old-fashioned glass bottle that I bet she found on the beach. I imagine Mum sending the bottle out to sea with a note inside to me saying:

Dearest son, I love you and although I had to go you're not to be sad. And you don't have to say goodbye...

"But I do, Mum," I whisper, my fingers tracing the shape of the bottle she's holding. Last year at my old school, Mr Kipling asked us to write a message-in-a-bottle to someone we admired. I wrote to Alexander Fleming, who was a Scottish biologist, pharmacologist and botanist and who accidentally discovered penicillin, which was the beginning of modern antibiotics. I wrote in my letter to Fleming that I was very grateful because when I had tonsillitis antibiotics made me feel better. Without him, my throat would have been very sore indeed. Others wrote about their mums and I felt bad when I heard their messages. I felt like I'd forgotten my mum. I got a gold star for Alexander Fleming. But I didn't want it.

With no one around to see me, I bring the photo to my mouth and kiss the glass and imagine I'm kissing Mum's cheek. Carefully I set the photo back on Dad's table and reach down for Dad's wallet. I open it, looking for the three pounds. To be honest, I'm half expecting a load of moths to fly out, because lately Dad's always saying we can't spend too much. A scratchcard and a few pieces of paper fall out. They're just receipts and, yes, I look at them. I haven't given up on SNOOP completely.

On the left of the wallet, Dad always had a photo of Billy, me and Pearl. But now he has neatly trimmed Pearl out of the photo. It looks wrong, as if Pearl was never even part of our lives. Another piece of paper flutters out of the wallet and I pick it up and read it. There is a woman's name and telephone number on it. Camille. We don't know anyone called Camille.

Camille sounds fancier than a fondant fancy.

Camille sounds more interesting than finding out the word "muscle" comes from the Latin term "little mouse" which is what Romans thought muscles looked like.

Who is Camille?

When I climb onto the school coach I can't stop thinking that Pearl has Naked Man and now it seems like Dad has Camille, but the worst thing is that Billy and I have been told nothing. It feels like when you're young, everyone thinks it's better not to tell you stuff. But they *should* tell you, because being young doesn't mean being stupid and I reckon we could handle being told the truth. Lies are the thing that hurt the most.

Earlier, when I went back to the breakfast table, I tried to ask Dad about Camille but I kept bottling it and saying "camel" and Dad thought I had a new-found interest in beasts of the desert. When I snapped that I didn't, Dad said I had the hump. It wasn't even funny, although Billy laughed so much he was almost sitting in a yellow puddle of his own making.

"Becket Rumsey, can you please take a seat on the coach?" says Mr Beagle. "We haven't got all day." We have, but I'm not going to be the one who says it.

After a student headcount, Mr Beagle takes a seat at the front beside Mrs Dixon, Mimi's mother. I overhear Mimi tell Nevaeh that her mum offered to come and help us. Mrs Dixon looks like she could be a model and when she starts chatting to Mr Beagle he laughs like a hyena reading a joke book. A small missile of saliva lands on Mrs Dixon's shoulder and she looks horrified. He shuts up pretty quickly after that and signals to Sam Swiss, the school's groundsman-doubling-as-driver to get going.

Everyone cheers. It's nine thirty and we're on our way. At nine thirty-two it is obvious that we're moving at the speed of a tortoise. Sam Swiss is muttering under his breath that the speed limit round here is thirty and you should never reach that point because then you might slip up and go thirty-one miles per hour and then you'd be breaking the law and you cannot break the law in front of children. Well, let me tell him, speed limits never bothered Ibiza Nana, because once when she found out there was a half-price sale at her favourite clothes shop, she strapped me into the car and we took off like a rocket.

Half an hour later, when we've travelled the one mile to The Garden of Eden garden centre, a man with a goatee beard shaped like a goat welcomes us off the bus and says, "I thought you'd be here ages ago. Where did you come from, the Arctic?" Mrs Dixon looks at him like he's something on the bottom of her shoe and he quickly smiles and says, "Welcome to The Garden of Eden, where you will find a paradise of plants." He sniffs (I secretly diagnose hay fever) and takes us into a section where there are loads of small trees in pots and tiny tubs of star-shaped flowers in every colour of the rainbow. Goatee Guy tells us we can look around. I look around. It takes thirty seconds. Yep, I'm done looking around. Half the class are the same. They've already skived off and gone to the gift shop to buy pencils.

"Out of the shop everyone!" shouts Mr Beagle, his face mottled like corned beef. "Plants first, pencils second, unless you're already in the queue and then you might as well pay."

I'm next at the till and quickly buy myself one of the Garden of Eden pencils and I have enough money left over for a small notebook with a picture of frogspawn on the front (which looks like a dessert Ibiza Nana once made called tapioca and I refused to eat it because I didn't eat tadpoles). When Mr Beagle drags us all out of the shop he plonks us in front of Goatee Guy again, who shows us a few plants called annuals with a wave of his hand. Donté Moffatt says he thought annuals were books no one wanted at Christmas.

"They live fast and die young," mutters Knuckles under his breath. I glance over at him and he flicks his eyes away. What's his problem?

"I want butterflies in my garden design," announces Nevaeh, pulling up her blazer sleeve and showing me a drawing of a butterfly she's done on her arm.

"Butterflies are so boring." Mimi's eyeballs do a three-sixty and she smoothes down her school jumper. Mrs Dixon glances over at Mimi and smiles and Mimi smiles back and gives her mother a micro-wave with her fingers.

Goatee Guy tries to hush everyone by saying he's very grateful for all this interest in plants. He says we're going to have to choose outdoor plants and some need certain types of soil. Knuckles is suddenly spouting on about acid and alkaline. Goatee Guy is clearly delighted and nodding his head. I nudge Knuckles and ask how he knows all this acid and alkaline stuff and his face falls faster than a yo-yo on the way down.

"Stop talking about my dad," hisses Knuckles, glaring at me. "I told you he's gone."

Thing is, I wasn't even talking about his dad.

Mr Beagle, getting fed up with all the talking and shuffling about, says we all need to give our mouths a rest because there's too much chatting and time-wasting. Instead we need to go and write notes about what plants we'd like to include in our garden design and, who knows, if we come up with some good ideas we might win. Mrs Dixon is off like a whippet looking at plants. Anyone would think *she* was designing the garden. Knuckles hurries off on his own and he's checking the leaves of the plants and writing a little list. Goatee Guy looks impressed and is nodding his head in appreciation. Well, not to be outdone, I start checking leaves and writing a little list too. (It's a mistake to check the cacti this way though.)

"Ooh, get you, writing notes," says Mimi, leaning over me, her plait dangling over my shoulder. I do a little shimmy to free myself and then I put my hand over my notebook because I don't want her copying me. Mimi says she couldn't care less what I'm writing. "Did you ask your mum about the mix-up? Because you said it was a mix-up even though it sounds like your mum is the one who's mixed-up." There's a mean glint in her eyes.

"It wasn't my mum," I mutter. "It was my dad's girlfriend, Pearl."

"Weird," says Mimi, clearly delighted that she's discovered a bit of gossip.

"Quiet, everyone, and gather around," says Mr Beagle, splitting Mimi and me up. "This is a special project we're doing here and it needs one hundred per cent commitment. It's not an excuse to dodge class and chat. This is going to be the best project the school has ever undertaken."

"Better than the project we did on the Romans?" shouts Donté Moffatt.

"Okay, maybe the garden can't quite compete with the Romans, but it is still important. We're going to learn so much from it." Donté Moffatt opens his mouth but Mr Beagle gets there first. "No, we're not going to learn more from it than we learned from the Romans. Can we please forget about the Romans for a moment? This is entirely different. What ideas can you get from the garden centre? And what can you bring to the garden design?"

"I can bring worms," says Donté Moffatt.

"We don't need anyone to bring worms," replies Mr Beagle. "The worms will bring themselves."

"Okay, I'll bring chocolate," adds Donté Moffatt. "My mum says gardens are for sitting in with a cup of tea and a chocolate bar. So if we're bringing something to the garden, I'll bring that."

"Right, we need to get away from the Romans and the chocolate bars," sighs Mr Beagle. "This is about things growing, let's remember that." While all this is going on, Knuckles is still scribbling in his notebook and as I glance over his shoulder I can see what he's doing. He's drawing a little tree covered in apples and beside it he's written DAD in bubble letters.

Unable to resist, I ask, "You said your dad has gone. Has he gone to a better place?" I remember how Ibiza Nana always used to say Mum had gone to a better place when what she really meant was that Mum was dead. Once, when I was little, I said I wanted to go to the better place to be with Mum and Ibiza Nana said

I couldn't. I was furious. Why were they stopping me going to the better place?

Knuckles glares at me and tightens his jaw and says his dad hasn't gone to a better place. In fact, he's gone to the worst place in the universe and if I'm mocking him I'm going to get a knuckle sandwich.

I say I don't want a knuckle sandwich, thank you, because I've already got a fish paste sandwich in my bag. As I walk away to look at the herbs, I know I've said something stupid but have no idea what it was.

ELEVEN

At midday Mr Beagle puts his hand in the air, indicating we're done, and before he even says a word everyone starts charging to the coach as if they're a herd of buffalo being chased by a tiger.

Everyone scatters, taking seats here and there. I hear Sam Swiss holler about Health and Safety, namely his. He doesn't want to be trampled by the stampede. By the time I get on the coach, there's only two seats at the front for Mr Beagle and Mrs Dixon and one at the back beside Knuckles. When I look at him, he turns away. Normally this would be enough to make me scarper but there's nowhere else to go, so I slope down the aisle and squeeze in beside him.

Outside I see Goatee Guy sneezing into his hand. A few people wave at him and then Mrs Dixon and Mr Beagle appear by the coach. Mr Beagle shakes Goatee Guy's hand. As Mr Beagle is looking at his soggy hand, everyone on the coach starts pointing and laughing. It's total quality.

Once Mr Beagle and Mrs Dixon are on board, Sam Swiss swings out of the garden centre's gates and starts shouting that we should all have a sing-a-long. How about "One Hundred Green Bottles"? While everyone else starts singing, I pluck up the courage to tell Knuckles that I'm sorry if I said something wrong about his dad. Ibiza Nana used to say I spoke before I put my brain in gear, only you can't put brains in gear anyway. Knuckles grunts and says he's still not talking about his dad, so I can stop fishing.

"My dad loves fishing," I reply, hoping to strike up a conversation. But Knuckles isn't having it; instead he turns away and presses his nose against the window. It leaves a greasy mark on the glass. "He delivers to all the local restaurants," I continue. "I bet you've eaten his fish."

"Only if it's frozen and comes in a box from the corner shop. We can't afford to go to restaurants. It's hard because Mum doesn't have much money coming in, what with Dad..." The words trail off.

"Oh," I offer. "You could catch your own fish. I've done that before." Once I've started talking about catching fish, it's like I'm on a roller coaster and can't get off, and I start saying how you need maggots and then how Dad always says you begin thinking you'll catch fish from the head but really it's from the heart and how that's like life because you start off trying to figure everything out with your head but sometimes you should just let your heart talk.

Knuckles turns around and asks me what I'm waffling on about. "Nothing," I squeak and Knuckles snorts and for the rest of the journey he pretends to be asleep, but I swear I see the tiniest glitter of a tear in the corner of his closed eye. I don't understand what I'm doing wrong. Was it because I talked about fish this time?

The coach crawls through the streets of Eden and I stare out the window. Knuckles gives a tiny snore as we pass the arcades at the far end of town, their bulbs blinking and the sequined discs on the signs fluttering and catching the sunlight. The bus passes the big supermarket and then Beans Coffee Shop. I see sunlight glinting on a bald man's head. After a double take,

133

I realize it is sunlight glinting on my dad's bald head. I'd recognize it anywhere, because I've had to look at it enough times and be reminded that when I get older that'll be me too. Luckily Sam Swiss is crawling along so I can see everything in slow motion, like we're in some action movie. Dad's standing outside the coffee shop (looking nothing like someone in an action movie) talking to a tall pencil-thin woman with blonde candyfloss hair. She's wearing this pale pink dress that looks like a small cake. They smile at each other and I feel like telling Sam Swiss to stop the bus, I want to get off.

But I don't. Instead, I just stare at the woman.

I don't recognize her.

In her pink dress, she looks fancier than a fondant fancy.

If The Garden of Eden hadn't charged me a full three pounds for a pencil and notebook, I would have bet my last fifty pence that the lady doing the smiling was Camille.

This is the apocalypse. Dad is meeting this Camille woman behind our backs. Sneaking out to Beans Coffee Shop and drinking frothy mocha-chocco-tino-lattes when we think he's delivering haddocks. Billy doesn't shut up the whole way through dinner, but I barely speak to Dad, and when he asks if I'm feeling okay I say "never better", which is what I've heard grown-ups say when they've never felt worse. Ibiza Nana used to say it all the time when she had a headache from drinking too much sherry. Dad says I am looking a bit peaky and did my school trip go okay?

"I learned a lot," I mumble through Mr Wong's prawn toast. "Some things I didn't want to learn." The toast does a circuit of my mouth before it reaches the palatine uvula.

Oblivious, Dad says, "Learning is always a good thing."

"Even if it's something bad?" I raise my eyebrows. Dad thinks for a second and says that we can't sweep bad things under the carpet. Like in history, many bad things happened but we can't pretend they didn't. "Oh," I mutter, wishing I could pretend seeing Dad and Camille together hadn't happened. And Pearl and Naked Man. I wish I could pretend that hadn't happened too. Dad asks if the food is okay. He says he won ten pounds on a scratchcard and thought we should have takeaway as a treat (although we still have takeaway every night so it's not much of a treat). I bring a forkful of noodles up to my mouth and nod but I can't even taste them. That's how bad I'm feeling at this moment.

My mood hasn't improved much after dinner either. I'm sitting in our bedroom reading my book on healing herbs when Billy trots in, saying I have a face like a wet welly. When I tell Billy it's a "wet weekend", he shakes his head and says in his world it's a wet welly. Next, he says he knows what will cheer me up, and he skips over to his box and brings out his robotic arm.

"Fat lot of good that is," I mumble sourly.

When Billy explains that the robotic hand will help us on the next SNOOP mission, I repeat, "Fat lot of good that is." Anyway, "We found Pearl yesterday," I snap. "We just didn't speak to her, so that means that SNOOP is doomed. We had the chance to complete our mission but we failed. What's the point in finding Pearl if we don't even talk to her? Spies have to complete their mission properly and then close the case."

Billy's eyes widen. "Oh no, no, no. SNOOP is not doomed." He waves the robotic hand in the air, narrowly missing the light bulb. "Once in SNOOP, always in SNOOP. We can't give up on our second mum. Not ever. The case is still open." Billy explains that it was his fault we didn't talk to Pearl at the church hall. "I was very silly and got all cross because I thought the rudey-nudey man was Pearl's boyfriend, but he wasn't."

I'm listening now. "How do you know?" Perhaps Billy has discovered something new. Maybe Pearl hasn't got a new boyfriend and Dad doesn't have a new girlfriend and the world isn't a complete mess with us in the middle of it.

"Well..." Billy pauses, his eyes glittering. "They're not a couple because the rudey-nudey man is an emperor."

Okay, I've stopped listening. This is another one of Billy's crazy ideas. When I say to Billy that the Naked Man is not an emperor, Billy says he is and he'll explain.

"Please, don't," I reply. "No, really, please don't."

Ignoring me, Billy begins. "The rudey-nudey man is an emperor because everyone knows that the emperor had these invisible clothes, and everyone also knows he was a horrible man and he thought everyone else was stupid. But really he was the stupid one. Anyway, Pearl wouldn't have a boyfriend that was stupid. So, they're not a couple."

Boom! Seven-year-old Billy's logic is so far-fetched a dog would have to go to the moon to bring it back. Obviously, I tell him there's no way I'm going back to the church to speak to Pearl. For Billy's information, one sight of Naked Man is all my stomach will take.

At this point I am tempted to tell Billy the truth about Pearl and Naked Man. They *are* a couple. I saw it with my own eyeballs.

"What if…?" I pause and nibble the skin around my nails. "I mean, what if…?" This is harder than the world's biggest sudoku puzzle, but I need to say it. "What if the Naked Man *was* Pearl's boyfriend?" I suck in the air, waiting for Billy's reply.

"Nah," says Billy flatly. "Like I said, I have a new mission for SNOOP and it is…" There's an internal drum roll going on in my head. "Ring Pearl!"

Seriously, this is getting silly now. I tell Billy we tried it before and Pearl didn't reply.

"No, we *texted* her and she didn't reply," continues Billy, being all smart.

"Well, Dad said we couldn't ring Pearl," I reply, being all smart back.

"We're not going to actually ring her," snaps Billy, being so smart I'm confused. He waves his toy robotic hand at me. "This thing could ring." I half expect Billy to say "I'm a poet and I didn't know it," but clearly he doesn't know it because he doesn't say it, so we just move on.

Billy slips out into the hallway, picks up the phone and returns with it. He looks at me and then the phone and nods. Clearly, it's all systems go on Planet Billy.

5... The phone is placed on Billy's bed.

4... Billy tells me to call out Pearl's number.

3... Billy begins to punch in the digits using the robotic hand.

2... We're through to Balti Towers. Billy wants poppadums. I make him hang up. I don't have any pocket money to pay for them.

1... Next attempt and apparently we're through to Killer's Kick-boxing. This time Billy hangs up and says he doesn't want to talk to any killers. I say I think it was probably *Kelly's* Kick-boxing. We're never any good at hearing names properly. Ibiza Nana says we don't listen. (Truth is, grown-ups never say anything interesting anyway.)

0... We have lift off! The robot hand, operated at a distance by Billy, has punched in Pearl's number correctly. Billy hisses that I should speak because

I'm the oldest. I say I don't want to. I say he should speak because it was his idea. Billy says it was Brian's idea. My mouth drops open because I can't put a snail on the line. Suddenly, we hear Pearl's voice. *Hello, I'm not here at the moment but if you'd like to leave your name and number I'll get back to you as soon as possible.*

I grab the phone off the bed and hang up as Billy's eyes fill like a paddling pool. "Why didn't you say it was you?" Billy snivels. He wipes his nose with the robotic hand and then winces when he realizes it hurts.

"I don't know. Maybe I just couldn't think of what to say."

"No worries," says Billy brightly, setting down the robotic hand. "Brian can do all the talking. He's very chatty."

As Billy is marching over to Brian's penthouse shoebox, the phone rings by itself. My first thought is: it's Pearl calling us back. Quickly I pick it up and connect before mumbling, "Hello."

My ears are nearly blasted off by Ibiza Nana's booming "Hello!" back. Anyone would think she needed to speak louder because she was calling from Spain. Ibiza Nana hotfooted it to Spain a couple of years ago after Granddad Albert's death for a "new beginning" and a "quiet life". I pointed out that Ibiza Nana was nearly seventy so it wasn't really a "new beginning" more a "new ending". But Ibiza Nana didn't listen because she was babbling on about how it was time to do her own thing even though she'd been doing her own thing since Dad left home which was over twenty years ago. Off she went to Ibiza, promising to keep in touch with us by phone. Sometimes I miss her but she rings us every week to talk about sun, sand, sangria and her sciatica. Normally I'd like to have a full conversation about sciatica because it's on page 32 of *Marvin's Medical Manual* but now isn't the time, so I yell to Dad to come to the phone.

Dad's footsteps patter down the hallway and I lean out of the bedroom and hand him the hallway phone, saying it's Ibiza Nana on the line. Dad rolls his eyes and wipes some custard cream crumbs off his T-shirt before taking the phone from me. I duck back into the bedroom to find Billy has started using my bed as his own personal trampoline. Out in the hallway I hear Dad telling Ibiza Nana not to worry because we're eating like kings. What, burger kings?

Billy is jumping so high now his head is nearly battering the ceiling, but that's not what's troubling me most. I swear I've just heard Dad tell Ibiza Nana he's made a bit of a mess of things with Pearl. Who would have thought you could actually strain your ears? I just have, trying to make out what Dad's on about. Thing is, when he mentions Pearl his voice goes all hush-hush and when he's talking about mackerel he shouts so loud they could hear him in Timbuktu.

Five minutes later I've grown bored listening and I'm looking at THE GOODBYE LIST again, noting what I've tried and what I haven't. The shrine was a failure when Billy demolished it. The tattoo nearly took my skin off because I had to use a nail brush to remove it. Even with scrubbing I couldn't get some of the letters off and was left with GOD on my hands for days. Mimi stopped me at school, pointed at it and said, "You wish." The seeds were pointless. The balloon was wrong too. The star was beautiful but not right. The sparklers were a lost cause because I couldn't buy any, and the poem... Well, let's just say:

I thought the poem would be ace
And would bring a smile to my face
But soon I knew, as a poet I was through
Because I couldn't really rhyme and it didn't say
goodbye to Mum properly anyway

There are only two things left on THE GOODBYE LIST. Number nine: just say "goodbye". And finally number ten, which is nothing, because I still haven't come up with a number ten yet.

As I'm muttering "Goodbye" over and over, Billy is attempting the world record for the number of bounces one small boy can do to annoy his older brother into kicking him in the shins. Let's just say my metatarsals are ready to take action.

The phone rings again in the hall.

"Five hundred and fifty-three," huffs Billy, bouncing up in the air. "Five hundred and fifty-four. Five hundred and fifty-five."

At first I think Ibiza Nana has probably forgotten to tell Dad something about her bunions and is ringing back. Tilting my head, I listen to Dad pad back to the phone. Only this time, when he talks to the person on the other end, his voice is less sing-song. In fact, he's all hush-hush again and I try to tell Billy to shush, only he's too busy counting and he tells me to go shush. I shush him again and it's like we're in a shushing competition.

Only because I've got bionic ears do I hear Dad hissing quietly, "Pearl, how did you get this new number? You are not allowed to contact me. You know this is serious."

TWELVE

IMPORTANT INFORMATION FOR SNOOP: Pearl has our Eden flat phone number.

DAD: Does not want Pearl to have our Eden flat phone number.

NOTES ABOUT HOW PEARL GOT OUR PHONE NUMBER: A robotic hand was the culprit. Billy and I were almost entirely innocent. I suspect Dad will not believe this if he asks me how it happened. Although judging by the way Dad is whispering, I do not think he wants us to know he is on the phone to Pearl.

SNOOP HAS WORKED OUT THAT: Pearl must have seen a strange number come up on her phone and rung it straight back and connected with Dad.

MORE IMPORTANT INFORMATION: Why did Dad tell Ibiza Nana that he had made a mess of things with Pearl? Does this mean he was going out with Camille before he left Pearl and we all ran away because of it? (I have seen this sort of problem mentioned on daytime TV shows where everyone has bad teeth and they always pull their chairs apart before saying they're stuck in love triangles. I am not one hundred per cent sure what a love triangle is, but it seems to involve at least three people who are all very cross.)

CONCERNS: Too many to mention, but the main one being that Billy has just broken my bed springs. When I tell him this, he says he can't stop now because he's showing Brian how to relax. I say Brian is always relaxed and Billy says I don't know Brian at all.

With all this new information to digest, I sit on Billy's bed and rub my chin in the manner of a spy trying to solve a puzzle. Nothing about Dad and Pearl is making any sense to me.

Twenty minutes later, when I'm still trying to figure things out, Dad comes into our bedroom and says Ibiza Nana was asking how we were both keeping. I pause, waiting for him to say that Pearl rang too, but he doesn't. Instead Dad rubs his eyes and says it's getting late and we should both get ready for bed. Then he asks why Billy is sweating like a long-haired guinea pig in a sauna and Billy says he's been exercising.

"Good-oh," says Dad, kissing him on the forehead and then wiping the sweat from his lips. When Dad kisses me I blurt out that I know all about love triangles. Startled, Dad says, "Well, you can just forget about those, because you're eleven and the only triangles you need to worry about are in your maths." It seems Dad has cut my conversation down with a great big axe before it even began.

When Dad leaves the room I tell Billy I'm sleeping in his bed tonight because I don't want a broken spring in my spine.

"No way," shouts Billy and adds, "what's yours is mine and what's mine is my own." Then he jumps into his own bed and goes straight to sleep. Apparently, all that jumping has worn him out.

As Billy lets out a little snore, I pad over to the window, pull back the curtain and stare out across the rooftops of Eden again. Each one looks like it has been dipped in silver oil and soft clouds like ghostly galleons sail across the sky. The star I picked out for Mum is still glistening.

I want to say goodbye properly so much, but the words are all tangled up in my throat, like Ibiza Nana's knitting wool after Billy has been pretending it's a wig. My eyes begin to go so blurry from rogue tears that it's hard to see properly and all I can do is mumble "Mum" over and over again. But the star above me, it keeps on shining, and even when I shut my eyes and let the tears spill like tiny rivers, it feels as though the star throws a veil of light on my sodden face. After five minutes of silent sobbing and thinking that if love could bring back someone who has died then Mum would be right here in the room behind me, whispering in my ear how much she loved me, I turn to go back to bed.

That's when it happens.

A paper crane spirals to the floor, right beside me.

The paper crane must be magical, I decide. It's definitely not one of my efforts because it has been folded perfectly. It's not the original crane either. That one is still on my desk. Nope, this is like something a magician would do. Abracadabra! Open his hat and pull out one rabbit and then a second identical rabbit would follow.

I bring it to school with me on Monday because I can't bear to leave it at home. For ages I stare at it under the table, not stopping even when Mr Beagle tells us to get out some paper and begin drawing our garden designs.

"You've had time to consider it. You've been to a garden centre. Now is the time for action," Mr Beagle continues. "And, Becket, can you stop staring at the crotch of your trousers, please?" There is a ripple of laughter as I snap my head upwards and nearly give myself whiplash. When the hysteria dies down, everyone gets out some paper and starts writing and drawing ideas for POOP.

Nevaeh nudges me with the point of a set square from her next-door desk and when I glance up she holds up her sheet of paper, on which she has drawn a load of butterflies. She gives me the thumbs up and points to my bracelet. I give her the thumbs down and point to my bracelet. I lean over and say bracelets are a girl thing.

"No way," hisses Nevaeh. "Not this one. Boys need good things to happen to them too. That's why you've got it on your wrist." She reaches across the desk and tries to grab my hand, only I pull away. "Seriously, remember what I said. My sister came back and she was a butterfly and afterwards I felt really happy and it was an amazing thing. So, now I'm spreading that amazing thing about. You just don't believe in good things, maybe because bad things have happened in the past, but mark my words, Becket Rumsey, I can feel something important is going to happen to you."

"What happened with your sister?" I ask.

"She came back as a butterfly, I told you," explains Nevaeh. "It was as if magic happened when I least expected it. One day a butterfly just landed on me. Oh, I know you'll think there's a logical explanation but there wasn't."

Yes, I do think there is a logical explanation because butterflies land on people sometimes.

"The thing is, the butterfly stayed on me for ages. When it eventually flew away I went straight home and looked up butterflies on the computer and it said that they were the symbol of a soul," explains Nevaeh. "It made me think about how I'd been sad about my sister for ages but I felt happy after seeing the butterfly because it was her. It was as if the time was right to move forward."

Knuckles turns around and tells Nevaeh something

weird happened to him too only a few days ago. "This snail flew down from the sky and landed on my head," he hisses.

"See," says Nevaeh. "Magic is all around us."

I have to bite my cheek really hard not to laugh. But then I figure it's no laughing matter, because a strange paper bird did exactly the same to me.

Mr Beagle bellows that a classroom is not the place for chatting and we're to finish up on POOP because it's time for lunch. With that the bell parps and I don't know what else Mr Beagle is trying to say, because the entire class are vaulting desks to escape.

The last thing I hear from our teacher is, "*Eden Echo*," but no one cares.

I'm standing by the wall in the playground, near the water fountain to be precise, when Knuckles walks past with a tennis ball in his ham hands.

"Hey," I say, staring at his wrist. "You've got one of Nevaeh's bracelets too." Knuckles throws the ball against the wall and then catches it. Quickly, I hold up my wrist to prove she's given me one as well. Knuckles stops and shrugs in a *So what?* kind of way. He puts the ball in his pocket.

"I sort of like it," I mutter, twanging the rubber bracelet like a guitar string. "Anyway, who wouldn't want a bit of magic in their life? If you could have a bit of magic happen, what would it be?" I reach down and scratch my leg.

"My dad back," Knuckles says as I bob back up again.

My eyes widen. "I understand," I reply. "I mean, I know what it's like when someone has passed on." I tilt my head, wanting to make conversation to prove that we're both similar. We've both lost someone.

Knuckles smirks at me and pulls the ball from his pocket again. "Passed on? You mean *dead*, passed on? So that's what you meant by a better place. You really don't have a clue about me and my dad."

And that's when Knuckles walks away, bouncing the ball up and down and then kicking it at a wall.

Oh man, I'm even more confused about him than I was before.

At three forty, Billy and I are walking home from school when we spot Dad's van outside a bubblegum-pink house. Not only is it very hard to miss the house, but it is also very hard to miss Dad's van due to the giant plastic cod on the roof.

"Why is Daddy here?" asks Billy, picking some mud out of his fingernails. He stops and stares up at the house, which has ivy strangling the walls and tiny windows that look like the top of one of Ibiza Nana's lattice pies.

"I don't know. Maybe he's delivering fish?" I explain, grimacing. A nanosecond of thought tells me he isn't actually delivering fish because Dad doesn't deliver to houses, only restaurants. I hoist my school bag back up onto my shoulder and stare at the house, as if I half expect it to provide some answers. It doesn't.

"We could go and knock on the door," Billy offers. To reinforce this idea he knocks on my head with his knuckles. And then I knock on his but it sounds hollow. "Then we would know why Daddy is in here," says Billy, ducking away from me.

"What if Dad doesn't want us to know he's here?" Billy hasn't thought of that. But I just have. What if this is Camille's house? My eyes widen and the words hula-hoop inside my head: what if this is Camille's house? What if we're not supposed to know Dad is here? Before I can say anything more, Billy takes off like a greyhound, dashes through the gate and then throws himself onto the grass like a splattered octopus.

I shout the first thing that comes into my head. "Get

out of there, you eejit." Then I shout the second thing that comes into my head. "Before you get caught." Billy isn't budging. He says this is where he's going to wait until Dad comes out the front door. Well, I'm not taking this lying down, even if Billy is. I march right over to him and try to drag him away by the arm. Unfortunately, Billy has managed to pull off the best trick ever and that is to assume the weight of a baby hippopotamus instead of my baby brother. As I give one final tug on Billy's arm he yanks me down until I'm sprawled beside him.

The door opens.

The door closes.

A woman with long brown hair appears on the pathway beside us, wearing a dark blue coat and red polka-dot scarf. The look on her face when she spots us is priceless. At this point, Billy's chin is balanced on the earth and he has a mouthful of grass clenched between his teeth. When the woman bends over and asks what we think we're doing, Billy mumbles that he's cutting the grass.

"What, with your teeth?" quizzes the woman.

"Donkeys do," says Billy, triumphantly.

"Donkeys do," I hiss as we walk towards home. "Man alive, why did you say that? She must have thought we were stupid, or at least you were." Billy just shrugs and says it's a shame we didn't see Daddy before we had to go. I say it was probably the best option, as the lady was going to ring the police.

As we turn into our road I realize this isn't a love triangle any more. No, this is a love pentagon. There's Dad, Pearl, Naked Man, Camille and now the lady in the polka-dot scarf who thinks we are human lawnmowers.

Dad arrives home shortly after us and throws his white jacket over the sofa before tickling Billy and asking if he had a good day at school. Billy says he's forgotten what sort of a day he had and Dad says that's okay because it's very easy to forget stuff.

After Dad has ordered takeaway and we're sitting at the table, Billy blurts out, "Why were you at the pink house today, Daddy?"

"What pink house?" Dad's head goes red as an embarrassed tomato and then he changes the subject. Obviously, Dad's right – it's very easy to forget stuff, especially when you don't want anyone to know what that stuff is.

THIRTEEN

Thanks to what Billy "big mouth" Rumsey said last night, Dad now knows that we know some stuff but what stuff we know, Dad doesn't know, and *we* don't know how much stuff we actually know. Basically all the stuff to do with Dad and Pearl is jumbled up and that's where we are right now.

At school, I draw a pentagon and add all the relevant names in at the points. DAD, PEARL, CAMILLE, NAKED MAN, SPOTTY SCARF WOMAN.

I try to draw lines across the centre to see who will end up with whom. I've drawn a line between Dad and Pearl and then paired the Naked Man off with Camille but the lady with the polka-dot scarf is on her own. Sitting back, I admire my quite excellent diagram, only for Mr Beagle to wander past me and bellow that it's a fine drawing of a pentagon but if I hadn't noticed we are actually talking about POOP at the moment.

"So, we are nearly at the end of the first phase of POOP," says Mr Beagle, wandering back to the front of the class and tugging on his tie. He looks over and ignores Donté Moffatt, who has his hand up. "The next phase is for you to finish your designs and I will announce the winner. Then we will plant the garden, and of course the final and most exciting phase is when we invite your parents to come and marvel at their offspring's talent."

Oh, fabulous! As if I wasn't feeling rotten enough, Mr Beagle has just reminded me that Pearl won't be coming to the POOP display. I glance over at Knuckles and he looks just as miserable as me. Maybe he's annoyed that his dad can't come too. As I catch his eye he looks away and pretends to be very busy, picking his nose.

Mr Beagle says we have probably noticed that there is a table with items on it that we could add into our garden designs. "You may not have considered things like this going in a garden. For example: CDs. They glint in the light, look amazing and keep birds away; practical and pretty. Please take a look and you may choose something from the table and include it in your design or not. You are the designer here."

Everyone gets up to look at the items Mr Beagle has brought in. They include:

- CDs from the nineties. Vintage, as Ibiza Nana would say. Old, as I would say.
- An old washing machine drum. Mr Beagle says we could put flowers in it.
- Used tin cans. Mr Beagle eats a lot of beans.
- A biscuit tin. Mr Beagle also eats a lot of biscuits.
- A toy yellow dumper truck. Again, for plants, says Mr Beagle.
- An old boot.

Knuckles strolls over to the table and picks up the dumper truck. Mimi is saying how she wouldn't touch anything here with a barge pole, which is lucky because there is no barge pole. She rises from her chair and then saunters over to me at the table and mutters in my ear, "Nothing here for you then?" I just shrug and she continues, "I'm going to win anyway. My mum says I'm great at everything I do because I'm just like her. I'm always top of the class."

That's when Knuckles accidentally knocks Mimi with the dumper truck and she squeals that he's a complete idiot. "Just like your dad! I read about him in the paper."

I see fury erupt in Knuckles's chest. Just as it's about to kick off, I get in between them. Suddenly, Knuckles's knuckles shoot forward and biff me right in the belly. Unfortunately, my belly does not have a sniff of muscle. Fortunately, I have about four folds of flesh that act like a trampoline and his knuckles bounce straight off. Without warning, my own hands fly forward and grab his wrists in a vice-like grip. Next, he twists around as if he's dancing and that's when Mr Beagle starts shouting that POOP is not about having a wrestling match and if we don't stop tussling we will be in big trouble.

"What's this all about?" snaps Mr Beagle, separating us.

"I don't know," seethes Knuckles. But he does know. It was because Mimi said Knuckles was an idiot like his dad. How could she say that about someone who has died? I don't like Mimi one little bit. Mr Beagle tells us to get out of his sight and I hurry away as quickly as possible.

Back at my desk, I pretend to be very busy finishing my design for POOP. Nevaeh, seeing my sad face, strolls past and before she can say a word to me about butterflies I say the bracelet isn't making anything amazing happen. In fact, it's making things go even worse. Look, I nearly got into a big fight wearing it.

"Haven't you heard that it's always darkest before the dawn?" whispers Nevaeh, before walking back to her desk, humming as she goes.

"Haven't you heard that butterflies are just butterflies and bracelets don't make amazing things happen?" I holler after her.

Nevaeh glances back and I can tell she's upset with me.

After school, when I switch on my mobile there is a text from Dad.

We need to talk. Dad x

I text back:

Is it about the 🐦 & the 🐝? Beck

No! It isn't! You're too young to know about the birds and the bees.

Okay, if it's not a talk about growing up then Dad's going to tell us what's going on with him and Pearl and why he didn't sound happy to get a phone call from her on Friday. He must have been spurred on because he knows we saw him at polka-dot scarf lady's bubblegum house.

Dad picks us up from the school gates and takes us to the park across the road from our flat. When Billy runs off and lunges at a swing, Dad turns to me and says, "We need this little chat. I've been meaning to do it for ages."

Okay... I inhale, thinking this is the moment the world will become clear again, like when you're in a car wash and one minute surrounded by foam and the next you can see better than ever before. I breathe out as Dad reaches into his pocket and removes his mobile phone, before rummaging around for a tissue and then blowing his nose. He sets his phone down on the bench and settles beside it.

Billy goes up and down, down and up, up and down, down and up on the swing.

"He'll be seasick," says Dad, grinning. I sit down

beside him and Dad takes the breath of a deep-sea diver before saying, "I wanted to talk to you because we've not had enough fun in this family recently."

Sweet Baby Cheeses! Is that it? Is that what the BIG talk was about? This is a bigger disappointment than when Ibiza Nana said she'd bought me a tablet and it turned out to be Scottish tablet, which was like hard fudge.

"Let's have a flat-warming party. How about next Tuesday? That gives us a week to organize it."

IS THAT IT? I'm screaming inside my head. Nothing about Pearl or Camille or the lady that trotted out of the bubblegum-pink house with the polka-dot scarf? There's a tiny thread on my school jumper and as I tug it it begins to unravel. In fact, I'm so annoyed that if I pull any harder I'm not going to have a jumper left. Dad continues, "It's exactly what we all need. So I'll arrange it for next Tuesday at seven thirty. I'll invite a few of the fish delivery blokes and you and Billy can invite anyone you like."

This is not a chat about what is going on.

This is nothing to do with why Pearl isn't with us and why he doesn't want us to make contact with her or for her to contact us.

This is nothing to do with Camille.

This is nothing to do with how Billy and I feel.

This is just like adding a cherry onto a cake that is already stale.

Dad furrows his brow when he sees my face is sourer than a super sour sweet. "Don't you want a party?"

I nod and say very carefully that I do want one but...

Billy has just run across the park and fallen in a heap on the floor because clearly he has no awareness of how his feet actually work and has managed to trip himself up. As Dad goes to help Billy, his mobile bleeps, and even though I think about calling Dad back, I can't resist reading the text first. Hey, I'm only human.

Hi Stephen, it's Camille. It was a pleasure to see you yesterday. Feel free to come back at any time. Orla will be here, if I'm not around. You could see her. Or if not Orla try Kimberley. I'll give you a ring at some point anyway.

Busted! Dad was most definitely with Camille yesterday and it sounds like there are loads of others too! This isn't a love pentagon, it's a love dodecahedron! When Dad comes back I pretend I haven't been looking at anything anywhere near his phone, oh no. In fact, all this time I've been staring up into the sky at a seagull flying overhead (and praying it hasn't eaten anything dodgy). Dad parks his bum back on the bench and picks up his phone, glancing at the message. His ears turn a funny shade of red and he clears his throat, before putting the mobile back in his pocket.

"Any messages?" I blink innocently.

"Nope," replies Dad. "I'm Daddy-No-Mates." It's on the tip of my tongue to say I doubt that very much, only Dad stops me in my tracks by saying, "Your mother loved a party." Billy is back on the swings now, going up and down, down and up. I'd like to shout at Dad: *DON'T CHANGE THE SUBJECT!* But at the same time I *want* him to change the subject, because we never talk about Mum enough. "Yeah, she was always at the heart and soul of a good party." Dad sighs. "Your mum and I came here before, right to this spot. Did you know that?" I shake my head. "We lived in the house in Honeydown Hills but came here for a little day trip to see a seal."

I swallow. "Did you see one?"

Dad smiles and ruffles my hair with his fingers. "No, but Mum found this old glass water bottle on the beach and said she wanted to do something special." I remember the photo I saw in Dad's bedroom in the flat where Mum was holding a bottle. "She wanted to send a message-in-a-bottle. Well, I told her it was pointless doing that because no one ever bothers with those things any more. Not now we've got emails and we can send phone messages." Dad lowers his eyes until his lashes tickle his cheeks. "But your mum insisted that she wanted to. She said someone out there would get her message. They might be very far away from her but it would reach them and maybe they'd get in contact if she gave her address."

"And did someone get Mum's message?" I swallow and blink rapidly. At this moment I don't care about parties or anything else; what I want most in the world is for someone to have replied to Mum's message-in-a-bottle.

Dad keeps his gaze steady and when I lick my lips, waiting for his reply, I taste the tang of salt. "No," Dad admits eventually. "She never did get a reply. A few years later we were looking at photos and we came across one from that day and I asked your mum if she minded that no one had ever replied and Mum said someone would. There was still time." Dad sighs and rubs his eyes.

But there wasn't time. I swallow again and it's like my stomach is on a helter-skelter whizzing downwards on a straw mat. "I wish Mum could come back and give me a hug," I whisper, more to myself than anyone.

"Oh, son, if she could she would. I could give you a hug in her place, if that would count. Mum would be happy with that." I nod and take the hug from Dad and I close my eyes and imagine it *is* Mum, even though Dad's about three times her size and he smells of fish and sweat and pine forests. And I imagine Mum smelling of vanilla cupcakes and flowers. For one pure and perfect second it almost feels real and I don't want to let Dad go. If I try really hard I can imagine Mum's heartbeat. Then Dad pulls away and just like that it feels like Mum has gone again.

FOURTEEN

Knock, knock...

Who's there?

Don't know – because Dad is playing musical statues.

We're just home from the park and have taken off our coats when Dad hears someone at the front door, and he stands completely still and doesn't move.

Knock, knock...

Who's there?

Still don't know – because Dad appears to be glued to the floor even though somebody is repeatedly knocking.

"Dad, what are you doing? We need to answer the door," I say.

"I'll do it," shouts Billy, although I think that might be tricky as he's sitting on the toilet at the moment. I hear the rasp of the toilet roll holder as it revolves.

"No way," hisses Dad, edging slowly towards the front door. He puts on the chain, then opens the front door a teeny bit to see who it is. After a second, he takes the chain off again, opening the door properly.

"Hello, boys," says Cat breezily as she wafts in, carrying a dish of bubbling molten lava which she calls lasagne. "I've brought you this because I guessed you're probably still finding your feet in the kitchen and a little bit of home-cooked food wouldn't go amiss."

Dad pipes up, "You must be psychic." Then his tongue literally unfurls and rolls across the carpet in the direction of the lasagne dish.

Cat laughs and wanders into the kitchen. "Yes, if a psychic also happens to notice an awful lot of takeaway cartons in the rubbish." She sets the dish down and tells Dad to be careful because it's fiery enough to serve to Beelzebub himself.

When Billy comes out of the toilet his tongue joins Dad's on the floor. Dad says Cat must stay because there's no way we can eat all this lovely grub by ourselves. Grinning, Cat ladles out great dollops of lasagne that squeaks and bubbles as she puts it onto plates and then she carries them to the table. Dad takes a bowl and fills it with cheese-and-onion crisps, saying he's sorry he has no garlic bread, so this'll have to do. Next, Cat suggests Dad should put on some music, because the flat has gone a bit gloomy again. "Hey, I thought you were getting the fun back after our evening of decorating. Come on, let's get the party started," she says, poking Dad playfully in the belly. There's a lot to poke. Dad says he's having a party next Tuesday for real and will she come? Cat says she'd love to.

Within minutes the music is on and Cat is laughing at Dad's stupid jokes and Billy is doing a little finger dance on the table. When I look around from one face to another it's like the flat is waking up again – maybe even our family too. Cat grins at me, shoves a big forkful of lasagne into her mouth and asks if I'm enjoying it.

Does the wood have trees?

Does the ocean have water?

Does hot lasagne take the roof off your mouth?

"I love it," I mumble through the boiling cheesy pasta blanket that slithers down my throat and nearly takes all my skin with it. After downing a glass of water I get a bit bold, happy on the atmosphere, like Ibiza Nana after a few drinks. I ask Cat if she's married. She hasn't mentioned a Mr Cat yet and since she's about Dad's age

I'd expect a Mr Cat somewhere in the background. Dad tries to make cutting hand signals but Cat ignores him, thinking he's doing a dance move to the eighties music he's put on.

"Why? Are you asking?" Cat leans over the table towards me. I smell cheese and onion on her breath.

"Oh no," I reply a bit too quickly. Cat laughs, leans back again and says it's all right because she thinks I might be a little on the young side for her anyway. And no, she's not married, she's been divorced a few years now. Billy tells Cat no one would want to marry me.

"No one would want *you*," I hiss.

"Brian would want me."

"You can't marry a snail, stupid. They'd never make it to the altar because they're so sluggish."

Dad tells us to stop bickering in front of guests and goes into the fridge and finds a few cans of fizzy cola and tells Cat it's all he's got. "I know I should have a bottle of wine but I'm not really organized at the minute."

"Ooh, I'm not sure I should drink anyway." Cat taps her nose with her forefinger. "I've got to be able to get back home in one piece. It's a long way."

Everyone laughs at the joke and Cat picks up a can and pulls the tab and takes a swig. For the next ten minutes we talk about everything from my garden design – which, when I show her, Cat says is amazing – to the park opposite, to what fish the restaurants are serving in town, to what's going on in Cat's hairdressing salon (mainly colouring). Cat tells us she set up her salon with an inheritance she had when she was younger. Then she says she likes to get out and cut elderly people's hair for those that can't make it to the salon.

I can tell Dad is impressed because he's gone a bit goggle-eyed as he picks up our empty plates and takes them to the sink. Billy jumps down from the table and disappears to our bedroom, coming back a minute or so later with Brian. He starts playing with his snail, piping up that Brian could be on a UK talent show. I say if that's the best we've got to offer I'm definitely moving to another country. Cat peers across the table as Billy plonks Brian near the salt shaker.

"I wouldn't do that," says Cat, reaching out. "You'll kill him – snails don't like salt."

Billy says that Cat has saved Brian's life and he'll never forget it. A few seconds later though he has already forgotten it, because Cat has to remind him once again to keep the snail away from the table.

Cat seems so nice that I seize my chance and ask her

about her mum. "When we were decorating the flat you said your mum likes lilies," I whisper. "What's your mum like?"

There's a huge clatter of dishes behind us and Cat excuses herself and rises from the table, dropping her square of toilet roll (which was doubling as a napkin – Dad said if it was soft enough for the bum, it would do just fine for the lips). Cat says she'll tell me about her mum later because Dad needs help. Dad turns around and gives her a sheepish nod.

A few seconds later there's an awful lot of laughter and rattling of dishes. Cat flicks a load of foam at me and it sticks to my hair like I've got a bubble wig.

"Don't ever lose the fun," laughs Cat. "It's the law according to me."

"What's the law according to your other superhero friends?" I ask.

Cat looks at me as if I have two heads, neither of them making any sense. With a name like Cat Woman, you'd think she'd know everything about superheroes.

Two hours later, after Cat has gone home and Billy has gone to bed, I settle down with Dad to watch *Monster vs Man* on TV. Every so often I look at him, studying his face. He doesn't look different, but I can't help thinking of all the women he's dating. It's like Dad is a woman-magnet. Just as I am distracted by gazing at Dad's long nostril hair, the phone rings. Dad and his nostrils trot away down the hallway.

On the TV, a troll whacks a man on the head with a fish as he tries to get across the assault course. A giggle escapes from my lips. *Ding ding!* The man makes his way to the punching wall next and gets biffed in the guts. What kind of crazy person would do this stuff? I ask myself. Over the sound of the TV, I suddenly hear Dad say Pearl's name. I rise off my bum and peer over the back of the sofa through the open door into the hall.

I strain my ears and hear Dad pleading with Pearl not to keep ringing him, to leave it. Suddenly it feels like the previous happiness in the flat has been vacuumed up. After a minute or two, I feel so awkward listening in that I go and hide under the kitchen table, where I find Brian, who clearly left the table two hours ago and has only just reached the floor.

"Becket!" I bang my head on the underside of the table with an almighty thwack. Painfully, I crawl out and tell Dad I was looking for Brian. That's when I stand up and hear a horrible crack under my foot. The sort of crack that makes you realize your internal organs can play their own wind instrument. Gingerly I lift my foot, praying to the gods of all things slimy, and stare at what is underneath. A cheese and onion crisp is stuck to my sock. Brian is still under the table. With much relief, I pick him up and say I'm going to put him back in the shoebox penthouse Billy made for him.

"Before you go, did you hear anything of my phone call?" Dad chews on his lip until I see a tiny split in the skin.

"What?"

"Did you hear who I was talking to?" asks Dad.

The lie tumbles from my tongue like a toddler on a gym mat. "No."

Dad says that's good and then he changes the subject, saying he can't wait for the party. He looks at Brian in my hand and says it's time I put him to bed and went there myself. Dad kisses my head and says, "I love you, son."

I tell Dad I love him too.

What I don't tell him is that I don't understand him.

Once I'm inside our bedroom, Brian goes straight back into the shoebox by Billy's bed. Billy has built him a proper little home out of matchsticks, bits of fluff, and a small patch of mud in the corner.

"You see, Billy..." I whisper, placing Brian carefully

back in the box. Billy gives a contented little snore. "I brought your friend home. I might have fired Brian number one into Knuckles's garden but I made a mistake. You need Brian. I can see that now." Billy's eyelids flicker gently, and then he turns away and lets out a little sigh.

I put on my pyjamas and climb into bed, but that's not the last time I see Billy before morning.

At five forty-three exactly Billy comes to me, saying he's had another nightmare.

"Do you want to get into bed with me?" I mumble through the sleepy haze of a dream about a giant troll whacking me in the face with a giddy kipper as I ran across cracked snail shells in my bare feet.

"No," Billy replies. "It's dark and scary when you close your eyes."

"But you close your eyes every night," I mumble throwing back the sheets and climbing out. I tell Billy we'll curl up in the armchair for a while. "I'll tell you more of the story," I say.

Billy nods and rubs his eyes briskly before following me to the armchair.

"When the first boy fell into the water," I tell Billy, wiggling my feet, "it felt as though he had escaped the storm. It was calm below the ocean surface. That's when he saw her, a creature so beautiful that he could hardly tear his eyes away from her. She had hair like long dark ribbons and her skin was wrapped in seaweed. And although she didn't open her mouth, she had the voice he had heard on the surface."

Billy asks for her name. I say I'm not sure but I'll come up with a name soon.

"When the second boy followed, hoping to save his brother, he too saw the beautiful creature," I say.

"Was she a mermaid?" Billy takes the swallow cushion and hugs it tightly.

"I don't know, but she was definitely from another world and the two boys wanted to stay with her more than anything. They decided they didn't want to go back to the storm because it was hard work trying to get through it, especially when they didn't even know what the land would be like if they reached it. No, they'd stay with her where it was calm. She swam with them through sunken galleons and she showed them things they'd never seen before: giant starfish that looked like they'd fallen from heaven, small shrines made from shells, and corals that grew like plants from the sand. She showed them fish that sparkled like fireworks and pufferfish that floated away like balloons and she drew pictures on the ocean floor."

Billy's eyes droop and he lifts his thumb and pops it into his mouth, snuggling closer into my dinosaur pyjamas.

There is a tiny snore and Billy is already asleep. Gently, I try to disentangle myself without disturbing him. Lifting his duvet from the bed, I gently cover his little body.

"I've never told you this, Billy," I whisper. "The thing is, it was so hard when Mum died...but we had you. And you're special." My eyes fill with tears and I let them go because there's no one to see them spill. Quickly I tiptoe back to my bed, hardly seeing where I'm going, and when I pull back the cover there's a paper crane there, waiting for me.

As I pick it up my tears soak the wing, making it droop a little.

FIFTEEN

Ever since Dad mentioned the party last week he has talked of nothing else. He's been saying: I'd better buy a million pork pies for all the guests that will be attending (in the end I found out it was eleven, including us, so by my reckoning he doesn't need 999,989 of those pork pies). He's bought spotty bunting and balloons too. We blew the balloons up earlier and I thought they'd been made of rhino hide, they were so hard to blow up. In the end I was grateful I was still alive to attend the party and hadn't burst the air sacs in my lungs. Right now those same balloons are floating across the floor like oily bubbles and the eleven pork pies that Dad bought are sitting on a paper plate in the kitchen along with quiche, crisps, buns and sandwiches.

All we need now are some guests.

"Everything is going to be brilliant," says Billy, stretching out his arms and looking up and spinning around until he drops in a heap onto the floor.

I don't answer him. To be honest, I don't think everything is going to be brilliant, not after hearing Dad on the phone to Pearl over a week ago. But I don't want to burst Billy's bubble. (Although, last night, I did accidentally burst his helium balloon from that shopping trip we had. Who lets a slightly deflated horse float about in the dark? I went to the toilet in the middle of the night and when something floated from behind the door I thought it was a ghost. It was only after I'd put my fingernails in its head that I realized what it was. This morning when I told Dad what had happened he just laughed and said it was your classic night mare.)

"You know why it's going to be brilliant?" Billy grins. No, I don't know but I have a feeling Billy is going to tell me. I pause as Billy continues, "Because I invited Pearl."

Sweet Baby Cheeses! If I was prone to fainting, I would be in a heap on the floor. I stutter, "Y-y-you are joking, amirite?"

"You are wrong."

I need time for this to sink in – and by time, I mean a millennium.

Then Billy corrects himself and says he didn't invite Pearl after all. Just as my body is relaxing he says, "I didn't invite Pearl, Brian did." Oh, for the love of Lego. Billy continues that last week Brian encouraged him to borrow my phone while I was in the toilet and Brian left a message asking Pearl to come to the party.

I bark, "Brian CANNOT talk."

"Brian said you'd say that."

Oh, I cannot speak to Billy any more. I have to actually walk away and bang my head on a wall, which is very hard and I have to stop because I cannot afford to lose any brain cells since I'm the only one in this family with any to start with.

Dad zooms past me and then begins dancing like no one is watching which, in my opinion, is a bad thing. All people should dance like someone is watching – that way they wouldn't be so awful. Right now, Dad is pirouetting like a baby elephant. He has accidentally pulled some of the bunting down and it looks like a triangular wig. In his hand is a can of beer and when his hand wobbles, wee-coloured liquid sloshes onto the carpet. When Dad realizes he mouths, "Whoops," and smudges the wet patch with his toe. Then he skitters into the kitchen, pulling down the sleeve of his jumper and using the fabric as an oven mitt to bring out a tray of steaming-hot baby sausages.

To be honest, I'm no Einstein (although I'm the closest this family has got to him) but I don't think the jumper will work as an oven mitt. This is confirmed when Dad slams the tray down and begins blowing on his fingers and dancing around again, only this time I think it's more pain than party.

"I think you're being very silly, Daddy," announces Billy.

"I am," replies Dad. "But it's all good. Why worry about a few tiny blisters on my fingers when there's a whole heap of fun to be had?"

"Daddy will stop being a big boo-boo when Pearl gets here," whispers Billy when we go back into the living room with a bowl of prawn cocktail crisps. "When Pearl gets here everything will be okay and SNOOP will be the winners and it'll be all because of Brian."

I lean over and whisper in Billy's ear. "You can't rely on Pearl to come. I don't want you getting your hopes up." I think back to Dad's phone call from Pearl over a week ago. There's no way that he's in any mood to meet up with Pearl, and definitely not by surprise like this.

But it's obvious that Billy's hopes are so high they're

on a ladder halfway to heaven. What's more, I've obviously made him angry by suggesting she might not show up, because he pushes me away and says no SNOOP member would say something like that. Then he snatches the prawn cocktail crisps, drags up a chair and plonks himself where he has a view straight down the hallway to the front door. "Pearl will come," he echoes.

At that very moment there's a knock at the door. Billy looks at me and I look at him. Dad yells that he'll get it and I have to yell back that I'll get it because Dad needs to look after those blisters he just got before they get infected and turn into big green pus-filled sacs of goo that could lead to impetigo which is very infectious and requires antibiotics. And sometimes antibiotics don't even work. Dad doesn't answer me back but I hear him frantically banging cupboards and muttering about antiseptic spray as I race towards the front door, Billy following me.

A millisecond later I reach for the door and fling it open.

It's Cat and she is all smiles and carrying a tray of funny little pastry circles. "Vol-au-vents?" she says.

Billy says he can only speak one language.

"English, you mean?" Cat says as she enters the hallway.

"No," replies Billy. "Snail."

Cat almost creases up and says, "Oh, Billy. You're one of a kind." She's got that right.

Today, Cat looks different. She's all smart and wearing a flouncy black dress dotted with these tiny red ladybirds, which Billy likes very much. Around her neck she's wearing a thin red satin ribbon and she's tied it in a dainty bow to the side. Her hair is all red and glossy like the newly washed bonnet of a car and she has got these funny little black flicky lines drawn on her eyes that really make her look like Cat Woman.

Dad wobbles towards Cat and says she's a sight for sore eyes. The scent of antiseptic is coming off him but everyone pretends not to notice. Dad glances down at Cat's tray and says how much he loves vol-au-vents, before leading Cat towards the kitchen, his bum cheeks doing a tiny salsa on the way.

Dad has propped the door onto the street open with a plastic haddock from the back of his van, which means everyone can come on up to the party without having to buzz. There are several more knocks at the flat door...

Ten minutes later, if I was writing up the guests we now have in attendance, it would take me about thirty seconds:

We have Dad, who is insisting on doing the "Hokey Cokey", only when he's supposed to put his left leg in he makes a mistake and uses his right, kicking Cat in the shin and nearly sending her plate of food into the air.

We have Cat, who is now limping around asking for ice. Dad asks, for her drink? No, apparently for her shin.

We have three fish delivery blokes, let's just call them Flounder, Skate and Sole. A fourth and fifth turn up and it's obvious the fourth loves himself because he talks very loudly. Let's just call him Brill. The fifth looks well shifty, with a dodgy haircut. Small-Eyed Ray for him. Although it was a toss-up between that name and Thick-Lipped Grey Mullet.

We have two women from a restaurant Dad delivers to. They are standing in the corner talking about mussels. Or muscles. I don't know which.

Then there's Billy, who is back on his seat, watching the front door. "Pearl's going to come," he repeats over and over.

And me. And I keep saying that Pearl might not.

"She will, because I said Dad had won the lottery."

I tell Billy we haven't won the lottery. Actually, scrap that, I *screech* that we haven't won the lottery. "Why would you leave Pearl a message saying that?" Okay, now I'm so angry I could punch a hole in a hole punch. "Are you completely doolally, Billy Rumsey? The flipping lottery? This takes the biscuit. Like, we're millionaires now who happen to be living in a crummy two-bed flat. Yeah, because so many millionaires do that and so many millionaires drive an old van with a plastic cod on it instead of a Lamborghini. Oh, and we eat from Mr Wong's or the Giggling Squid chippie or the Burger, She Wrote burger van and we're beating off those other millionaires to get to the onion rings first."

"Daddy won ten pounds," says Billy, frowning at me. He pauses and then continues, "On a scratchcard."

Sweet Baby Cheeses! The penny drops from the height of Kilimanjaro. "Oh," I reply, piping right down. "I suppose he did, *but* it was ages ago and it was only ten pounds and we spent it on takeaway."

"Oh yeah," replies Billy. "I forgot to tell Pearl that. I liked the prawn toast though." Billy adds that we might win the lottery again soon. Does that count? No, it doesn't. I glance over at Dad, who according to Billy should be holding one of those giant cheques with loads of zeros on it. Instead he's headbutting balloons and doing the can'tcan't, which is Dad's own version of the cancan.

I hear the door go again and sprint down the hallway,

followed by Billy. As I open the door, Billy's mouth drops open and he shouts, "Pearl, I knew you'd come!"

"Fancy seeing you here and how lovely that you're having a party," says Pearl, smiling at me and handing me a bottle of wine. "Trust your dad to have a party on a Tuesday – he always was daft. I suppose it's to celebrate your lottery win." She plays with a large ring on her little finger that looks like a spoonful of amber-coloured jelly.

"Oh yeah," says Billy, rushing towards Pearl and clinging to her like a spider monkey. "I got mixed up. We won—"

"Exactly ten pounds," I finish Billy's sentence for him. "But you're here now, so it doesn't matter." I feel a rush of excitement when I reach out to hug Pearl. She feels warm and smells of coconut and summer sunshine. I remember how it used to be, having her around the house. I think about how Pearl would let us paint pictures using her special tubes of paint that Billy called goo-ache and how she'd pick us up from school and take us to the sweet shop on a Friday. And if we were sick she'd give us white syrup on a spoon and tuck us up in bed. She'd come to school nativities too, even the time when Billy was the inn keeper and told Joseph and Mary there was room at the inn.

But Pearl pulls away. "I didn't know where you'd run off to until I got Billy's phone call last week and he left me a message about this party above Crops and Bobbers. Anyway, I took down the details and I drove straight here after my painting classes at Tower Point." Spluttering, I try to tell Pearl that we texted her but she didn't respond. Pearl looks vaguely surprised and says she didn't get the texts, but I don't believe her because there's a tiny twitch at the corner of her lip. Billy is so excited, it's like he's drunk ten fruit squashes all at once. He wants to show Pearl his pet snail who helped him contact her, but Pearl is telling him she doesn't want to see the snail unless it's on a plate and covered in a herby butter sauce.

"Oh," says Billy and then his face brightens as he realizes it was probably a joke. Only judging by Pearl's face now, I don't think it was. "I knew you wouldn't leave us," adds Billy, hopping about from one foot to the other. I can see a spark of happiness in his eyes and I feel the same until Pearl grimaces.

Her voice is as dry as a flip-flop in the Sahara. "I didn't leave you. You left me, didn't you? Now where's your father?"

There's a big whoop from the living room. That's our father; I'd know that whoop anywhere. Pearl marches straight into the living room and sees Dad hand-in-hand with Cat as they limbo under a kitchen broom. I didn't even know we had a broom – we've never used it. They're both snorting with laughter as they fall onto the floor together in one big mass of frothy red net from Cat's skirt.

Someone changes the music and suddenly Dad, whose arms and legs are tangled up octopus-style with Cat's, looks up and sees Pearl towering over him, arms folded. There's a moment when his jaw drops so low he could fit the world's biggest gobstopper in there. And still have room for a watermelon.

SIXTEEN

I've never seen Dad move so fast unless it's for the remote control when we want to watch kids' TV. He's up off the floor in a flash and starts saying that the party is over because he's got an early appointment in the morning. There are groans and grumbles until Dad says everyone can take a bottle with them. No need to feel shy. Apparently no one does, because it's like a plague of locusts have just cleared our kitchen. Someone even took Pearl's wine bottle from my hand. It was probably Small-Eyed Ray. I knew he was shifty.

Five minutes later it's just Dad, Pearl, Billy and me. Billy swings his legs against the sofa and Dad doesn't say a word but his shoulders are slumped and his fingers locked together. Pearl is telling Billy how much she loves Dad but was very disappointed that one night everyone just disappeared and left her no forwarding address or phone number. "I went out for fresh air and when I got back you'd gone. Packed up and left no contact details. In the end I had to move out too." Pearl's mouth twists.

"Come live with us." Billy claps his hands together.

"It's up to your father," says Pearl, staring around at the flat and clearly not liking what she sees. "But we'd have to get rid of those cushions and I can't stand fake lilies." I swallow, thinking: *Not the lilies, they can't go.* "Your father just doesn't appreciate that you have to work at relationships and it's all about give and take. I told him this when we spoke recently." It's weird how Pearl's talking as though Dad's the Invisible Man. But *I* can see him, and I can see that Dad looks defeated, confused and more broken than a packet of reduced-price biscuits.

"You know why we left, Pearl," he whispers, his hand skating over his head. "Let's not do this in front of them." He nods towards Billy and me and runs his hand back again – nope, still no hair. "They've already put up with such a lot. They don't need this. You know what happened. You know everything."

I swallow again, deeper this time.

"It's all your fault," hisses Pearl, leaning into his face and waggling her finger. Her nails are scarlet and I don't like the colour. "You broke up a happy home. You were always daft, Stephen Rumsey. I don't know how your wife ever put up with you."

My heart feels like a Slinky going downstairs. Mum didn't have to "put up" with Dad. Why would Pearl say that? Mum loved Dad and I don't care what anyone says.

Dad agrees with Pearl that he can be stupid sometimes. Actually nods his approval like a nodding dog you see in the back of old people's cars. I want to say that Dad isn't stupid. The words roll around inside my head like a meatball on a plate but they never quite make it to my lips. Next Dad begins telling Pearl he's sorry over and over.

All I hear is that Dad's sorry, which is what makes me think he's totally to blame for all this mess. That's why I say it. "This is all because of Fondant Fancy, isn't it?"

Dad's eyebrows make a question mark. "Isn't that a little pink cake?"

"Camille," I spit. There's a burning in my stomach as I continue, "The Fondant Fancy lady I saw you with the day I was on my school trip; the one who texted you."

It feels like I've unleashed a Fondant Fancy Armageddon as Pearl squeals the question I've asked myself many times: "Who is Camille?"

Well, Dad suddenly has more bluster than a blustery day. "Oh, um, er..." Three pairs of eyeballs stare and glare at him. "It's not what you think." I'm thinking of the love dodecahedron, I don't know what Pearl's thinking. Whatever it is, it's not great, judging by the way she's narrowing her eyes. To be honest, I'm surprised she can still see. Thing is, I'm glad I've said it and it's out in the open. I've wanted to ask Dad about it for ages and now he *has* to answer. "Camille is, um, er..." Dad eventually manages to splutter out that she's a work acquaintance.

"*Pffttt...*" wheezes Pearl, her cheeks flushing pink. "Was that Camille you were frolicking on the floor with just now?"

"That was Cat," offers Billy.

"Oh, so there's two – Camille and Cat."

"And polka-dot scarf lady, and Orla and Kimberley," I add.

Dad's eyeballs nearly fall out of their sockets because they're bulging so much. He hisses that I've been reading his texts. I say the phone happened to bleep that day we went to the park and my eyes happened to

191

fall on it and I can't help it that I can read. He should be glad I've had such a good education.

"Pearl," pleads Dad, addressing her directly, "honestly, it's not what you think. I don't know those other women and Cat just owns the hairdressing salon downstairs."

"Next, you'll be telling me she cuts your hair." Pearl's eyes fall on Dad's bald head and she growls, "You've changed, Stephen Rumsey."

Billy starts kicking the bottom of the sofa with his heels. *Thump-thump-thump.* Me, I'm staring at the fake lilies in the vase and thinking: imagine a lovely family evening. Now scrap that and imagine us. We're like a row of sad ducks at a funfair waiting to be knocked down one by one.

Thump-thump-thump.

"I don't think you know what you've done," says Pearl, her voice buzzing around our ears like an annoying drone.

Thump-thump-thump.

Frustrated, Dad asks me to get Billy ready for bed and for us both to stay in our bedroom. He needs to talk to Pearl without little ears listening. As I softly close the bedroom door and get Billy into his pyjamas, he says that everything has worked out how Brian planned.

That's when the arguing starts for real. It's soft at first, with only the occasional raised voice. Billy tilts his head, trying to hear what they're saying. A few seconds later and Pearl is getting louder. Balloons are bursting and I'm telling myself parties aren't supposed to end like this. Dad is trying to calm Pearl down but it's not working because Pearl is shouting about Camille and how she doesn't like Fondant Fancies.

The only safe place to go is the armchair and Billy and I curl up together and I pull the duvet over our heads to try and drown out the shouting but it doesn't work. Even our safe place isn't feeling so safe. Pearl is shouting about how everyone warned her. "Oh, they said I shouldn't take on a bloke with a ready-made family. But I thought I knew better."

Billy is all elbows and knees and whispers, "Becket, I don't like it. Pearl is very cross with Daddy. Did I do a bad thing telling her to come to the party?" I assure him he didn't.

Now Pearl is shouting about playing the field. Billy says Pearl can't be cross now because this sounds like fun and he'd like to play the field too. Only Pearl has gone on to say men that play the field are horrible and cowardly. Billy's face darkens again and he says actually he wouldn't like to play the field after all. I can't hear what Dad is saying in reply. He's very quiet and there's a dull thrum like a kettle boiling. Without warning, Pearl starts shouting that now isn't the time for tea. I hear a door slam and then open again.

"Tell me the story," whispers Billy. "I don't want to hear them shouting." He sticks his fingers in his ears.

My voice trembling, I say, "The boys stayed underwater with the beautiful creature for a long time and they loved her with all their hearts and she loved them. They forgot about the others of their kind who were still in the storm on the surface. They forgot about the land they needed to reach. And they forgot they had been invisible, because she saw them and they saw her. She sang them songs too and told the boys stories about her ancestors and how they had travelled through storms. But then one day, just when they had almost forgotten the life they had before, she told them that the storm had passed. She said they had to go back. But the boys did not want to hear that."

There is a small knock at my bedroom door and we throw off the duvet. Dad pokes his head into the bedroom and says he's sorry if we heard a bit of shouting. It's all over now and we don't have to worry. It was just a silly disagreement, all forgotten. Billy looks like he's been in a wind tunnel, his hair sprouting off at different angles. Dad sighs, adding, "Would you mind if I went for a tiny walk with Pearl? She needs a breath of fresh air."

"There's air here, Daddy," says Billy. He sucks some in to prove it.

"I know, son," replies Dad, easing into our bedroom and ushering us from the armchair into our beds. "But Pearl wants to nip out for a second. I wouldn't ask but I'm only going outside for a few minutes and I'll come straight back in time to give you your goodnight kiss."

Before I can stop him, Dad is back at the bedroom door and blowing us a kiss. The door closes behind him. "Oh," says Billy. He coughs. "That was quick."

The front door closes quietly. The second it happens the flat feels different – scarier, somehow. I spend ages listening for Dad to come back. I even get up fifteen minutes later, pretending I need a glass of water, but really to check if Dad has sneaked back in and I haven't heard. The living room is littered with crisps and there are vol-au-vent pastry cases scattered on tables, all the filling licked out. Dad hasn't come back.

When I return to the bedroom, Billy perks up and asks why Dad hasn't given him his bedtime kiss.

"I surrender. I'll do it," I reply, holding my hands up and padding towards his bed.

"No thanks," says Billy. "I'd rather kiss Brian." So that's what he does.

At first I think I'm dreaming but then there's a sharp elbow to the lumbar vertebrae at the lower end of my back (page 72 of *Marvin's Medical Manual*) and it makes me jolt awake. I sit up in bed and in the sliver of moonlight that slices through the gap in the curtains I can see it's Billy and he's not in bed where he's supposed to be.

"My belly is sore," he moans.

I glance at my phone and see it's stupid o'clock again. "I'll get Dad," I mutter, throwing back the duvet and rubbing my eyes.

"You can't," wails Billy, flopping down on top of my bed. "Dad's left us."

SEVENTEEN

No word of a lie; my eyes have just zinged open like someone squirted lemon juice in them. Dad can't have *gone* anywhere. There's only one place dads should be in the middle of the night and that's in bed, snoring their heads off and dreaming of what nice things they can do for their kids. Billy clutches his belly and I can hear it gurgling louder than a geyser. Next, Billy leans over me and says he's feeling sick. Sweet Baby Cheeses! Don't lean over me then.

Billy's right about Dad. I've just checked the flat and Dad's not in his bed and he's not in the toilet either. I even open the cupboard doors, although I know Dad squeezing into a cupboard would be like an orang-utan squeezing into a monkey nut.

"This is all wrong," I mutter, more to myself than Billy. "If Dad's still talking to Pearl he must have a very dry throat by now."

Billy reaches out for my hand and gives it a squeeze. I squeeze back but, nope, this isn't okay. On a scale of one to ten, ten being okay and one being not okay, this is a 0.0001.

"Becket!" Billy wails, rising from the bed like a zombie. "There is a fire-breathing dragon living in my belly." He's up and clutching the bum of his pyjamas with his hand. "Ohmyflippingactualgod!" I scream, because now Billy is running towards the toilet, shouting that the dragon is coming out to play. The toilet door bangs against the wall as Billy flings it open and then there is the faint rumble of something unpleasant. I wince slightly as the toilet roll holder rasps as it revolves. The toilet flushes.

It flushes again.

And again.

Billy is back with a face the colour of an uncooked pasty. His hair is like tiny damp snakes and he says it must have been something he ate at the party. Surely it wasn't the:

Five burned cocktail sausages
Two pork pies
Three mini pizzas with pepperoni
Prawn cocktail, pickled onion and salt-and-vinegar crisps
One prawn vol-au-vent (licked and put back on plate)
Six mushroom parcels
Four cupcakes with deep swirls of rose frosting
Five cheese sandwiches cut into triangles, with fluorescent yellow piccalilli that made the white bread look nuclear
Four bottles of fizzy pop, blue in colour
Three slices of ham quiche
Six chocolate-chip cookies

Without trying to panic, I encourage Billy to get back into his bed (basically I don't want him puking in mine), but no sooner have I tucked him in and said he should get some sleep than he's up and running to the toilet again, screaming it's the dragon that needs a snooze.

While Billy's in there I try to ring Dad on his mobile, but he isn't picking up.

Answer the phone, come on, Dad

Billy is ill, it makes him feel bad
Answer the phone, before I get mad
Why am I rhyming, it's really sad

After I put the phone down, I think about two things. Firstly, why do I keep making up poems when they're utterly rubbish? Secondly, whatever has poisoned Billy's belly will find one of two ways out, it always does when he's sick. For the record, I think Niagara Falls has relocated to our bathroom.

Actually, now there's a third thing I'm thinking and it's this: sick is more slippery than sliding down a slope in slippers. I know this because I just ran into the bathroom and, holy guacamole, I nearly skidded into tomorrow. Billy is a mess; a sick-splattered, bathroom pebble-dashing mess. As I'm giving him a wipe with one of the new flannels Dad bought at the shopping mall, Billy unleashes yet another avalanche which I have to hide under the fluffy bath mat.

The last time Billy was this sick, we were on the ghost train at a fair. It was easier then though. Firstly it was dark and we couldn't see the sick. Secondly, we were in our own carriage and moving. That definitely helped. Thirdly a fan blew it away from us. Mind you, there were a lot a screams behind us, which we thought were babyish because the ghost train wasn't that scary. When we got out we realized the people in the carriage behind us were splattered in Billy's sick but they seemed to think it was all part of the spooky experience and we just ran away laughing.

One sickly, miserable-as-Mondays hour later, after failing to get hold of Dad, I get Billy back into bed. He looks up at me with the eyes of a spaniel watching a sad movie and says, "I wish Cat, I mean Pearl, was here."

"Yes, I know," I reply, smoothing down Billy's damp hair as he falls asleep. "But it would help even more if Dad was."

Next morning Dad still hasn't appeared, but I tell Billy I spoke to Dad while he was asleep – all a lie. Then I convince Billy that Dad said I was supposed to get him ready in his uniform and we'd walk to school by ourselves as usual, and then Dad would be home later on. Billy nods and says he's hungry, but after looking around I realize there's nothing healthy and the nine pork pie leftovers from the party are probably not a good idea. That's when I remember I didn't eat the apple in my packed lunch yesterday. I find it and hand it over to Billy and tell him to eat it. For a second it feels like I'm taking over Dad's job and that isn't good. For starters, I have too much hair to be Dad.

While Billy's biting into the apple I get myself into my school trousers, shirt, tie and jumper and every few seconds I check my phone for messages from Dad. Nothing. There's a little yelp from Billy and I go running to him in case he's being sick again.

"Something terrible has happened," says Billy, clutching at his throat.

"Are you feeling sick again?" My eyes widen and I look around wildly for something to catch the puke in. I find Dad's good shoes in the hallway. They'll do.

"It's worse, much worse," says Billy, clawing at his neck as I hold a shoe under his chin. "I'm growing a tree in my belly."

Note to self: relax, set down the shoe, Billy is okay. I stare at him and tell Billy he is not growing a tree in his belly or anywhere else. Turns out he'd swallowed an apple pip. As I'm explaining how digestion works and how if you eat a monkey nut you won't suddenly grow a gibbon in your belly, the phone rings and I run towards it, certain it has to be Dad.

It's not Dad.

The line is spluttering and fizzing but the voice belongs to a woman. "Stephen?"

"Uh," I mutter. "Huh?" I can't hear properly because there's more crackling than on one of Ibiza Nana's pork dinners. The woman continues talking and says she's glad I'm here because she tried to reach me on my mobile but I didn't pick up.

"It's me," she adds. "Camille."

I think I've just swallowed a snooker ball hidden inside a bowling ball. I nearly stutter out that she's the Fondant Fancy lady who has caused all this trouble and made Dad and Pearl argue.

"Camille from Dovedale House. I said I'd give you a call when I texted last week. I tried your mobile first but couldn't get you so I thought I'd try this other number you gave me. I'm actually available next week, so if you want to come over to visit again you can. You know the address."

The line crackles again.

"Can you hear me? This line is terrible. Are you okay, Stephen? Is everything okay? It's just you sound a trifle..."

"I'm not a trifle," I manage to squeak. "I don't like jelly." The line fizzes and crackles.

"Sorry... I can't hear you very well. What did you say? Did you hear me say you sound a trifle strange?"

Oh.

"I think I'll ring you another time, Stephen. But yes, next week, I'm free if you're free."

There is a yell from the bathroom and I have to hang up, pronto. Billy's only gone tobogganing using the bath mat. That's when I remember where I hid the sick last night. I have to pick Billy up off the floor and tell him he's not supposed to be having this kind of fun without me. That we don't want to discover any more patches of hidden sick today. Billy grins and says there aren't any.

"Except on your school jumper," he adds, pointing to my sleeve.

Ibiza Nana used to say bad luck came in threes. Well, 1) Dad was gone. 2) Billy was sick. And just as I am wondering what three is, someone knocks on the flat door. Billy says it's Dad and I say it isn't because Dad has a key.

Gingerly, I open the door slightly and peep out. It's Cat and she proffers us a dish, saying that she's glad she didn't miss us before we went to school. "Thank you for the lovely party last night." I wonder if Cat heard Pearl shouting afterwards; if she did, she doesn't say so. "I brought you a shepherd's pie. I needed to make space in the freezer and thought you'd like it. Is your dad in?"

There we go, that's number three.

Confused, Billy says, "But I don't eat shepherds."

Bursting out laughing, Cat says, "There aren't any shepherds in there. There aren't any cottages in cottage pie either. No mud in mud pie. And definitely no spots in spotted..." Cat stops herself and repeats, "Is your dad in?"

"Dad," I yell, turning behind me and shouting the words as loud as I can. "Cat has brought shepherd's pie." There is silence, as I knew there would be. Billy tugs on my sleeve and tries to remind me that Dad is missing.

"Missing his alarm clock," I mutter, my teeth clenched into a smile. I prise the pie dish from Cat's fingers and close the door behind me, resting my head on it. That was close, I tell Billy – but he's not listening, because he's too busy supposing that you don't get bangers in bangers and mash either.

Mr Beagle is saying how impressed he was with our garden designs. It seems he thinks we are all very talented, some more talented than others, granted – those being the ones who didn't use the backs of cereal packets and crayons. To be honest, I'm not really listening and it doesn't take long before Mr Beagle points at me and says that school isn't a place for daydreaming.

"Yeah," hisses Donté Moffatt, leaning over to me. "You need to be more like orange juice." When I mutter that I have no idea what he's on about, Mr Beagle yells, "Concentrate!"

"As soon as I open my mouth, you stop listening, isn't that right, Becket?"

"Hmmm?" Unfortunately, I wasn't really listening, because how can I listen when my life is a whirlpool and everything feels like it's going down the plughole.

"Becket, please wake up. Becket, can you please pay attention to what I'm saying about POOP? Becket, the moon is made of margarine."

"Is it?" shouts Donté Moffatt. Mr Beagle says it isn't but at least someone is listening.

At any moment I could disappear too. Poof! No one would notice me fall down the plughole. I feel my cheeks flare as I look over at Nevaeh, but she's not interested in me. I think it's because I said I didn't believe in butterflies and bracelets didn't bring good things. Ever since I said that she's been a bit funny with me. I tried to make eye contact in assembly but she looked right through me. Pretty impressive though, considering she hasn't got X-ray eyes.

"Okay, class – and the daydreamer over there, Becket – I want you to get your listening ears on. I have some very exciting news that I did mention to you a while back but you were all in such a hurry to escape that I don't think you heard me." Mr Beagle's bum perches on the edge of the desk. He is wearing comedy socks with little cartoon characters on. "I said that POOP was going to have some very special visitors, other than your parents." I sigh and use my maths compass to clean out my fingernails. "And since you weren't listening the last time I mentioned it then I'm going to repeat it. The *Eden Echo* newspaper are coming to do a piece on our project. I can see the headline now: *Bleeding Heart's POOP*. It'll be magnificent." Mr Beagle claps his hands together so loud they can probably hear it on the International Space Station. "They'll want an angle, a heart-warming story to go with it. Perhaps they'll interview one of you."

There is a lot of whooping, most of it from Mimi who says she's been in the paper before. "I won a baby beauty pageant and got a crown and sash." Mr Beagle thanks Mimi for the information. But Mimi is on a roll and when Mr Beagle says a photographer will be present she says she'll be ready for her close-up. Mr Beagle says she needn't bother because the photographer won't be doing any. "Anyway," explains Mr Beagle, "I imagine the *Eden Echo* will be most interested in the winner of the design competition and that leads me nicely on to the big announcement."

The whole class is waiting. Admittedly some are waiting with their eyes closed because they're less interested in who's won than being in the paper. Mr Beagle pauses all dramatically like he's on some imaginary TV show...

"And the winner is Robert Absolom." Mr Beagle claps. "I loved his DAD GARDEN. And I loved how he put everything in it that reminded him of his dad – such a super personal touch. The apple tree and the little dumper truck to pick up fallen apples was genius." Mr Beagle wants Knuckles to stand up and take a bow. At first Knuckles goes as red as a baboon's bum but when Mr Beagle says his dad garden was so special that his dad must be special too a small smile plays on Knuckles's lips. As he gets up to take his bow, I spot the bracelet on Knuckles's wrist get caught on the corner of the desk. Knuckles doesn't realize and pulls himself up until the bracelet snaps and is lying like a tiny rubbery snake on top of the desk. I turn to Nevaeh and point at it and she turns away, her nose in the air.

Mr Beagle says, "I haven't finished yet." Teachers never have. Just when you hope they'll stop talking, they keep going. "There is another winner. I realized that the two gardens could work in harmony."

Mimi's up off one bum cheek and getting ready to

take a bow. Clearly she wants to win and appear in the newspaper. *"Eden Echo's Next Top Model,"* she mouths.

As I'm sniggering at how eager she is, Mr Beagle shouts, "Becket Rumsey and his wonderful healing HERB GARDEN. I had to pick this garden too because Becket had researched it so thoroughly. From my point of view, it was amazing to learn about nature's medicine and I think the whole school will benefit from Becket's knowledge. What's more we can bring the herbs into class and discuss how plants such as lavender were not only used as antiseptic but also in ancient Egypt in mummifying bodies." Mimi's bum cheek goes right back down again and she's shooting me eye-daggers. Hardly top model material with eyes like that, if you ask me.

"Thank you to everyone for all your hard work, and special congratulations to Robert and Becket," adds Mr Beagle, encouraging me to take a bow. "This garden will look fantastic. Your parents will be proud, you will be proud. I will be proud." Clearly everyone is going to be proud. Mr Beagle says, "I just have to consider what we'll do with that boring white wall behind. But that's not something you need to worry about. Leave that to me. I have an idea."

I've just won POOP. But unlike Knuckles, my bracelet is still firmly on my wrist.

EIGHTEEN

Dad is sitting on the sofa when we get home. It's as if nothing ever happened, he didn't go AWOL and I didn't need to spend all day at school worrying about what I'd do if Dad never returned. In fact, I had planned for Billy and me to move to Ibiza and live with Ibiza Nana. I'd even written her a letter in class:

Hola, Ibiza Nana,
We have decided that we would like to come live with you in Ibiza. We know you said that when you left it was time for you to think of yourself, but we think you've been doing that for a couple of years

210

now and so it's time to think of us. Therefore we will help you by coming on the next flight. I am also prepared to massage your feet when I get there, for a fee. I am afraid I cannot do this for free any longer because there is a law against children working. We are not living in the days of children going up chimneys. Although I know you were alive in those days and so you don't think anything of it.

Dad will not be with us. Of course, I realize this is a surprise but you did say that anyone over twenty-five should not still be living with their parents. So, that means Dad will not be coming to Ibiza. Please don't be sad about this because you'll have us and unlike Dad we do not smell of kippers. By the way, we will be bringing a snail in our suitcase. He doesn't take up much space. He does like a freshly-made bed at the end of his travels, probably yours. I've already had him in mine so it's someone else's turn. Brian will not like being in the sun, or sand, or the sea come to think of it. Actually we don't think he'll like Spain much so we won't ask his opinion.

Adiós,

Becket Rumsey, Doctor-in-training

Billy Rumsey, Snail Whisperer

When we walk into the living room I realize we won't be needing Ibiza Nana's letter after all. Dad looks up and says "Hello", as casual as an old man's pair of trousers. Near his feet there is a Santa-sized black sack of rubbish. Dad's cleared up the remnants of the party.

With a giant leap, Billy flings himself at Dad's belly like it's a massive marshmallow.

"Hello, Daddy, I was sick as a cat last night," says Billy proudly, bouncing right back off again. When I mutter "dog", Billy ignores me and snuggles up beside Dad. He continues, "Everywhere. I thought it was the squish and then I saw square carrots but I didn't eat square carrots at the party, Daddy. I didn't."

"It's quiche and I had to clear it up using the underneath of the bath mat." My jaw tightens and I fling my school bag in a corner before standing in front of Dad, arms folded. "Why didn't you answer your phone? Dad, what's going on? You need to tell us."

Dad's hands tremble slightly and his Adam's apple moves about so much it looks as if it's on a marble run. "I'm sorry I didn't get in contact with you. By the time I got home you'd gone to school. That's all I've got to say."

"But you could have used Pearl's phone to ring us."

Dad smoothes Billy's hair and says softly, "No, I'm

afraid I couldn't use Pearl's phone. Anyway, Pearl had gone by that time and then they took my phone away. They said they'd look out for any important messages left on the mobile but there weren't any." When I ask Dad who "they" are, Dad swallows and uses up his entire day's worth of blinking in about ten seconds. All 28,800 of them. "The police," whispers Dad.

"The police?" I echo. "Why did the police take your phone?" Okay, I'm seriously lost with all this now. And it doesn't help when Dad admits that he was arrested and put in the cells. "Put in the cells?" I echo. I'm beginning to feel like a repeating parrot (and as sick as one too).

Dad reaches for my arm and I can feel sweat on his fingers. "Don't jump to conclusions." I shake my head but really I already feel like I'm on a trampoline, I'm jumping to so many conclusions. "It was a mix-up about something and nothing."

Let's get this straight. "Nothing" does not get you arrested. I do "nothing" a lot and no one has arrested me yet. Ibiza Nana does "nothing" and calls it "retirement" and no one has thrown her in a cell. That's when Dad asks Billy to go and check on Brian before dinner. "And wash your hands straight after," shouts Dad, as Billy disappears down the hallway.

I think this is code for: *I want to talk to you alone, Becket.*

I'm right.

"I wanted to talk to you alone, Becket. Please understand, I'm so sorry about this. Honestly, it was the last thing I meant to happen..." Dad clarifies that he only meant to be out for thirty minutes max. When I ask Dad what actually happened, he swallows and says it was a small disagreement, an argument if you will. He tries to say it was "nothing" again.

"Who did you fight with?" As Dad doesn't look badly injured, I'm thinking the other bloke must have been smaller. More weedy. Thing is, I can't imagine Dad fighting anyone. That's not really Dad. Or at least, not the Dad I used to know.

There is a long silence before Dad says, "It was Pearl."

Pearl?

"Seriously, Becket, you have to believe me. I didn't hurt her. Pearl was just shouting and I asked her to stop. She grabbed my phone but I tried to grab it back. She ducked out of my way and used my phone to ring the police, saying I was attacking her. But I wasn't."

This has got to be one of the worst things ever. It couldn't get any worse if I found myself sitting on a public toilet only to realize there was no toilet roll. I stare at Dad, thinking: *My dad attacked Pearl and the police put him in prison.* But then my brain switches over and thinks: *My dad has never got that angry, not even when Billy busted the TV by throwing a brick at it. (Not a plastic brick either, but a brick he'd discovered in the garden and thought needed bringing in and giving a home.)*

"Pearl's dropped the charges," explains Dad.

My head slumps until my chin rests on my chest and my stomach feels like it's on a catapult. "Do you hate Pearl that much?"

"Oh no, Becket, you've got the wrong end of the stick. I love Pearl."

Love? Hate? I'm so confused.

Dad asks me if I'd like to choose something from the Chinese takeaway for dinner. He says he'll even throw in a few fortune cookies for dessert. As if a few fortune cookies are going to make this mess turn out okay.

After we've finished eating, Dad brings out the little crescent moons and hands them round.

Dad's fortune cookie says: *You will learn a lot from your mistakes.*

My fortune cookie says: *Everything happens for a reason.*

Billy's fortune cookie says: *To be old and wise you have to be young and stupid.*

When Billy's taken what's left of his fortune cookie to show Brian, I tell Dad I've been thinking about what he said. "I have ideas," I offer. "I mean, if you did get angry with Pearl." Dad shakes his head vigorously. "Okay, but if you did you can get all these books that will help with it. There are medical books for everything and so I bet there's a book out there that would suit you. Um..." The words get tangled in my throat. "What I'm saying is there must be a book to teach you not to be so cross with Pearl."

"I wasn't and there isn't," sighs Dad. "But thank you, son."

"Okay." I pause, my tongue doing a circuit of my lips, before adding, "Just stay away from Pearl then. If she makes you so angry that you end up in prison, then you should definitely stay away from her..." I think about how this is all down to Billy and me. We needed Pearl so much but we never thought it would end up like this. I feel worse than when I made a daddy-long-legs that Billy brought home a daddy-short-legs by accidentally standing on it.

"Seeing Pearl and talking to her again last night made me realize that I've made a mess of everything. You both looked so happy to see her." Dad eases back on the sofa, stretching his arms out. "I know she's sorry about everything. She promised she'd never go back to the way..." The words trail off. "You're right though, Becket. For now, I probably should let the dust settle. Not speak to Pearl."

Later, I'm just sinking under the duvet when the phone rings. I hear Dad's footsteps and the bleep as the phone connects. Then:

"Pearl, I'm so glad you've phoned. I wanted to talk to you."

A tiny teardrop escapes from my eye. "Oh, Dad," I mouth. "What are you doing?"

As I turn towards the wall, I feel something scratchy under my cheek. Cursing to myself that Billy has left Brian on my pillow, I use my mobile to light up my bed.

The light falls on a paper crane waiting for me, as if it knew I needed some more magic in my life. As if it knew I needed something to believe in.

NINETEEN

When Billy and I get home from school, there is a letter with Dad's name on it sitting on the hall mat. Carefully, I pick it up and stare at it. On the front, Dad's name is written in swirly purple ink, and on the back it says DOVEDALE HOUSE.

I think back to Camille's phone call. She said she was from Dovedale House and I reckon I've just had a thought worthy of SNOOP: if you were dating someone and you were ringing them up, would you say, "Hi, it's Becket from Flat B, above Crops and Bobbers?" No, you wouldn't because your girlfriend or boyfriend would already know where you lived. Sweet Baby Cheeses!

I need to look up DOVEDALE HOUSE on the internet.

DOVEDALE HOUSE
CENTRE FOR COUNSELLING
12 CHERRY BLOSSOM WAY
EDEN
Serving Eden and the surrounding areas since 2001
Appointments available at short notice because
IT'S GOOD TO TALK.
Camille Ogdon
Orla O'Brien
Kimberley Laing

IMPORTANT INFORMATION FOR SNOOP:
I don't think Camille Ogdon is Dad's girlfriend after
all. And my suspicions have been confirmed by what
I've just read.

DAD: Has been seeing Camille Ogdon to talk.
Maybe he's talking about how much he loves Pearl.
I mean, he's just told me as much. He doesn't hate
her, he loves her. And that's why we saw him at the
bubblegum-pink house, he was telling Camille or Orla
or Kimberley (perhaps one of them is the lady in the
polka-dot scarf?) all about it. For years after Mum

219

died Ibiza Nana said exactly the same thing: it's good to talk. Don't bottle it up because then the bottle gets all full of pressure and explodes.

ME: I told Pearl about Camille Ogdon and got her all cross. That's why she argued with Dad after the party and he was arrested. It was just a big mix-up and completely my fault for getting it wrong in the first place.

NOTES ABOUT HOW TO PUT IT RIGHT: When Dad gets home I need to borrow his phone.

SNOOP HAS WORKED OUT THAT: Dad loves Pearl and Pearl must love Dad more than The Naked Man or why else would she be so angry that he was going out with Camille Ogdon (even though he wasn't going out with Camille Ogdon).

MORE IMPORTANT INFORMATION: I got it all wrong and I made Pearl suspicious. I have to do something to bring Pearl back for good. I have to put it right and when Pearl does come back we'll have our almost mum again. We'll get hugs like we used to; we'll paint pictures and eat green things (not bogeys, even if Billy likes them) instead of takeaways. Pearl will be able to attend our nativities like she used to. We'll get 768,800 km of love too. What's more we'll have lots of fun because without Pearl things haven't been much fun. Billy's sad, Dad's sad and I'm sad because everyone else is sad. I have an idea.

An hour later Dad has come home from his fish delivery rounds and is in the shower singing about heartbreak at the top of his lungs. While Billy is urging Brian to walk a tightrope in the snail circus, I nip into Dad's bedroom and take his mobile phone from his jeans pocket. I feel a bit guilty when I look over and see Mum's photo on the bedside table. "I have to do this, Mum," I whisper. "I'm not stealing it, just borrowing." I sit on Dad's bed and punch in the message to Pearl.

I am not dating Camille Ogdon, the Fondant Fancy lady. I am just talking to her because I miss you. I was wrong to leave our house in a hurry. We want you back. Let's forget everything that has happened.

I think for a second.

And start all over again.

I put three kisses and then figure it might be too many for Dad and just put one. I hit send. Almost instantly the phone bleeps back with a message from Pearl.

Okay, Sugar Plum. Sorry about last night. Let's forget it. X

Sugar Plum, ugh! I wipe both messages in case Dad sees them and realizes what I've been up to. As I leave Dad's bedroom, I could almost hug myself with my own genius.

The rest of my Thursday night could be summed up like this:

- Dad got out of the shower and said he'd brought home some leftover cod from his delivery round and he'd cook it for tea because he's figured out the oven. Billy said he didn't like cod unless it had fingers and Dad said fish didn't have fingers. Billy said they did because he'd eaten fish fingers many times. Dad didn't argue but I heard him mutter "Oh my cod" under his breath as he went into the kitchen. I wasn't bothered what we ate because I was too busy spending the whole time smiling to myself because I had a secret and Billy got fed up and asked if my teeth had been glued together and I said "Nnnnn", and Billy said he couldn't understand me and I said it was because my teeth were glued together.

- Cat came round and said she hoped we'd enjoyed the shepherd's pie and Dad said it was lovely and stared at me. I went very red when I remembered I'd left it in the fridge and it was probably still there. Cat asked if I wanted to make some extra pocket money by helping her on Sunday evening on one of her special rounds to the old people's home. She needed assistance carrying her hairdressing kit and then I could entertain the waiting clients while she was busy. I said yes because even though I had no idea how to entertain anyone, I like money, I'm not going to lie.

- Billy didn't speak to Dad the entire evening. Later, when I asked him what was wrong, he said he was doing a sponsored silence. When I asked for which charity he said there wasn't one because he'd sponsored himself.

- Brian ran away from the circus – which is strange because I thought everyone ran away *to* the circus – and I found him in my fluffy sock slippers, but only after I'd put my bare feet in them.
- Later on, Dad knocked on our bedroom door and asked me what I was doing folding paper and I told him I was making paper cranes like the one he found but I didn't say I had to make one thousand to get a wish. Dad said I reminded him of Mum because she was always making things. I felt sad but proud at the same time. Sad that Mum wasn't here and proud that Dad said I was like her. Then Dad told me it was probably the time to stop as it was nearly midnight. He said the light would wake up Billy. I said, "You're in for a surprise," and Dad asked what it was. Then I had to think really quickly because I didn't want to divulge that I'd sent Pearl a text pretending I was Dad so I said I'd left Brian in the kitchen earlier and he was trying to make a friend. Dad pulled a face and said he hoped there weren't any other snails living in the kitchen. I said his "friend" was a sticky tape dispenser.
- I got up to go to the toilet and I found an even bigger surprise than the surprise I had for Dad.

There was something white in the bowl, when white wasn't the colour I was expecting. After some inspection, I realized there was a paper crane in there and I was one hundred per cent certain I hadn't started pooping folded bits of paper.

"Why are you drawing an armchair on water?" hisses Mimi the next day, looking over at my weekly science paper. "You're not supposed to be drawing pictures on your test paper. I'm going to tell." Mimi sticks her hand up to get Mr Beagle's attention.

As Mr Beagle approaches with a face like thunder he asks if I've answered all the test questions and I say I have and he takes my paper. When he looks over at Mimi she says she was just stretching her arm and Mr Beagle says it would be much better if Mimi stretched her fingers and actually wrote down the answers. "Look at Becket, he's already finished his science test." Mr Beagle claps me on the back. "Now his time is his own while everyone else finishes."

There is a tiny groan from the rest of the class.

Mr Beagle says groaning won't help with the answers.

I take THE GOODBYE LIST from my blazer pocket

and look at it. There's nothing left. Since I got all caught up in the Pearl situation I've not done anything for Mum and I feel guilty. Trouble is, I can't think of any new ways to say goodbye. On the back of the list I draw a little storm cloud and the sea below and then I draw the armchair and two boys on it. I draw teardrops and then I draw a paper crane and then Mr Beagle shouts, "Time's up!" and I put the list back in my pocket, still with no ideas what to put for number ten.

After collecting our science tests, Mr Beagle says we're going straight to the garden patch and we're actually going to start planting. "Remember, the *Eden Echo* is coming so we want to make it—"

"POOP," shouts Donté Moffatt.

"'Amazing' is what I was going to say," retorts Mr Beagle. He lines us up like soldiers and marches us through the playground until we reach the garden patch. The earth has already been prepared by Sam Swiss and all the plants have been bought. There is a criss-cross of trowels and Mr Beagle instructs us how and where to dig. When I glance over at Nevaeh, she's standing by the white wall, just staring at it, and she doesn't even turn around when Mr Beagle tells us to pick up our trowels.

After five minutes of digging little holes, I see

something small and white in the soil and I know exactly what it is, having seen the same thing in the toilet bowl last night. Now, this is getting really weird. Paper cranes are following me all over the place. One of two things is happening: 1) The cranes are magical like I first thought; 2) I am folding cranes and they're getting caught up in my clothes and then falling out at a later stage. Thing is, I've made one hundred paper cranes now and not one of them is perfect. That only leaves me with one option: the cranes are magical. Back to square one. I hold the crane up in the air and Mr Beagle waves his hands and asks what I've got. I tell him it turned up in the soil.

"Don't be ridiculous. You didn't find that in the soil. It's the paper crane from your show-and-tell."

"No, sir, it isn't," I argue. "Mine is at home. I don't know how this one got here. I found one in the toilet last night too." Okay, it was a mistake to announce that, because everyone around me starts laughing. Annoyed, I say, "Is there something else to the story, sir? Something you didn't tell us, like the cranes can turn up anywhere?"

Mr Beagle stifles a giggle. "Like a bad penny that always turns up? No, there's nothing I didn't tell you. But since this paper crane seems to be causing such a stir and stopping everyone from getting on with work, I think I'll just keep it on the bookshelf in the classroom and you can collect it later."

After lunch, Mr Beagle returns our science papers and as he delivers Mimi's I hear her take a sharp breath. She mutters, "No way." After a second she hoists up her hand and asks Mr Beagle if there was some mistake.

"With your science test?" asks Mr Beagle. "No, you did well. You can go into the weekend knowing that you did a good job."

"But I didn't get them all right," says Mimi, looking shocked. "And I have extra tuition after school."

"You did well," repeats Mr Beagle.

"'Well' isn't good enough," says Mimi, slouching back in her chair. "'Well' won't make my parents happy. I do lots of after-school clubs – French, ballet, kung fu – and I want to be on *Top Model* and I'm—"

"Not yet an A* student in science but that's okay because it gives you something to work for. I don't expect you – or anyone else – to be perfect all the time," explains Mr Beagle, setting my test paper in front of me. "Well done, Becket. You did get one hundred per cent.

Is there anything you don't know about the human body?"

"Not really, sir."

Mimi throws herself back on her chair, her lower lip jutting out. She sighs, leans down, pulls up her sock, throws her plait over her shoulder and then puts her hand up. "Yes?" shouts Mr Beagle. Mimi says she needs the toilet. "Are you sure you're desperate? Or is it just that you're upset about your results."

"It's Donté Moffatt's fault, sir." Mimi points at Donté. "I've got a sore belly. He recommended getting something from Burger, She Wrote."

"It's not my fault," pipes up Donté Moffatt. "It was Becket who recommended it."

Mimi glowers at me and gets up out of her chair as Mr Beagle says she'd better go because the last thing he wants is an accident in class. Mr Beagle goes on handing out the science tests as I look at mine, marvelling at my own genius. Knuckles points at his and says he's done pretty well on the questions about the bones in the hand and Nevaeh just draws butterflies on her arms as if she's not bothered what her score was. Out of the corner of my eye I see someone at our classroom window, hands pressed flat and making stupid faces. When I look up, it's Mimi, and she sees me and gives a smile worthy of a comic book villain. Something tells me she's in no hurry to get to the toilet at all. Something tells me Mimi was lying.

Later when the home-time bell goes and Mr Beagle shouts that we're to have a lovely weekend, I hang back and after everyone has gone I ask if I can have my crane back, please. Mr Beagle moves towards the bookshelf and his eyes scan back and forth. Books are moved, rearranged, pulled out and the pages fluttered.

"I'm sorry, Becket," says Mr Beagle, scratching his head. "The crane appears to be gone."

TWENTY

Sunday evening comes and I'm taking a large black holdall bag from Cat's hand as she locks the front door of Crops and Bobbers. Humming, she takes out her car key and flicks the button and then tells me to get in.

"I feel a bit guilty being paid to carry a bag," I point out.

"Not a bit of it," says Cat briskly, starting the car. "You'll be doing more than that. And it's worth every penny of my five English pounds." We whiz through a blustery Eden before parking outside the Green Acres Old People's Home, where Cat jumps out of the car and negotiates her way along a pathway, either side of it overgrown with tangled weeds. There's a jigsaw puzzle of moss on the grey stone of the old Victorian house and Cat gives me a little salute before ringing the doorbell. A buzzer sounds for us to enter.

When we get inside, Cat signs us in and waves to all the staff. Then she beckons me into a large living area with pink floral wallpaper and giant draping curtains like you'd find on a stage. There's a big bay window at the back and lots of elderly people sitting in armchairs. "Haircuts one hundred," shouts Cat. "And I'm not talking about that eighties pop group, but the average age of everyone here." There is tittering and nodding of heads. "And don't all hurry to get your purses because it's on the house, as usual." I'm not sure anyone could rush to get their purses, because they actually *are* all about one hundred, even if Cat was just joking.

Cat pulls a red velvet armchair up to the window and sets up a small mirror on a table with wheels and asks for her first willing victim. Then she points at an elderly lady and says she doesn't want to show favouritism, but if no one else minds she'll start here with this beautiful woman.

As instructed by Cat, I try to entertain those waiting, but all I can think to do is talk and I've never been any good at that. An old man in the corner tells me about the war and his memories of it and a woman tells me about her bloated belly, which I love – not because she has a bloated belly, but because I can help her think of new ways to make it better. I talk about how the herb peppermint might help and I tell her all about my winning garden design. I talk about the magic of paper cranes and show them all the bracelet with the butterfly. All the time the queue for Cat gets shorter and there's an Everest of silver hair on some newspaper she has laid on the floor. After an hour and a half, I realize I've talked non-stop.

"Until next time, Nana," says Cat, kissing the first lady whose hair she cut. "Don't tell anyone else, but you're my favourite customer." Cat winks.

Back in the car, I tell Cat how much I enjoyed it. "And your nana was lovely. I didn't realize she lived there."

Cat turns the steering wheel. "I'm glad you liked it so much. I like going there too, and especially seeing Nana. Everyone is so much fun and they've got fascinating stories to tell if you take the time to talk to them."

"I'm not good at talking."

"It looked like you were doing a pretty good job to me," says Cat, swinging the car left at a junction. I catch sight of the lily tattoo on her wrist and notice there's a little date underneath it. "In fact, I'd say you were both a good talker and a good listener and that's a great mix."

"Cat, you said lilies were your mum's favourite flower. Does your mum live in Eden too?" I ask. Condensation has built on the inside of the car window and I turn to it and draw a tiny heart. The water runs down from the point like a tear running down a cheek.

"I suppose she does. I'm very happy to talk about Mum now, but it wasn't always that way," explains Cat, stopping at some traffic lights. As we wait for them to turn green, she faces me. "You see, my nana, the lady you've just met, brought me up because I lost my mum when I was thirteen."

I gulp. "You lost your mum too?"

"Yes, sadly I lost her when I wasn't much older than you. It was my inheritance from Mum that meant I could open my own hair salon. Don't look so surprised," says Cat, driving on again as the lights turn. "You're not the only person in the world that it's happened to, even if you feel that way. There are lots of us about. You just can't tell by looking at us, because we're normal. Maybe if we were wearing a sign it would help."

"But..." I hesitate. Then the words tumble out. "I feel different to everyone else."

Cat takes the first exit at the roundabout. "That's okay," she says. "We all feel like that about something. But there is always someone who has gone through the same thing." She turns right and then left and then pulls up at a cemetery.

"It's locked," I point out. "They don't open at night."

"You're right," says Cat. "But I stopped here because I wanted to tell you that my mum is buried in here. However, I didn't bring you here to make you sad. Don't be. I brought you here to say my mum's not really in there. Not really."

"Where is she then?" I feel my throat burn and my stomach does a little somersault inside my ribcage.

Cat leans over and points at my drawing on the window. "You already know where she is. She's in my heart. Just like your mum is in yours." I stare at my hastily scribbled heart on the window and I know what Cat is saying. She pauses and lets it sink in before adding, "I know it's hard to grow up without your mum."

"I don't want to grow up without her."

Cat touches my shoulder and her hand feels warm and comforting. "Even if you don't want it, growing up will happen no matter what."

Cat starts the car engine again and I ask her if she'll

do something for me and stop by the ocean for a few minutes. Even if it's dark and I can't see anything, I don't care. I just want to be there, I tell her. Cat promises and ten minutes later she pulls the car up by the edge of the road overlooking the sea.

"I miss my mum," I say, looking out across the ocean. "Dad told me he'd scattered her ashes on the sea. I didn't go because I was too young. Dad said it was sad letting go but then a gust of wind came and carried Mum off to the sea. Well, most of her. Dad said a tiny bit of Mum blew backwards and landed on him."

"Oh."

"It's okay. Dad said he thought it was Mum's way of saying a tiny bit of her would always be with him.

"I'm sad I couldn't be there with Dad." Here I am talking about Mum. Stranger still, I'm talking about Mum with Cat and somehow it feels right and Cat understands what I mean. I could never have done this with Pearl even though I always thought she was easy to talk to.

"I know, it's hard for those left behind," replies Cat quietly and she presses a button and the windows glide down. A gust of sea air fills the car and when I lick my lips I taste the tang of salt. When I ask Cat if she had the chance to say goodbye to her mum, she says, "Would it make it better for you if I did? Would it make you feel better if I didn't? No, I don't think it would. And that's why you have to find your own way, Becket. My story is the same as yours, but different."

"At least your nana lives nearby," I offer.

"Sometimes she doesn't know who I am any more," says Cat. "And it feels like I'm losing my mother all over again, only this time slowly. But there's one thing I know for certain and that is I've been very lucky and no matter what happens in the future I'm going to carry the people I've lost with me for ever."

Staring out to sea again, I say, "One day I'm going to say a proper goodbye to my mum. I've been trying – I've got THE GOODBYE LIST and I've written all these ways to say goodbye, but the trouble is none of them have been any good."

Cat nods and says there's nothing wrong with me writing things down if it helps me. She starts the car again and drives towards our flats.

"I just don't know how to do it," I add.

"Yet," points out Cat. "You just don't know how to do it *yet*."

TWENTY-ONE

When we get back to the flat, I feel as light as a feather in an anti-gravity chamber, because as we drove away from the ocean Cat said she'd like to throw us a party. She said she wanted to invite us all around to her flat, since we invited her to ours. There would be lasagne again and she was very good at making home-made chips from sweet potatoes. And her Knickerbocker Glories were famous.

"With who?" I asked.

"With myself," replied Cat, laughing.

And that was good enough for me.

Truth is, I don't want the evening to end, so I ask Cat

to come into our flat and say hello to Dad because he's always happy to see her. In fact, I say she has to tell Dad about the party invite herself. I'm still chatting to Cat when I turn the key in our front door, and then I hurry down the hallway, calling that Cat is with me.

When I reach the living room, I stop. Pearl is sitting on the sofa with Dad, and Billy is between them. Dad beckons me on and says it's great to hear I've enjoyed myself. He thanks Cat for letting me come with her on the job.

"My pleasure," says Cat, giving me a tiny punch to the arm. "You were mighty, Becket."

There is an awkward moment when Pearl shifts on the sofa and says nothing. She smoothes down her frilly skirt and tucks her feet underneath.

As Cat turns to leave, I remind her that she was going to ask Dad something. "Oh yes," says Cat, a nervous smile dancing around on her lips. "I'm throwing a tiny party." A strand of hair falls over her eyes and she pushes it back behind her ear. She's wearing earrings shaped like tiny scissors. "It was kind of you to invite me to yours and I thought I'd say thank you. It'll be nothing fancy, mind."

Dad looks at Pearl for approval but her face stays totally straight, not a smile, a frown, nothing. "Er...I'm not sure," replies Dad, turning back to Cat. "Could I let you know?" The temperature in the flat has dropped a few degrees and I pull my coat closer to my body and shiver. Maybe Dad hasn't put the radiators on.

Billy, sensing something is wrong, pipes up, "Can Pearl come to your party?"

"Thank you, Billy," replies Pearl and she makes a huge fuss of him. It's not how she treated him at the party though. Now she's all over him like a bluebottle on poop. "I never seem to get invites to all these parties you two throw for each other," says Pearl. "Perhaps I'm not as popular as I thought I was."

Cat, her cheeks two red apples, says of course Pearl can come, and she'd better get back to her flat and sort out her hairdressing kit because all the combs and scissors need cleaning. "Thank you again, Becket," Cat says, pushing a crumpled five-pound note into my palm. "We must do it again sometime."

"It's a wonder she's a hairdresser," mutters Pearl as Cat walks into the hallway with Dad. "Her hair is atrocious – she looks like she's been in a wind tunnel."

I think of our evening together. Cat's hair didn't matter because she was too busy doing everyone else's, and when she wound down the car window so I could see the ocean, she wasn't bothered about how it might mess up her hair.

When Dad returns I don't feel as confident about Pearl being here as I thought I would when I sent that text. This was supposed to be a lovely surprise but it feels like Pearl's angry, only she doesn't say so. Instead she plays with a strand of beads that look like boiled sweets around her neck, saying, "Well, isn't this lovely? Since we're all getting along so well, perhaps you'd like to come to my exhibition of nudes, Stephen?"

"Oh," says Dad. "'Kay. I guess I could come and see it."

Pearl dips her head and rests it on Dad's shoulder and tells him it's going to be a lot of fun. She follows this with a tiny kiss on the cheek, like a chicken pecking corn. Dad brightens and he says maybe it would be good and he's never been to a proper art exhibition before.

"You were too busy with fish," says Pearl. "But since you texted me and begged me to come back, I'm prepared to give it a whirl if you are." Dad looks confused, his eyebrows rising up his forehead like two caterpillars in a glass lift. "So, from tomorrow we can start again. Put the past behind us. Never mention Cat or Camille again."

Dad pauses, looks at Billy, who nods. He looks at me and I don't know whether I'm nodding or shaking my head. After a moment Dad agrees with Pearl, before adding that since it is dinner time, maybe we could get a pizza in. He orders ham and pineapple and when it arrives we all eat it sitting in front of the TV like we used to.

Pearl dabs the side of her mouth with a paper napkin. There is a smear of red lipstick on white. "You know you can't do without me, Stephen. Not really. Look at you, living here in this horrible grimy flat with horrible fake flowers." The lilies are not that horrible and I want to say so, but I don't. All of a sudden I feel a wave of sadness that maybe I won't want to talk about Mum to Pearl like I've just done with Cat. "And you've got that awful woman with the screechy voice from the flat next door."

"Cat." I do correct Pearl this time, chewing on the crust of my pizza. "And she's not awful." I couldn't ignore her saying that, not after the evening I've had with Cat. Not when Cat listened to me talk about Mum.

"Like I said," says Pearl without catching my eye, "the awful woman with the screechy voice from the flat next door. You'll need to get away from her as soon as possible." She glares at Dad, daring him to disagree with her. He doesn't, even though he knows Cat doesn't have a screechy voice. She is softly spoken and I don't think I've ever heard her say anything horrible. I think of how Cat was today, cutting everyone's hair and telling jokes, making them laugh. And I think about how she was with me, making me feel better. Pearl continues, "I could paint my nudes anywhere. Perhaps we could go to the city and soak up the art scene there and you could get a desk job instead of that awful fish delivery job. Yes, Sugar Plum?" She pouts as prettily as she can.

A desk job isn't Dad. He loves fish. He can recite an A-Z of fish from Adriatic salmon to Zambezi parrotfish.

Pearl smiles and grabs the last piece of pizza from the box, just as Billy reaches for it. I wait for her to offer it to him, but instead she takes a huge bite right in front of him and then throws the rest of it back down in the box, saying she's full and didn't want it anyway. Next, she eases her body away from Billy and rises from the sofa. "So, four o'clock tomorrow at Saint Bartholomew's church hall. I'm usually at Tower Point on Mondays but not tomorrow."

"Okay," says Dad softly. "We can talk things through afterwards. I think we need to talk about all this properly. Things need to change."

Pearl doesn't respond. Instead her green eyes flicker like the inside of an emerald. If it was possible to bore through someone with your eyes, Pearl would have just drilled a hole through Dad, the wall behind, the street, the town, the world.

"I'll show you," says Pearl finally, "that you're no good without me." She smiles dreamily. "There would be many men who would feel privileged to go out with me." It's on the tip of my tongue to say Naked Man, for starters. "And think of Billy. He needs a mother and I suppose I'm the only person left to fill that position." Pearl tuts and shakes her head. "If only the birth hadn't killed his own mother things would have been so very different."

Dad's eyes explode like millions of tiny fireworks.

"Oh, I'm sorry," says Pearl quickly. "I didn't mean it like that. Ignore me. I'm sorry, Billy, it slipped out. I'm silly. Please forgive me. You weren't involved in your mother's death at all. I was just thinking aloud."

On the outside Billy's smile appears to be flaring brightly, but inside I can see it flicker and begin to die.

"Sorry," repeats Pearl, her eyes not meeting mine – which is just as well because my eyes are very angry with her. The rest of me is too.

"I'll get Billy and Becket to stay with Cat in the

salon after school tomorrow," Dad sighs. "That way I can come."

"I don't think we should keep worrying about your neighbour." Pearl looks up again and gives Dad a smile. Dad doesn't smile back. "And anyway, Becket doesn't need a babysitter. I think he's grown up enough to watch Billy for a couple of hours after school. Aren't you, love?"

I nod quickly, wishing Pearl would just go away now. As if she can read my mind, Pearl stands up and waits until Dad finds her pink coat and helps her put it on. "Four. Don't be late." Then she leads Dad into the hallway.

Once their footsteps fade, Billy, legs banging against the sofa, looks at the half-chewed piece of pizza. "It wasn't my fault that Mummy died, was it, Becket?" he says quietly. "It wasn't anyone's fault, right?" Billy stares at me, the water level in his eyes rising. "I didn't kill Mummy, I didn't. No one will put me in prison for it, will they?"

"Ignore Pearl," I hiss, reaching out to him. I give Billy a hug and when I pull away I say, "You heard her. She said she was sorry and she didn't mean it that way. I think she just got things confused. You know Mum had eclampsia and that it had nothing to do with you."

"But if I hadn't been in her tummy then she'd be okay."

"It's not like that," I tell him.

"You're telling fibs," Billy cries. "I can see it in your eyeballs."

The awful thing is…Mum *would* be alive if she hadn't been having a baby, because eclampsia only happens when you're pregnant. I could kick myself for even letting Billy ask me the question. Billy flicks the remote control and stares at a cartoon on the TV. I want to say: look at me. But he doesn't. Every so often he laughs, clear and sparkly like a little silver bell, but it doesn't fool me.

From the hallway I can hear Pearl repeatedly telling Dad that she doesn't like Cat and why did he bother texting to tell her to come back if he's still interested in someone else. Dad says he didn't text her at all and hasn't a clue what she's talking about. That's when I jump up like a flea attempting the high jump. I skitter across the living room and fling open the hallway door, thinking I'll pretend I wanted to say goodbye. Any excuse to stop the pair of them discussing the text that I sent from Dad's phone. But when the door swings open, I see something.

Something I don't think I should have seen.

Something that makes my stomach flip like a pancake.

Something that makes me question everything.

My knees buckle a bit. Pearl notices me from the corner of her eye and says firmly, "Be there," before opening the front door. As she's leaving, she gives Dad a peck on the cheek. The lipstick mark is shaped like a broken heart.

"It wasn't what it looked like," says Dad quickly after he shuts the door.

"What did it look like?"

"I don't know, but whatever it looked like it wasn't that." Dad leans against the wall in the hallway, his bald head crowned by the roses on the wallpaper.

I don't say anything else, I just go into the bathroom, glad it's all over. I vow I'll never go out with someone who makes me raise my voice, or get cross. I lock the toilet door and stand for the longest time staring in the mirror. Is this what it looks like to be mixed up, confused, sad, scared? Is this what it's like to start growing up? If it is, I want to go back and be little again. If love is about hurting each other, I don't want any part of it. I wish I'd never sent that stupid text now. I wish I didn't know that grown-ups argue and say and do things they don't mean. I wish the world wasn't so confusing. I wish I'd never been born. I swallow, feeling guilty for thinking that. I tell myself over and over that I'm glad I was born and I'm glad Billy was too.

At bedtime I'm walking towards our room and I can hear Billy talking to someone. I peep in through the open door and then duck back again and rest my head against the wall, listening.

"I think my mummy would be alive if it wasn't for me, Brian," says Billy.

"Why do you say that, Billy?" says Billy, making his voice deep and clearly pretending he's a snail. Although if it was me pretending to be a snail, I think I'd talk a lot slower than Billy is.

"Pearl said if only my birth hadn't killed Mummy things would be different, Brian. Pearl wouldn't say so if it wasn't true," replies Billy in his own voice again. "I think that's why Pearl and Daddy argue. They are very cross and Daddy is very cross because Pearl says Mummy died because of me. But I was very little and I don't remember it. I must be very bad, Brian."

"Hmm... I don't think you are. Could Pearl be wrong?" Billy replies in his Brian tone.

"Awww. I don't know, Brian. She's a grown-up and they know everything."

"We snails know a lot too, Billy." Billy's voice changes again.

"I know, Brian." I hear a pause and I want to punch through the wall like a superhero and save Billy but I can't. "But I want a mummy and it's very hard when it's me who keeps losing them. Maybe if I wasn't around, Becket could have a mummy for himself."

TWENTY-TWO

On Monday, Dad is up and down from the breakfast table like his bum is doing a Mexican wave. He says he won't be at the exhibition long. He makes tea, he sits down and then he gets up and walks over to the window. He stares at the grey clouds and says it's freezing out there. He comes back and sits down. We're to go to Cat straight after school and then he'll be back and pick us up from Crops and Bobbers. Dad sips his tea and adds more milk. He says everything will change when he gets back. It will be the beginning of a whole new chapter.

I bring a spoonful of chocolate cereal to my lips. I'm still feeling uneasy about what I saw in the hallway. Last night I tried to figure it all out but it hurt my head so much that I fell into an uneasy dreamless sleep, until Billy woke me at five forty-three. Only this time he didn't come into my bed. I heard him get up and sit in Mum's armchair, and I heard him mumbling something, but then I fell back asleep so I have no idea what it was.

This morning Billy doesn't speak to either Dad or me at all. He's got tiny little purple half-moons under his eyes and when Dad asks if he's tired Billy just shrugs and says he slept all the way through the night.

On the way to school I challenge Billy. "What's wrong?" I ask. "Is it what Pearl said? You know she's not right. It was a stupid thing to say."

"Nothing is wrong," Billy replies and for the first time ever on our walk to school he doesn't bend down and poke through the mud in someone's garden. He doesn't tell me that he's seen a ladybird or a millipede, or a spider with six legs (because he accidentally stood on two of them). When we reach the playground, Billy says goodbye. I don't answer because the bell rings just then and I have to join my line. Out of the corner of my eye I see Billy and his class trot away to their classroom like tiny ducklings wearing backpacks. He turns back and waves at me so I wave in return. Then Billy is gone.

At lunchtime it is obvious Dad had a lot on his mind

this morning because he has forgotten to put fish paste in my sandwiches. All I've got is plain white bread.

"Nice simple sandwiches you've got there," scoffs Nevaeh, from the table next door. I lean over and say I'm sorry about what I said about butterflies. Nevaeh says she knew I would be.

"How?"

"Because you're still wearing the bracelet." She points at my wrist. "If you really thought it was stupid then you'd have taken it off, but you haven't. I was just waiting until you said sorry and now you have."

Knuckles butts in and says the bracelet worked for him. He won the garden competition and got to plant an apple tree for his dad. I shrug and say it still hasn't done anything for me and maybe nothing is ever going to happen.

Nevaeh leans across and passes me a cheesy biscuit and says she's sure it will because she can feel it in her bones. I want to say that I hope she can't feel anything in her bones because I've read about bones in my medical manual and if they start hurting it's not a great sign, but now we're back to being friends I just take the biscuit instead.

The one person I'm definitely not friends with though walks past and shoots me a smug smile. I can't figure out why. When I ask Nevaeh what Mimi's problem is, Nevaeh shakes her head. "Perfection is her problem." You could knock me down with an ostrich feather. How is being perfect a problem? "Okay, you're looking at me as if I'm stupid," says Nevaeh, "but listen. Mimi might live in a perfect house, with perfect parents, and her mum might look like a model, but they expect her to be perfect at *everything*. Didn't you see how annoyed she was at not doing well in her science test? She was fuming at you for getting everything right."

"I can't help being good at science," I bluster.

"And you won the garden competition."

"I can't help being good at…" I scratch my head.

Nevaeh explains that Mimi is probably a bit envious because she was used to getting the gold stars for everything until I came along. "Did you know we used to be best mates and I'd go around to her house all the time?" I shake my head. Nevaeh continues, "But her mum didn't like us messing up their perfect house. And her mum made her do all these after-school clubs. We kind of drifted apart after that. I don't think she's got any real friends any more."

"She could have us," says Knuckles, chewing the last of his tuna sandwich. He shrugs.

I bite my lip. Mimi hasn't been all that nice to me

253

since I started at Bleeding Heart. Knuckles, seeing my face, says there's no point in being annoyed with Mimi any more because it won't get us anywhere and let's face it, none of us are perfect anyway. So, the girl who thinks she has to be perfect is about to get three imperfect friends, whether she likes it or not, Knuckles suggests. After a moment's thought, I tell Nevaeh she should make Mimi one of her special bracelets and Nevaeh smiles and says she might just do that, because Mimi probably needs something good to happen to her too.

"Maybe we could be the good thing," Nevaeh muses.

"Like the garden was my amazing thing," says Knuckles, opening his lunch box. He takes out a carton of apple juice and pierces it with a straw. Nevaeh asks him why he thinks the garden made the bracelet snap, because he never really said. "Well, you know it's for my dad." Knuckles takes a slurp of apple juice and sets down the carton on the table. A tiny drip dangles on the end of the straw. "I miss him so much and I wanted to do something that would make me feel a bit closer to him, despite everything that happened to us. Dad loved gardening and once told me apples were a symbol of love and happiness and I wanted to try to remember Dad with love and happiness even though it was hard so I thought of planting an apple tree. Seeing the dumper truck on the table made me think about how Dad and me used to play together." Knuckles pauses. "And then all that was gone."

"Was it a memorial garden?" I suddenly wish I'd thought of that for my mum. It was better than planting seeds. I could have designed THE GOODBYE GARDEN. Why oh why didn't I put that on the list? It could have been number ten, the one I didn't have an idea for. But I can't hijack the idea now, not since Knuckles has taken it for his dad.

Knuckles stares at me. "What are you on about? My dad isn't dead. He's in prison."

I nearly choke on Nevaeh's cheesy biscuit.

I spend all afternoon thinking about Knuckles's dad and how hard it must be and I realize that even though his dad isn't dead like my mum, it's sort of the same thing. It explains why he didn't like talking about his dad in the beginning and why the garden was so important to him. I'm glad the bracelet broke for him. I don't care why his dad's in prison and I'm glad the apple tree will grow in his garden, blossom and bear pretty apples for all to see. I stare down at my bracelet.

But why does it feel like nothing good is ever going to happen to me?

An hour later, something so incredibly bad happens to me that it makes me wish I'd never even believed anything good might happen. And it's all because I am late to the school gate.

I'm talking to Nevaeh and Knuckles when I get there, five minutes late. After the bell rang we got talking about the garden again and Knuckles was saying that he'd love to do an interview with the *Eden Echo*, if they asked. Knuckles says he used to feel bad talking about his dad because when he said his dad was in prison it made others treat him differently. Either they stopped being friends with him or they felt sorry for him. So he kept quiet. But the garden made him feel better. It was as if his dad wasn't gone, as if he was right there in the garden and everyone thought the garden was amazing. It made Knuckles feel special and feel that his dad was special too. I didn't notice how slow we were walking and at first I don't notice that Billy's not there at the gate waiting for me. But when it becomes obvious that his whole class has gone home, I begin to panic. I tell Nevaeh and Knuckles to wait at the gate for Billy while I run around the school, checking the classrooms and the toilets, checking the muddy patches. I can see the teachers sitting in the school assembly hall and there's a man on the stage giving a talk. They can't see me press my face against the glass. They can't see I'm in a flap about Billy. Sweat blooms on my shirt, leaving grey flowers.

"Billy hasn't come to the gate yet," shouts Nevaeh as I run back towards her. "But he can't have gone that far. I'll just text Mum and tell her I'm helping you look and I'll be home soon." She starts punching the words into her mobile phone.

"I'll help too," says Knuckles. "Billy will turn up, he must be around here somewhere."

No matter what they both say, there is a horrible feeling in my stomach that won't go away. Billy said goodbye this morning, and I didn't say a proper goodbye back. Did it mean something? At the time I didn't think. Dazed, I say, "Maybe he's gone home already. Maybe I just missed him and he thought he could walk by himself."

That's where we go first.

I fling open the flat door and Nevaeh and Knuckles follow me into the hallway. I shout Billy's name but he's obviously not here, because I know he would come running. He always comes to me. In our bedroom there are paper cranes all over the floor, like the crumbs leading to the witch's house in *Hansel and Gretel*. Carefully, I pick them up and put them in a large envelope along with the ones I've made. I know I wasn't able to make one thousand in the end, nowhere near. But for some reason I want all the paper cranes with me, because I'm hoping their magic will bring me my biggest wish of all: finding Billy.

Billy has to come back, I tell myself.

Nevaeh stops and looks around and says our living room is lovely and the lilies are pretty. I look at our living room again. Maybe it's not so bad after all, I think, before making my way down the hall and opening the front door.

This time SNOOP (including two new honorary members) is on the mission of a lifetime: to find Billy Rumsey. This mission cannot fail. My first thought is he'll have gone back to our old house at Honeydown Hills.

"Is that where you used to live?" asks Nevaeh. I nod and say we moved recently and perhaps Billy was taking Brian back to look at the old house. "Is Brian his friend, maybe we could ring him first and ask?" replies Nevaeh.

"Brian," I say, slamming the flat's front door behind us and running down the steps, "prefers snail mail."

258

Before we all go to the bus stop, I want to try to speak to Cat. The last time we were talking she seemed to have such sensible ideas about everything and made me feel calm inside, like she was throwing a tea towel over my flames. Plus she seems to have the right answers, like a mum would. Maybe she's seen Billy and I'm worrying about nothing. But the Crops and Bobbers door is locked and there's a tiny notice in the window saying, *Back in five minutes*. Thing is, I haven't got five minutes.

Eventually the bus arrives and we all jump on board and hurry towards the back. I set down the envelope of cranes and tell Nevaeh and Knuckles how Billy was sad about us leaving our old home and how Dad's girlfriend didn't come with us. I tell them how things have been all muddled up recently. "I think Billy wanted it to be the same as it was before." I look at Nevaeh. "I mean he wanted us to stay the same. But sometimes things change even when you don't want them to. Even if you want to take a moment and stick it in a bottle and put the lid on it to save it."

"You can't," whispers Nevaeh.

"But it doesn't stop Billy wanting us to go backwards," I reply, staring out the bus window. "He's only seven and he doesn't understand."

"If the bus went backwards though," says Knuckles, thinking, "then we'd never get anywhere other than where we started. I think that journey sounds pants. Back at the beginning every time. I'd rather go someplace new."

"What if you had a time machine? Would you go back then?" I blink.

"I would," says Nevaeh. "I'd want to change history so my sister lived." She pauses. "I never told you what happened, did I?" The words explode around me like bubbles in a fizzy drink. "I'm a twin. It was me and my sister. Mum picked names for us. I was Nevaeh and my sister was Mariposa. It's Spanish for butterfly. My mum has Spanish heritage. Only, I was okay when I was born but Mariposa wasn't. She was so tiny and had a problem with her heart which meant that she didn't survive more than a few days. Mum never talked about it again. Then one day years later a butterfly landed on me, like I told you. It was Mariposa. I looked it up and started drawing butterflies everywhere but I kept the reason why a secret from Mum because I didn't want to upset her." Nevaeh shrugs. "I made the bracelets too because I wanted good things to happen, because the worst thing that could ever happen already had."

"But I don't think I can believe in butterflies."

"You don't have to believe in butterflies," says Nevaeh. "That's just what I believe and it works for me. Maybe there's something else for you."

"I'm sorry your sister died. My mum died too." It's the first time I've told any of my new friends about my mum. The first time I've ever felt brave enough to do it.

Next, the craziest thing happens that makes me wonder if Nevaeh really does have a point about butterflies being souls. A Red Admiral butterfly flutters onto the bus window and stays there.

"Look! My sister has come to visit to say things will be okay." Nevaeh is jumping up and down in excitement on her seat. "It's Mariposa."

I nod and inside my head I'm saying: *Do you think your sister could go back and tell my mum to get in contact?*

TWENTY-THREE

We stare at it for a moment before it flies away. But then it comes back again. Nevaeh is up out of her seat, her hands pressed flat against the window now. The butterfly waits for a second before flying away and coming back again. "It's telling us something," shouts Nevaeh, her cornrows bouncing. "It is. Honestly, it is."

"I don't understand butterfly," I reply, picking up the envelope of paper cranes.

"Well I do," says Nevaeh and she grabs me by the arm. "We need to follow that butterfly." In movies they always say "Follow that taxi" but never "Follow that butterfly". And there's probably a good reason for that, because when Nevaeh rings the bell and we jump off the bus, the butterfly has done what butterflies do: flown off.

"Okay, what happens now?" I ask as the bus trundles away down the road towards Honeydown Hills without us. My nails make crescent moons in my palms.

"Oh," says Nevaeh, her head drooping. "The butterfly has gone. I thought we could follow it and it would lead us to Billy."

There's a volcano building inside my stomach as I storm off down the street, shouting that I'm going to have to go back to the bus stop and catch another one now. I've lost valuable time thanks to Nevaeh's butterfly. Undeterred, Nevaeh and Knuckles follow me and Nevaeh is shaking her head, saying she can't believe the butterfly got it wrong. "I was sure it was a sign," she sighs. "I thought it would take us straight to Billy and we were going in the wrong direction on that bus. It was like it was trying to lead us somewhere else."

"We're definitely going in the wrong direction now," I mutter. "We're going away from our old house. That's where he'll be." We walk along the pavement that passes candy-coloured houses. Every so often there's a little break and you can see down towards the harbour where the sun is trying to squeeze itself through the clouds and throw golden pennies across the water. I shout back that Nevaeh and Knuckles can go home now and I'll find Billy by myself. I shout that the bracelet is stupid. They pretend they can't hear me and slope along behind me like two shadows. This is totally useless; I'm going to have to stop and text Dad and tell him Billy is missing. But Dad's at Pearl's exhibition and things are going to totally kick off when he gets this.

I sit on the wall at the end of the row of houses and pull out my mobile to type in a message: *Dad, I've lost…* Knuckles and Nevaeh sit on either side of me.

At that point a butterfly flutters past all three of us and then into one of the gardens behind. I turn to look at it. Nevaeh turns to watch too as it settles on a bush and scolds the butterfly, saying that this isn't the time for eating. It's the time to find Billy.

"It's just a butterfly," I yell, getting angry. "I don't believe the universe cares about us enough to send help via butterflies, otherwise we'd never lose the people we love in the first place."

Nevaeh looks at me, her eyes glittering. "You're just saying that because you're worried about Billy."

"Here, take your stupid bracelet," I spit, shoving the envelope of cranes under one armpit and tugging at the bracelet on my wrist. "I knew it was a daft idea wearing it. I'm sick of it. I wish I'd never put it on. Nothing amazing's happened, just loads of bad things." The elastic stretches between my fingers but doesn't snap and then the bracelet springs back, catching the hairs on my arm and making my eyes water. I tell myself: *I'm not crying, I'm not crying, I'm not crying.* I *am* crying though. I'm crying inside, because I want my mum, I want my dad and most of all I want my Billy back.

Embarrassed, I plan to storm off to hide the tears that are already spilling down my cheeks, only Nevaeh storms off before me, rising from the wall and walking towards the path that leads to the harbour. I get all uppity that she's storming off before me and start to follow her. "Where do you think you're going?" I ask.

"Why should you care? You don't think my butterflies are important so that means you can't think I am either. I thought you and I were similar but we're not. I believe that we haven't lost our loved ones and you believe we have."

There is a fireball rising up my chest and I wipe away any lipids, water, sodium and potassium from my cheeks.

Knuckles catches up and walks along beside me. After a moment he says, "I saw you in reception on the first day of school, you know. You hugged your dad and...I wanted that for myself. I felt bad about it, but I couldn't help it either. After that I could hardly look at you, because I thought you had everything I didn't have. I was jealous because you had a dad who was there for you when mine wasn't. When I got home I felt sad and I wanted to cry and I remembered how Dad told me: *Trees need water to grow strong and people need tears to do the same*." Knuckles gives me a faint smile. "I'm sorry, and what I'm trying to say is: crying is okay, it'll make you stronger. My dad says so."

I sniff a bit but manage a smile.

When we catch her up, Nevaeh is staring out across the harbour, which looks deserted except for one small person standing on his own on the harbour wall. "Who's that?" asks Nevaeh, lifting her hand to shield her eyes against the late afternoon sunlight. "They're standing close to the edge."

I follow her gaze.

It's hard to make the person out.

But I know in my gut that it's Billy.

I scream at Billy as I run all the way down the winding road towards the harbour. It's not a long way but it's too far for him to hear me. Nevaeh and Knuckles race after me and no matter how much we shout, our voices seem to be carried away on the chariots of wind. Hypnotized, Billy leans closer to the water. Too close, in fact. There's something in his hand only I can't make it out. Billy's mouth seems to be moving. I propel myself forward as fast as my legs will go.

Screaming: check.

Arm-waving: check.

Panicking: check.

Stressing: check.

Wishing for stronger underpants: check.

If there isn't a law about how far to lean over harbour walls, there should be. I watch in horror as the wall under Billy's feet seems to disappear and Billy, in a rainbow smear of clothes, topples forward. There is a plop like a pebble breaking the surface of the water. Then there's the whoosh of wind in my hair as I run towards the edge of the harbour wall, screaming. But I'm still too far from him. I can't reach. Nevaeh and Knuckles are running after me, shouting that we need to get help from grown-ups and we can't do anything stupid. As I look behind me, I see Nevaeh on her mobile.

That's the last thing I see – on land anyway.

I jump in after Billy. The envelope in my hand flies

into the air and lands on the water beside me with a slap as I break the surface.

Let me say this: falling is a funny business.

Hitting the water is not.

Down I go, dropping like a stone, down into the darkness.

TWENTY-FOUR

I feel small.
Losing Billy feels BIG.
The world is dark without him.
I think about Billy's nightmare.
I think I'm in it.

TWENTY-FIVE

Like a pebble I plunge down into the water. It feels like some unseen giant has found me and covered my head in a cold black wet blanket and no matter how much I try to shake it free it won't leave me. Worse still, I don't even know where I'm going, but wherever it is I can't leave Billy behind when I get there. Not my Billy. Not the baby who came home when Mum didn't. Not Billy, who, when he was only a few days old, clutched my finger; and he still does it now, waiting for me to squeeze back.

Not Billy, who I didn't say goodbye to.

"Billy." My mouth is full of bubbles and my voice

doesn't carry anywhere. I am light as a feather and heavy as a brick. My arms and legs jerk at odd angles as if I'm a puppet, controlled by a puppetmaster. The envelope I was carrying has spilled all its paper cranes and it's as though they're flying around me in the water. When I realize I'm sinking deeper, fear sweeps over me. But it's as if I'm fighting a monster I can't really see. The more I kick out, the less energy I have, and the monster is so big that it makes no difference how much I fight. He wins.

Above me everyone is doing everyday stuff: coming home from school or work, going to art exhibitions. They don't even know I'm here. And I want them to know I've slipped into another world but they don't. They won't come. Dad won't come.

I am sucked deeper.

I wish I was sitting in the armchair now.

My mouth makes a swoosh sound as I try to scream, but more water gushes into my throat. Blindly, I push forward, searching for Billy in the blackness. As I propel myself with my arms, I suddenly feel as peaceful as a school at five o'clock on a Friday. Then I see someone. It's not Billy though.

Mum.

She was here all along. I shake my head and tell

myself, *This is not happening, it's only my imagination,* but I'm so happy I don't want it to stop. Mum smiles through the water and I can see the gleam of sunlight on her teeth and her hair float behind her like dark ribbons of seaweed. I reach out my hand but it sags through the water without touching her. *Mum, you were in the ocean all along. Why didn't you say?* I think she's going to swim away from me and I frantically battle to bring her back. She tells me she knows I've been worrying about Billy and Dad and she's right. I can feel I'm crying. No one can see. Mum tells me that Dad will sort it out in the end and I try to ask her why she can't help him to sort it.

I can't, he has to do it himself.

Why? I think.

He doesn't know I'm here.

Does Billy know?

Billy knows. You know. I'm all around you. I'm in the air and in the raindrops. I'm in the rustle of the trees and the ocean. I'm in every living thing. You already know that. You can speak to me any time because I am everywhere. You don't need to say goodbye to me. You never did. Can you catch the air in your hand?

I know you can't.

Can you hold the ocean in your palm?

No.

Can you hold memories in your heart?

I know that you can and when I try to smile Mum looks behind me and as I spin around in the water I see Billy. His eyes are closed, his face a pale moon. His hand floats towards me, ghostly white, and I desperately need to reach it to give it a squeeze, but the more I flick and flap my body, the further apart we are.

Mum, I do need to say goodbye. I really do.

Why?

You have to say goodbye. It feels like the story has no ending if you don't say goodbye.

Maybe the story should never end, my son.

When I try to ask Mum what she means, she's gone. I spin back again towards Billy and then I see them, together. Mum and Billy, Billy and Mum. Small bubbles of life float from her mouth to his and his eyelids flutter like butterfly wings.

Exploding like a shaken bottle of fizzy pop, I break the surface of the water, gasping, with Billy clenched under my arm. The sky is grey now and as endless as for ever as I stare into it. I can hear the wailing of seagulls. As I stare upwards they circle overhead and I think about how I might have stayed with Mum a moment longer, how I should have said goodbye but I blew it again. THE GOODBYE LIST has been totally useless. A warm tear eases from my eye and joins the saltwater of the sea and you'd never know which was which.

I pull Billy to where the water meets the sand and Knuckles helps drag us up the beach. Billy's like a sodden sponge of ice and he collapses on the sand, with me joining him. Knuckles quickly takes off his blazer and puts it over us to keep us warm but I already know that it's not going to help because Billy's not breathing properly.

Once, a long time ago, Dad took us to a waxwork museum and although they looked real their skin had a funny colour. That's how Billy looks now. Knuckles and Nevaeh are standing over us, both of them hardly able to move. I bend down to check if Billy's breathing and I can't hear anything except my own breath, which is thundering.

Heart massage – I know how to do it. Although even after reading loads of medical books and watching it on TV, I can't move. Marvin never mentioned this in his medical manual; how your fear of losing someone can be so big, you can't move your muscles.

The seagulls are properly weeping above me now.

I can't save Billy.

I'm afraid.

I'm afraid he'll die.

I know what it feels like to lose those you love.

Inside my head I hear Mum saying she has just slipped around the corner. I'm not to be afraid. It feels as though Mum might be watching me now, urging me on. Without thinking, I lean down and place my hands on Billy's chest. It's cold. I retreat, my heart a galloping horse. Then I bend forward again, pushing down, exactly as I saw it done on the TV.

Live, Billy. Live, Billy.

I try again. I feel a tiny movement beneath my hands. A twitching; like a goldfish out of water. Billy's breathing again.

When I'm sure he's okay, I roll him onto his side, to the recovery position, and I fall back onto the velvet sand. Above me, the clouds are shaped like teardrops.

My fingers feel their way across the sand until they reach Billy's hand. I give it a squeeze.

Billy's hand twitches slightly in mine but he doesn't squeeze back.

Nevaeh crouches down beside us. She must have called an ambulance because I can hear its sirens and they're close now; then I hear the paramedics talking

275

and covering us in tinfoil. I want to say we're like frozen turkeys going into the oven, but the words don't come out.

"Look after them," shouts Nevaeh as we're lifted into the ambulance. "It's my best friend and his brother."

We're taken to Eden General Hospital and I won't let the doctors separate us, even though they want to. I'm not leaving Billy. They take away our wet clothes and put us in gowns and we cling to each other, not even enough room between us to fit a sliver of tissue paper.

"Billy," I whisper, thinking about what he said last night when he was pretending to be Brian. "Is this all because you thought you should go away so I could have a mummy? I don't want a mummy if it means losing you."

Billy's voice is hoarse and dry. "Nope, I went to the sea for Brian."

"Brian?" I'm confused.

"I brought him to school with me because I wanted to show him around. Then he disappeared, but I found him again in the garden patch. When you weren't at the school gate, I was telling Brian the armchair story and he wanted to see the beautiful creature from it." Billy gives me a little smile. "I only went to show him the surface of the ocean, but he jumped in saying he was a diver and then I lost him, so I was leaning over to see if I could find him again. I'm not as good a diver as Brian, Becket."

I pull Billy tight to my body and say that I'm sorry about Brian diving into the sea like that, but he shouldn't lean over the water again because it's dangerous.

There's a small knock at our door and the doctor enters and says we're very lucky. There's nothing seriously wrong with either of us and it's a good thing we had friends that helped us and called the ambulance so quickly. "It was Nevaeh and Knuckles who rang them," I explain to Billy. "My mobile phone is still in the water somewhere and I dropped the envelope with the cranes too."

"Since you had no identification on you, could you please give us your mother's number," says the doctor, preparing to write it down. "We will contact her now so she can come and get you."

"She's dead," says Billy.

The doctor says he's sorry to hear that, but a guardian's number will suffice. His nostrils flare a little and I can see the hairs inside his nose that filter germs.

"We've got Dad," I say, my voice tight like a stretched catapult. I give the doctor the number and he disappears out the door, before returning five minutes later. Apparently, Dad didn't answer. He's probably still at Pearl's art exhibition, I tell the doctor. Maybe he's got his mobile phone switched off.

"I want Dad," whispers Billy.

The doctor says he'll get a staff member to keep trying. In the meantime, he asks if I have any other relatives that could come and get us if we were discharged, but I say there isn't anyone. We're on our own. It was a mistake saying that, I know it the second the words spill from my lips. The doctor makes a grunting noise before leaving.

Half an hour later the doctor is back and fussing about how it is still impossible to contact our father on the number that I've given him.

This time when he leaves, I tell Billy we've got to get out of here. When Billy asks me why, all wide-eyed and trusting, I tell him I imagine Dad is missing us. Billy seems satisfied with my answer. Trouble is, the real reason we need to do a runner is because I think the hospital staff are getting suspicious about why they can't get hold of anyone and why no one is coming to get us. What if they ring social services? I heard about something like this happening on the news once, only in that case the mum ran off and didn't come back for her kids. Social services came for them instead and they were going to look after them.

The doctor looks back in through the glass porthole in the door, smiles and then moves on. Dad must still be at the art exhibition. Maybe Pearl is persuading Dad they're a perfect match, or maybe they're talking about what I thought I saw in the hallway the other night.

I explain to Billy that we have to go on another SNOOP secret mission: escaping the hospital without being seen. Billy says he doesn't have his balaclava and I say it doesn't matter this time. Anyway, I don't have my sheep hat either.

Staring through the glass porthole, I see a nurse at the far end of the corridor, but she's busy writing notes and looking at her computer. She hasn't been in our room yet, so she probably wouldn't recognize us if we slipped away and went back to the flat by ourselves. Even if Dad's not there, I can look after Billy until he turns up. I did it before when Billy was sick. I can do it again.

I can make everything right.

Slowly I ease Billy's soggy shoes on, put a heavy blanket over his hospital gown and I put my soggy clothes back on. They're freezing and make my teeth chatter. I tell Billy to be ready to run when I say so. First,

I'm going to go out and check the coast is clear. Billy nods and his jaw is set firm. He promises me he'll be the best spy I've ever known. Since I don't know any, the level isn't set that high.

There is no sign of the doctor outside so I grab Billy's hand and drag him, feet squelching, down the corridor and then turn into another. There are signs for everything: cardiology, oncology, gastroenterology, haematology and neurology – but no exit sign. I'm lost in the hospital maze and I'm dragging around a boy who looks terrified but determined (since he's on a secret mission). A few people turn to stare at us but I brazen it out. If you hold your head up and match their stare, they usually look away first. Hurrying down the corridors, I'm glaring at every person we meet. Until I turn the next corner. Our doctor is in the distance and talking to a police officer.

We've been rumbled. The SNOOP secret mission is going to be over before it began. The police officer is going to take us away if I don't think of something fast.

I think of something fast.

To start with, I pull Billy's blanket as far over his head and mine as I can and mutter to him that the blanket is the new balaclava, and then I open the first door we come to. It's a cleaner's closet – otherwise known as SNOOP's new den until the coast is clear again. It's not much of den and Billy's not impressed. It's full of mops and brushes, buckets and bottles of pine-fresh disinfectant. We crouch down on the floor as I tell Billy we just need to be quiet for a little while and when the doctor buzzes off we can escape properly and go back to the flat. But Billy has other ideas and wants to know why we can't just go straight home. As I'm trying to tell Billy we wouldn't be good spies if we marched out and everyone saw us, a paper crane falls softly from the blanket.

We stare at it.

We stare at each other.

"Maybe it stuck to me when I fell in the water. I mean, I dropped the envelope of cranes into the ocean so perhaps this one was tucked into my clothes."

Thing is, my clothes are completely wet and it's completely dry.

Billy says he'll hold the crane while I tell him what happened to the beautiful creature, because I didn't finish the story. There's nothing much else to do in this cupboard, so I pull the blanket closer around us and say I'm going to tell him the ending.

"Close your eyes. This is what really happened to the two boys and this is how they got through the storm and

281

took the longest journey of their lives." I take a deep breath. "The beautiful creature said it was time to go back to where they belonged. The storm was gone and the seas calm once more. She had enjoyed swimming with them, she had drawn them pictures, sang to them, showed them sparkly fish, coral plants and starfish brighter than any stars in the sky. But she said now was the time they must leave. One boy asked how they could say goodbye when they loved her so much. She said, 'I drew my goodbyes, I planted them, I whispered them on stars, I spelled them out in sparkly fish.' One of the boys said he didn't realize they were goodbyes so how could they count? She told them that each time she did something with them they thought of her and they smiled, and so each one counted. Each smile, each memory, she would leave with them. But one boy was not satisfied."

"Why?" asks Billy, his little body shivering until I snuggle up closer to him.

"He thought goodbye was more important than all the times they'd spent together. He thought saying it would make a proper ending to everything. The beautiful creature shook her head. 'Saying goodbye will not make you happy,' she whispered. 'What will make you happy is remembering the times we had and keeping

282

me alive in your heart. There is no ending.'" Tears are prickling my eyes now. "She was right, and at last the boy understood because her words danced inside his heart and he knew, he just knew. At that moment the two boys held hands and were propelled back to the ocean surface. The armchair was still waiting for them and they climbed back on board, thinking of the beautiful creature who they'd shared happy times with. The storm had passed and the travellers saw them now and waved because they weren't invisible any more. Each and every person made it safely to shore, and began happy lives in the new land. But the two boys never forgot the beautiful creature. And she never forgot them."

"I wish I'd seen the beautiful creature when I fell in the water."

"I think she saw you," I reply.

"What was her name? You never told me."

"It was Rebekah."

"But that was Mummy's name."

"I know."

TWENTY-SIX

After that, I think we must have fallen asleep. Next thing we know, we are being guided from the darkness of the cupboard and into the light of the corridor by the police officer. I don't know what time it is but I do know that the lady police officer is now asking if I'm Becket Rumsey and if this is my brother, Billy.

I nod.

Billy nudges me and says spies don't give their real names. I tell him we don't need to be spies any more because we've been caught.

"We thought you'd left the hospital and we'd lost you," says the police officer. I squint up at her, expecting her to tell us we're in terrible trouble and we will have to go into a home.

"Dad didn't turn up for us," I whisper, clutching Billy to my chest. He's shaking again and his cold fingers are gripping my wrist like a vice. "I think he's with Pearl."

"But not Naked Man," says Billy even though I try to shush him.

"And this would be..." The officer flips open her notebook. "Pearl Kinnerton, formerly of 22 Cavalier Approach and now residing at 40 Carlton Terrace."

"Yes," I say meekly. "That's her. She's an artist." Clearly, I've given up on being a spy and all the information is spilling from me like beans from an upturned tin. The officer looks at her notebook again and makes a small smacking noise with her lips. Bet she has information that Dad attacked Pearl and she's probably thinking he might attack us and we'd be safer without him. I half expect a social worker to appear in a puff of smoke behind her and then whisk us away to an orphanage, like the ones in Victorian novels.

"Let's get you double-checked by a doctor," says the police officer. "You've clearly been hiding in that cupboard for a little while. You've got strange marks on your cheeks."

"Bristles," I say.

"I'm not sure you're old enough to have bristles." The officer smiles at me, pleased she's made a joke. I smile back. Billy does too. I don't think he understands though, he smiles at a lot of daft things. Billy's hospital gown is filthy and covered in fluff and we smell of pine disinfectant and salty seawater. The officer tightens the blanket around Billy and he asks if she's going to be his new parent. She clears her throat. "I'm sure that would be very nice but you've got your own father for that, Billy."

"Dad?" I swallow. Did she just say we've still got Dad? Are we not being taken away and put into care? Doesn't she know our dad was in prison for attacking his girlfriend? I bet it's on record. Surely, she thinks we won't be safe with him. We trail after the police officer down the corridor and I ask millions of questions, but the officer tells me to shush until we're settled in our room.

"You are not being removed from the hospital until a lady comes to get you. I've just had confirmation, I've got her name here somewhere..." The police officer looks at her notebook again. "Here it is, Cat—"

"Cat Woman!" says Billy.

"Well, that's not—"

"Cat gives us lasagne."

"Okay."

"And she does fancy orange chips too, Becket said so."

"Okay."

"I think she gets the picture, Billy," I say.

"Well, this Cat Woman, who sounds like a great cook, is on her way to pick you up. Apparently she will take care of you until your father is finished at the police station." The officer shows us back to our room.

I blink. Until Dad is finished at the police station? Nothing is making sense. The officer asks us to sit on the bed and she says that Dad was involved in an argument. My eyes start to fill up. "Don't worry," says the police officer. "We're just finishing talking to him and he'll be back with you again soon." The officer looks at her notebook again.

"Did he attack anyone?" I can hardly ask the question but I have to know. "He was going to an art exhibition."

"Attack anyone? Not that I know of," says the officer. "And I hope not. There was a little incident at the exhibition, an altercation." I want to ask what an altercation is but the officer continues, "All the paintings got ripped and destroyed and someone called us out because there was a lot of shouting coming from the church hall." The officer closes her notebook again.

"Did the paintings of the Naked Man get ripped?" Billy asks; his face is all crunched up like used tinfoil.

I'm not thinking of Naked Man though. An icy chill goes through me as my mind trots back to the moment when Pearl and Dad were in the hallway. I saw them arguing then too. I ask the officer if it was Dad who destroyed the paintings, was he the person shouting? The officer shakes her head and says all we need to know is that Dad is fine and will be released without any charge. Pearl on the other hand...

If I was writing up SNOOP notes now, I would write:

SUSPECT: Ms Pearl Kinnerton.

MOTIVE: Unsure. Could it be jealousy? Was Pearl so angry that Dad had a life before her with Mum, and did Pearl think he had another girlfriend after her, even though I texted to say Camille wasn't his girlfriend? Did she not believe the text?

OPPORTUNITY: She was with Dad at the art exhibition. In fact, it was her art exhibition.

IMPORTANT THINGS TO NOTE: Aggressive nature was seen by me in the hallway. Pearl had Dad by the wrist and her face was twisted and it was almost as if she was surrounded by a horrible black cloud of anger. I felt confused. Dad was trying to pull away but her scarlet nails dug against his flesh, stopping him. The whole thing felt menacing and wrong and weird. My stomach flopped to the floor right there and then and my mouth was as dry as the floor of a hamster's cage. It only lasted a second but I know what I saw. Yes, I ignored it because at first I couldn't believe it. But now, I'm certain Pearl was attacking my dad and not the other way around.

The officer won't divulge any further information. All she says is that Dad will be with us shortly. That's it. She won't say how the "altercation" happened.

Out of the blue, Billy whispers, "I don't like Pearl any more. She told me I'd killed my mummy. It made me sad."

The officer stops and looks at him. I have to explain that Mum died in childbirth, and I can see the officer visibly relaxing that there isn't another crime to deal with. She reminds us that we must never mess about at the harbour again. "It's dangerous," she says, flicking her eyes towards Billy. He mentions Brian and the officer asks if there was another person lost in the water. Her hand is already on her radio.

"No," says Billy. "He was my snail and it was very dark down there and I didn't see any beautiful creatures but Becket says the beautiful creature saw me."

And I saw Mum.

"She gave you the bubbles of life," I point out.

"Then I saw heaven," says Billy.

If Billy doesn't stop talking soon, the police officer is going to take us away for being totally crazy. I laugh nervously and say Billy's being silly, but he insists he isn't. "First of all I saw the darkness and then I saw heaven," he repeats. As I titter with fear, there's a small knock at the door.

In walks Cat and I'm so happy to see her. We both run to her and cover her in hugs and she smells of wet grass and roses all rolled into one. She tells us she was so worried when she got a call from Dad and he was in a police station but he explained everything. He said the hospital had also left him messages and she was to come and pick us up while he was finishing up at the station. The police officer smiles and says that the three of us can go home straight away.

"Oh, Cat Woman," exclaims Billy after he's practically hugged the life out of her. "You came for us."

"Excuse me?" Cat stares at him.

"You came," says Billy nervously. "You did come for us?"

"No, what was the bit before that."

"Cat Woman?"

She laughs for so long that tears run down her cheeks in tiny rivulets. Even the police officer looks amused. I repeat "Cat Woman" and look at her quizzically. I know it's a daft name but she should blame her parents. At least I never laughed at it. Not to her face anyway. The police officer eventually puts her notebook back in her pocket as Cat stops laughing long enough to be able to speak.

"It's not Cat Woman," she says, swallowing back more laughter. "It's Cat Womack. Cat, short for Catherine. I'm afraid I'm not remotely like a Cat Woman, even though I wish I was. What gave you that idea?"

"I thought it said that on your door label," I reply, squirming.

"I'm good with a pair of hairdressing scissors but useless with a pen. My handwriting is terrible." Cat grins. "Have you been calling me Cat Woman all this time?"

"Nope," I reply, lying. "As if!"

Billy laughs and says it was my fault for getting her

name wrong. Cat tickles him in the ribs and says she's so glad to see he finds it funny.

I love Cat for it.

We went to Cat's flat so we could get cleaned up and get something to eat, and on the way Cat put on the radio and we all sang along to the songs. Cat made us a quality dinner at her flat – potato smiley faces, chicken goujons and corn on the cob drizzled with chilli butter. Billy dribbled butter all over the carpet but Cat didn't get angry. It was ace.

Now we're picking up Dad and he's sitting waiting for us outside the police station. When we arrive, he says he was so worried about us and we're never to lean over the harbour again.

"If I lost you two, my life wouldn't be worth living," he says, grabbing us both into a massive hug. "You're my everything."

Dad asks why I didn't ring him before the hospital did when it happened and I say my mobile fell in the water along with my paper cranes.

When we all climb into Cat's car, Dad sighs and says, "What a day it's been. I didn't mean it to turn out like that. I'm just glad you two are okay."

I say I'm just glad Dad is okay.

When we get back to the flat, and say our goodbyes to Cat, Dad asks Billy to go watch TV for a bit which, in my mind, translates to: *I want to talk to Becket alone again.* "You know, don't you?" Dad sighs, closing the kitchen door so Billy can't hear our conversation.

I nod. "I saw Pearl grab your wrist in the hallway. I felt funny inside because I thought she did it to hurt you. I just couldn't figure it out, Dad. I was confused. Why would Pearl want to do that?"

Dad fills the kettle and pulls out a chair and sits down. "I was confused too, son. Pearl was the loveliest person, most of the time. I don't want to make you think she was all bad because nothing is ever black and white in this world. But Pearl had a temper and lots of little things would set her off and it was as if a switch had been flicked. When that happened she'd get so angry and it would spill out from destroying things in the house to attacking me. At times she'd hurt with words and other times she'd lash out, scratch me with her nails, push me."

"It's wrong to hurt people," I whisper.

"Yes," says Dad. "And I lied about everything because I felt awful about it. Whenever Pearl lashed out she said it was my fault because I made her angry. Sometimes

I wondered if she was right. Afterwards she'd always say she was sorry that it had happened but I drove her to it and I had to forgive her, so I did. I forgave her over and over, but I hated how we couldn't talk about Mum. In the end it felt like I was treading on eggshells and a big bloke like me can't do that for long because he'd only break them."

"Why didn't you leave her sooner?" I ask.

"Because I thought I loved her. But she didn't love me, not really. You don't hurt people you love like that. I tried over and over to please her but it was never going to work. In the end, the day we moved out, there was a massive argument – she was so angry she destroyed her own self-portrait, the one over the mantelpiece. You two were in bed and I was glad you were asleep and didn't hear her. After she'd gone storming off, I threw the portrait in the garden. I knew she'd come back after she'd cooled down but I decided I needed to get out – get us all out – and quick. I needed to leave her straight away. So I woke you both up, threw everything in boxes and us in the van. I'd already organized a flat for us to go to if we needed it. I left and didn't want to look back."

"You should have told us." My voice is soft, like candyfloss.

"I should have," replies Dad. "But you've been through so much. I thought I'd make it an adventure – only it wasn't. It was a complete mess and the more you asked about Pearl, the more I wondered if I'd made a mistake leaving her behind. When Pearl first rang I was shocked."

"It was our fault. We went looking for her without telling you," I reply. "Then we rang her from the flat and she must've seen a strange number she didn't recognize and rung back."

"Nothing is your fault," says Dad. "And when Pearl turned up again I thought it might work out if we both tried. I thought this was the right thing to do because you both needed her too. But that night, after the party, she attacked me and then rang the police and said it was the other way around. I felt so lost."

"You weren't lost, Dad, because we were here." I swallow. "We were here with you."

"I know." Dad smiles at me and says, "I think you're right, Becket. I wish I'd told you all this earlier and maybe it would have worked out so much better. I just didn't think it was fair to worry you. I wanted to try and protect you both from all the bad things, like a good parent should. When you were little and worried about bogeymen in the cupboard, I was there for you, and I wanted to make this situation go away too. I wanted to make your lives perfect. But I couldn't."

"I don't want things to be perfect," I say, thinking of Mimi.

"I'm glad," replies Dad. "Nothing is ever perfect. Maybe imperfect is perfect, for us. From now on things are going to be good. And now I've got someone to talk to when things get difficult it will help. It was your nana's idea. She phoned up one night and said I should talk to someone impartial."

"Camille?"

"Yes, she was someone I don't know who would listen," explains Dad. "I searched for places I could go to talk to people who would understand the situation and not judge. I found Camille Ogdon, as you say. I took down her number and arranged to meet her. After that I felt strong enough to arrange going to Dovedale House, which was a centre where you could talk."

"I'm a terrible spy. I made everything worse by being nosey," I admit, hanging my head in shame.

Dad shakes his head and says he couldn't tell me who Camille Ogdon was in front of Pearl because he wanted to protect me and it was easier to say she was just a work acquaintance. "And how are you a spy exactly?"

Ignoring Dad's question, I continue, "We saw Pearl with another man."

Dad reaches his arm across the table and gives my hand a squeeze.

"He was naked," I explain.

Dad shakes his head slowly and says, "I saw the paintings of him before Pearl destroyed them. Pearl hated me talking to other women but she did what she wanted most of the time. It doesn't surprise me that she got herself someone else immediately. Anyway, she's gone for good now. From today onwards, we're going to heal."

"Yes, we are," I whisper.

None of this type of healing is in *Marvin's Medical Manual* but that doesn't matter one bit. And I bite my lip as another thought comes into my head. I don't care one bit about saying goodbye to Pearl. It's the easiest thing I've ever done.

TWENTY-SEVEN

The next day, when Billy and I are back at school, we catch up with Knuckles and Nevaeh in the playground before we go to lessons. Suddenly Billy shouts, "Heaven."

Heaven? I stare at Billy who says, "Yes. Heaven. I said I saw Heaven."

"This isn't Heaven, it's my friend Nevaeh," I reply very slowly.

"No," says Nevaeh, laughing. "I sort of *am* Heaven. Nevaeh is 'heaven' backwards. He's pretty clever to work it out. It's a sweet name when you think about it. Mum picked the names butterfly and heaven, to go together. Like twins." Nevaeh smiles.

"Did you tell your mum about how the butterflies helped us find Billy?" I ask.

"Yes," replies Nevaeh. "I got around to explaining why I'd been drawing them everywhere. I thought she'd get upset if I told her the truth, but she wasn't. She said it felt good to think about Mariposa. It kept her alive in our minds. Mum said she'll always look for butterflies too because she thinks I'm right, it's Mariposa saying things are okay."

Nevaeh smiles as I give Knuckles a friendly punch to the stomach. "Thanks," says Knuckles. "Just what I needed this morning; a nice sore gut." He nudges me and I say he's got to watch it, because I'm half water. "Eh, did you swallow that much when you fell in?" Knuckles's eyes are wide.

"Nah," I reply, laughing. "It's just a fact I found in my medical manual. Everyone's body is at least fifty per cent water." When I stop laughing, I say, "Thanks, Knuckles, for getting us out of the water. If it hadn't been for you, we might have been one hundred per cent water."

I feel the heat off Knuckles's red face.

"It's okay. You're a mate," says Knuckles quickly. "Anyway, my dad used to say you should always help others if they're in need. My dad gave me lots of good advice and I haven't forgotten any of it. Do you think the newspaper would be interested in writing about how you fell in the harbour and how it all worked out okay in the end? It sounds like the sort of story a paper would love."

"I think they will," I reply. "We could tell them how your dad inspired the garden and how he told you to help others. I mean, your dad is pretty special because of all that, isn't he?"

Knuckles smiles and gives me a friendly punch to the arm.

When the morning bell goes, Billy trots off into school while Mr Beagle ushers our class up to the garden patch. When we reach the garden, we see there are a few new shoots on the plants we put in on the first day we worked on the garden. My herbs are growing well and Knuckles's tree looks a lot stronger than it did. It even has a tiny bit of white blossom beginning to appear if you look really close up. Knuckles smiles and says it just needed a little bit of love and attention. It'll bloom properly in another few weeks.

Mr Beagle appears behind us and says, "I'm really pleased at how well the garden is coming on. We just have a few final things to plant and then it'll be complete and all your parents and the people from the *Eden Echo* can come."

Everyone whoops and this time they mean it. The garden really is something to be proud of. We've turned a boring, unused patch of ground into a green space that's not only lovely to look at but when you brush past the herbs they give off a heavy scent that fills the air. Mr Beagle rolls his sleeves up and helps us plant the very last herb, which is sage. He says, "Looking after plants is like looking after friendships. Remember I said this would work on different levels?"

There are a few titters because we can't see what Mr Beagle is getting at.

Seeing everyone's confusion, Mr Beagle explains, "If we water friendships they will grow. If we turn our backs on them will they begin to wilt and perhaps die. I think we all have it in us to learn a lesson from growing plants, about how to love and care for our friends. And recently I have seen how my wonderful class have looked after each other."

Blimey! Mr Beagle is really deep. I just thought it was about giving us a job to do to keep us busy. Thinking about it though, Mr Beagle is right. There's just one thing still niggling me.

"Sir." I put my hand up. "The white wall at the back still looks a bit boring."

"Ah, well, I'm glad you've mentioned that," replies

Mr Beagle. "I will hire a fabulous painter to bring it to life. What I want is a professional job by a true artist, someone who has an eye for colour and can execute a piece of art that we will want to look at for years."

Nevaeh makes a tiny arc in the mud with her shoe.

At lunch break I find her and say no artist will be able to make a good job of it. It'll probably be rubbish. But as I'm in the middle of telling her this, Mimi catches up with us and tells us to stop, she has something to say.

"I'm a weed! A beautiful weed, but still a weed." We look at her as if she's gone bonkers. Mimi explains, "I haven't been looking after my friendships, like Mr Beagle said. I've sort of pushed my way into every corner and I look like a flower, but I reckon I've been taking over. And that sort of makes me a weed, doesn't it?"

"No," says Nevaeh. "You're not. Well, not really."

"Thanks," replies Mimi, giving Nevaeh a tiny punch on the arm. Nevaeh looks surprised and mouths "Ouch". "Sorry, I've started at Kelly's Kickboxing as a new after-school club. I dropped French and ballet. To be honest, I was only doing them to please Mum, but I stood up to her and said from now on I was going to pick my own hobbies. Anyway, that's not what I'm talking about. I know I've not been the best friend. I'm really sorry for everything, Becket. I didn't like you when you came into our class because everyone liked you and it was as if everything you did was perfect. Your crane was better than my object, you were better at science, you won the garden competition. I was jealous and got so caught up in trying to be the best at everything that I've forgotten how to be myself."

"Thanks for saying sorry. Yourself is good enough," I reply, shrugging. I mean it from all four chambers of my heart.

The garden is finished, and on the day the parents are coming to look at it, Knuckles and I go to make sure no rubbish has found its way in before they turn up. I find a tiny snowdrop just below the apple tree. When I show it to Knuckles, he says we didn't even plant snowdrops but look how one has found its way here anyway. He says it goes to prove that no matter what we think we have, sometimes something completely random turns up and that's okay too, because it makes us stop and think differently.

"Anyway, it's a sign," says Knuckles.

"Of what?" I stare at the tiny snowdrop. It's so delicate that it looks swamped by herbs and I imagine the tiniest puff of wind might blow it over.

"Winter is over," replies Knuckles, grinning. "This snowdrop proves it. The darkest days are gone and spring is here." It reminds me of something Nevaeh said about it always being darkest before the dawn.

There's a tiny flutter in my belly because, yes, I really feel like winter is behind me and now I can look forward. Knuckles says we'd better go and greet all the parents because they've probably started arriving.

"I wonder what's on the wall," I say as we slope away. Mr Beagle has covered it with tarpaulin and wouldn't tell the class a single thing about the artist or what was being painted. The artist also seems to have painted it at the weekend because we've never seen anyone working on it.

Mr Beagle is waiting in the playground with the rest of the school and parents. We give him the thumbs up to say the garden looks great and we're ready. Mr Beagle tells the parents they must come and see what wonders have been done, and we all troop towards the garden. I'm walking with Dad and Billy. Cat has come too. It makes me smile.

Knuckles's mum is there and I hear her telling him how proud she is that he designed the garden. She says Knuckles reminds her of his dad, in a good way. I can feel the glow of her pride. And Knuckles is so happy, he's gliding along like he's on a hovercraft.

Mr Beagle is talking to the reporter and photographer from the *Eden Echo* and they're taking snaps of the garden and the parents. After a few claps to get everyone's attention, Mr Beagle announces, "This is what your children have made. But it's so much more than just a garden. They've learned a lot this term. Look at the plants and how they've grown. Each plant in the garden may be slightly different, but they all share the same soil. None of them are competing with or destroying the other; no, they all live in harmony. It is the same with your children. They're all different but they've all come together for this project. I'm very proud of them. Each one is special."

There is a little round of applause. Knuckles grins and says, "We did that. We made something good from nothing."

Mr Beagle goes on talking for at least five minutes about the planting process we went through and how we went to The Garden of Eden. He says he thinks we would all do it again because we've enjoyed it so much.

Everyone in the class lets out a little cheer.

"Well, if you're all so keen on this garden, perhaps we *could* do another. I've been giving this some thought. There isn't anywhere left at school, but maybe you have some ideas on what patch of ground needs our help next."

It takes me a few seconds to put up my hand. "Please, sir, I know a place that would love a new garden." When Mr Beagle asks me where, I tell him Green Acres Old People's Home. "It's such a lively place, sir. But the garden isn't. I think everyone there would love to look out the window and see plants growing rather than weeds."

"Well, Becket. This is a great idea which I think we should look into."

The reporter from the *Eden Echo* nods and writes it down. There is another round of applause from the audience and when I look at Cat she's clapping the hardest. She makes a little heart shape at me with her fingers and I make one back.

Finally, Mr Beagle says he just has one last job to do and that's remove the tarpaulin on the wall at the back of the garden. Explaining that he found a brilliant artist to paint a mural, Mr Beagle reaches for a cord and begins to pull. The photographer is poised.

"This is going to be complete rubbish," I mutter, glancing over at Nevaeh.

As the tarpaulin slips to the ground I see the best painting ever. It's a huge butterfly flying above Eden and the harbour. Below it you can make out the Bleeding Heart School and above there's this rainbow and the artist has painted lots of paper cranes too. If I look really hard I can see loads of children in the school playground but five really stand out. In my mind it sort of looks like Billy, Nevaeh, Knuckles and me. And the other person looks a bit like Mimi. As I look at Mimi she nods, her face full of happiness and she gives me the thumbs up.

As the photographer takes lots of pictures, Mr Beagle continues, "I think you'll agree that the artist has done a fabulous job and the artist is none other than our very own, Nevaeh, who I have seen drawing butterflies on many occasions and have always admired her work. When I asked Nevaeh if she'd like to try painting a big butterfly on the wall she jumped at the opportunity. But we promised to keep it a surprise for everyone. I think you'll agree that Nevaeh's done an incredible job."

Donté Moffatt says it's no Van Gogh and then says that's okay because Van Gogh lost his ear and Nevaeh doesn't want to do that.

I clap for so long my palms smart and the butterfly charm on my wrist flaps up and down. Only when the clapping stops does Mr Beagle say thank you to all the parents for attending. Before they leave, Dad and Cat say they're very proud of me. I give them both a hug and then I hug Billy.

Back in the classroom, when the people from the *Eden Echo* and the parents have gone, Mr Beagle says we all did a brilliant job and so we're all getting a gold star for our efforts. Then he turns and says there's one more thing. "Mimi, you wanted to say something." Mimi rises from her chair and walks to the front of the class and holds up a big plastic bag.

"Yes, sir." Mimi's eyes dart around the classroom at everyone. "I just wanted to say that the story we learned about the paper crane was amazing. I didn't say so at the time because I was a bit envious it wasn't my story but I really think it was. I borrowed Becket's crane, the one that was in the classroom, without asking permission. When I was going to the toilet I sneaked it into my pocket."

Mr Beagle nods and waits for an explanation.

Mimi says quickly, "But there was a reason. At first I wanted to see how to make them so I could make one thousand and get a wish for myself. I made loads and loads until I got to one thousand. I even tried to get them to look perfect. But then I heard that Becket lost all his after he fell in the harbour, and so I want to give him mine. That way he can get his wish because, whatever

it is, I think it's probably more important than mine is."
Mimi brings the bag to me and hands it over and then
sits down. "I was just going to wish to be myself and
make real friends in my class, and I think that's kind of
happened anyway," she whispers to me.

I'm sort of gobsmacked. I sort of mouth "Thank you"
and Mimi sort of mouths "You're welcome".

Later that night I offer to tell Billy another story
in Mum's armchair, but he says he doesn't need one
because the one I've told can't be beaten. Anyway, he's
not scared about things any more.

"I'm sorry you lost Brian in the ocean," I reply. "I feel
like it's my fault that Brian jumped."

"It's okay. It was Brian who jumped. He was a bit
crazy like that sometimes. I think he took after you. I
still miss him though," says Billy, biting his lip so he
doesn't cry.

After Billy goes to bed and Dad has just nipped next
door to have a quick word with Cat, something weird
happens. I hit my toe on one of the boxes that we
brought with us from the old house. I've never looked
in the box of Mum's stuff. Dad has moved it around a
bit when he was tidying up and now I see there's a hole
in the side. As I bend down, I spot a book on origami,
and when I pick it up I notice someone has turned the

corner over on a page about paper cranes. As I set the book down on the side and move some things around in the box, I come across dozens of little cranes.

"Oh, Mum," I whisper. I think about how Mr Beagle said paper cranes were given to new babies for a lucky life, and I wonder if she made these ones all those years ago for Billy before he was born. The first one Dad gave to me must have fallen out of this box when he moved it around. I pick up a crane and blow it and it flies from my hand and floats down onto the carpet. "Dad said you folded a star a long time ago, Mum, so I should have known it was you who folded the cranes. I should have known it wasn't left by someone else who had lived in the flat before us. It really was magic all along."

The cranes were my butterflies.

I just had to believe.

Well, I believe now.

I reach into the box again and find a book on flowers and one on baking cakes. There's a wallpaper sample with blue swallows on it and a pressed lily which no longer looks like a creamy trumpet but like yellowing tissue paper. Underneath it there's a photograph of Mum looking happy standing by the water's edge, like the one in the frame in Dad's room. I lift the photo and hold it in front of my face. This one must have been taken a little later on in the day, because Mum has the message-in-a-bottle and she's holding it up in the air and standing at the water's edge. If I close my eyes I can almost imagine her firing it out across the ocean. But Dad said Mum didn't get a reply.

That's when I see something. How did I miss it before? I place the photograph right up to my eyes and look inside the bottle. It's not a note at all. At least I don't think so. My eyes grow wide. Inside Mum's bottle is a folded-up paper crane.

At that moment there's no doubt in my mind that Mum has been with me all along.

TWENTY-EIGHT

Dear Mum

For ages I wanted to say goodbye to you.

I even wrote a list called THE GOODBYE LIST, although I think you already know that. I tried every way I could think of to say goodbye to you but nothing felt right. It was as if saying goodbye was the biggest deal in the entire world and nothing would be good enough. Even if I hired a plane and it trailed a GOODBYE banner behind it for the whole world to see, it still wouldn't be enough. I had nine ways to say it. All nine were wrong. I had a tenth one and the tenth one was nothing because I couldn't decide on a tenth way to say goodbye.

I am attaching THE GOODBYE LIST to this letter. I've never written you a letter before. Ibiza Nana used to say that no one writes letters any more. So here I am, writing a letter, which means Ibiza Nana is not technically correct (then again she's not technically correct on a lot of things, like when she says you'll be laughing on the other side of your face or you've got eyes in the back of your head).

So many times over the years I've wanted to tell you things, Mum: like when I rode my bike for the first time. I wobbled for ages but I did it. When Dad let go of me it felt like I could do anything. And I wanted to tell you when I got a gold star for a story about a dog with no tail. I was seven then and I cried for ages when I couldn't read it to you.

I cried a lot.

And in school, when everyone made Mother's Day cards, I pretended I needed the toilet so I wouldn't have to make one and that made me cry even more.

My friend, Knuckles, said recently that tears are water and you need water to make things grow,

so I figure that all my tears were a good thing.
I bet I make a few more. I'm okay with that.

Billy is happy too. I just thought I'd throw that
in here. He looks just like you. I look like Dad,
without the bald head, the big belly and the tattoo.
By the way, Dad got the tattoo for you. Koi carps
mean you've overcome a struggle and when you
died Dad had a lot to overcome. But he's done
okay, and we love him even if we annoy him
sometimes. Dad says it's us children that made him
tear his hair out in the first place. He says he used
to have more hair than an angora rabbit, which I
think is very unlikely because I looked it up on the
internet and Dad never had that much hair even in
his dreams. Anyway, I think he's joking. I like it
when he jokes.

I think Dad is happy now too. There was a little
while when he wasn't. I didn't notice because I was
sad too. But everything is okay now. Dad has a
new friend. Her name is Cat. We thought she was
Cat Woman but she isn't. I think you'd like her. She
said you were very pretty when I showed her your
photo. Cat also said it was an honour for her to be
able to spend time with your children. I think she
means Billy and me.

No one has ever said that before.

Your armchair is in the living room now. It was Cat's idea for it to be put there. I think your armchair is the best. I didn't know it at the time, but your armchair has carried me on a journey when I felt all at sea, when I was under the darkest cloud. Your armchair was a safe place to go to and it has helped me realize that you can come through a storm and survive. You'll be stronger for it too. Maybe you'll be different though, a bit more grown up. But growing up is okay, even if it feels scary at times.

As for the paper cranes, well, I know you were sending me those. Nevaeh said our loved ones try to get in contact whatever way they can. I guess you already know I found a whole load of paper cranes in your cardboard box in the living room. Maybe they just fell out when the box got disturbed but maybe you made them fall out. That's what I'm going to believe. As I was making them, you were sending them, and it felt like I was wishing to make contact with you as you were wishing to make contact with me.

Boom! If you believe, things happen.

I asked Dad if he knew your box of belongings

was full of paper cranes and Dad said he didn't because he'd never looked in the box. He was so sad after you'd died that he couldn't bring himself to. Now I've told Dad everything about the cranes he believes in magic too.

Another thing I'm going to believe is that I saw you when I fell in the water. I know the brain does funny things when the body gets cold – maybe it even sees things that aren't there. But I don't care what my medical books say about it. I know I saw you and I know what you told me. I'll never forget, Mum.

I'm going to have to finish my letter now. It's not really a long one. The main thing is everyone is happy here in Eden and I think that's what you'd really like to know most of all. I'm going to post this note in the morning. You don't have to reply. I don't expect you to, so don't worry. A long time ago you sent out a message-in-a-bottle and you knew you'd get a reply. You believed. You didn't know when it would come but I think this is the reply you were waiting for.

By the way, I used to think the one important person in my life who I didn't get to talk to was you. But now I know I can talk to you every day.

Because the last thing, Mum, number ten on THE GOODBYE LIST, was the right way to say goodbye. Number ten said do nothing, and I've had to do loads of goodbyes and go through a big storm to realize that doing nothing, not saying goodbye at all, is actually the right thing for me. Because you're in my heart, Mum.

Becket x

The final SNOOP secret mission

This was SNOOP's last secret mission and I am writing up the notes now because Billy says if I don't write them down I'll forget. But Billy's wrong. I'll never forget what happened an hour ago, even if I live to about forty. This is what happened on that final mission:

AT 5.43 A.M.: Billy woke me as usual. I wasn't surprised. But this time he said he had a lovely dream about Mum. A few days ago I mentioned to Dad that Billy had been waking up at the same time every day and when Dad replied he sounded like he was swallowing jelly even though he'd just been eating a biscuit. Dad said five forty-three was the exact time that Mum died. At first I was shocked and I thought I'd feel sad but I didn't. It was just another thing that convinced me Mum was all around us.

THE FINAL MISSION: This was my idea and I told Billy I wanted to go.

For the record, Billy said, "Okay."

I wrote Dad a note in case he woke up and found us gone. I explained we wouldn't be long.

CARRYING: I had three items in my hand – a bag with one thousand paper cranes inside, a letter with a list attached and an empty plastic bottle. My thoughts were that the paper cranes should be set free.

WEATHER: The sun was rising and washing away the traces of night. Temperature was okay but a bit breezy. A small gust of wind tugged at the bag and made it whip around my knees. Billy and I wandered through the park and just as I went to speak to him I realized he was down and poking in the mud.

Billy said, and I quote, "Look! I've found Brian." Billy held up a small snail and waved him about.

I said this was great. "He must've followed you

again. We can take him home and put him back in his lovely house."

For the record, Billy held the snail up to his ear. "No," said Billy, setting Brian back in the mud. "Brian says he's not lost. He has travelled all over only to realize that he belongs at home with his family. This is his home in the mud and he's happy now."

MY MOOD: Surprised but over-the-moon. I even waved goodbye to Brian (I checked there was no one else around to see me first).

As we walked down towards the water's edge, I told Billy I had written Mum a letter.

Billy asked if she'd get it because she was actually dead. I said she would. He asked if she'd reply because she was still actually dead. I said I thought she already had.

I opened the bag and told Billy to help himself because we were going to let all the cranes go.

Together we took fistfuls of cranes and threw them into the air. We watched as they flew up into the sky. I said I thought things would be okay from now on. I was saying it to Mum really. Then I said I was going to get on with my life.

WHAT HAPPENED NEXT: The butterfly bracelet must have caught on something because it snapped and fell off my wrist into the sand. I picked it up and put it in my pocket. That's when I knew something amazing was going to happen.

Billy fired paper cranes higher and higher.

White birds in a blue sky.

I reached into the bag too and tried to throw mine higher. A breeze carried some birds far from us and others went to the ocean and bobbed there. Some tickled my arms before falling on the sand. It felt like we were standing inside a shaken snow globe. That's when the strangest thing happened. I realized what it was. There was no other place in the world I was supposed to be.

This was me.

Eleven-year-old Becket Rumsey, who used to be a big fan of reading medical books but now likes books on origami; older brother of no-longer-a-bug-collector Billy; son of The Codfather fish delivery man; grandson of Ibiza Nana; and who thinks of Mum every day and is happy.

Billy reached into the bag one final time and pulled out the last of the paper cranes and threw them into the air. The bag was empty. I tipped it up, double-checking we'd let all the cranes go. We watched as they floated away on the breeze.

Billy raced across the sand, waving at them and shouting "Goodbye, lovely birds!" at the top of his lungs. I followed him, my toes ploughing furrows in the sand. Then I stopped, spread my arms out wide, closed my eyes and spun around. The wind whipped my hair and, dizzy, I opened my eyes again and looked at the letter to Mum.

I quickly folded it into a crane, and then placed it inside the plastic bottle.

"For you, Mum," I whispered.

"For Mummy," Billy echoed as he ran towards me.

I told Billy that we had to hold the bottle together, before we let it go. "We've both touched it. I think Mum would like that," I said. Together we launched the plastic bottle far across the waves and we watched as it bobbed about and then got further away, far out of our reach. Eventually we couldn't see it any more and Billy asked if it had gone to the ocean.

"I think it has. It's definitely gone to Mum," I explained. "She knew I'd get her message and reply." I faced the ocean. "I never needed to say goodbye, no matter how much I wished I had. Our story won't ever end with a goodbye. How can it, when you're all around us? When you're in the sun and the rain and when you're in my heart and Billy's. You see, in the end I got your message. And our message back is that we love you and we'll never forget you."

In the distance a church bell tolled and Billy and I headed back across the sand. Billy did a cartwheel and I thought of Mum and I was happier than ever before. The sun came up fully and the sky was completely cloudless and it was a new chapter for us all.

TIME: 6.45A.M.: Billy reached for my hand and gave it a squeeze. I knew it was Billy's way of asking if everything would be okay from today onwards.

I squeezed back, my hand tightly furled around Billy's. And I meant "okay" with all my heart this time.

Billy looked up at me and asked, "Is it really okay?"

"Yes," I replied. "It really is."

How to Make a Paper Crane

Join Becket Origami Rumsey Esq. and have a go at
making a paper crane of your own!

You'll need a square piece
of paper, (15 x 15cm)

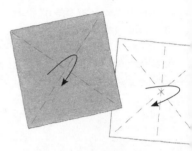

1. Take your square and
fold the bottom right corner
up to the top left corner.
Crease and unfold.

2. Fold and unfold the bottom
left corner to the top right
corner. Turn it over. Fold the
side edges together. Unfold.

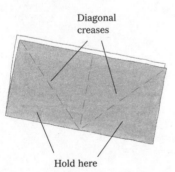

Diagonal
creases

Hold here

3. Fold your square in half
from bottom to top. Hold the
bottom edge at both sides just
below the diagonal creases.

4. Bring your fingers
together so that the
diagonal creases meet in
the middle. Four triangles
stick out, as shown.

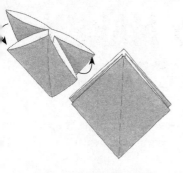

5. Fold the flap at the front to the right, and the flap at the back to the left. Press the paper flat. Turn the square so that the open ends are facing you.

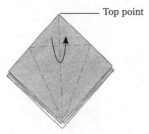

Top point

6. Fold the sides of the top layer in to the middle so that the edges meet. Unfold them again.

7. Fold the top point down and crease where the paper meets the top of the two diagonal creases. Unfold.

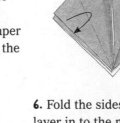

The edges will lift up.

Put a finger here to keep the layers underneath in place.

8. Lift the bottom corner of the top layer of paper over the top point, bending along the crease made in step 7.

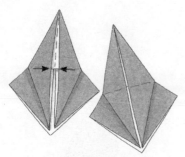

9. Then, fold the two sides into the middle, along the creases made in step 6, creasing from the bottom.

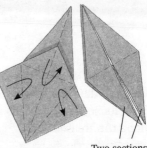

Two sections

10. Turn the paper over and repeat steps 6-9 on this side. The bottom half of the paper has two sections.

This edge touches the end of the middle crease.

11. Fold the bottom points up so that they stick out at an angle. Crease the folds well and then unfold them.

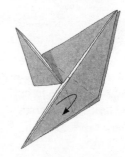

12. Turn the paper over and repeat step 11. Then, fold along the creases made on the other side of the paper.

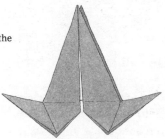

This makes the
bird's neck.

Bottom point

13. Open the right flap. Bend its bottom point up along the creases you have just made. Squash the paper flat.

14. Now repeat step 13 very neatly with the flap on the left. This makes the crane's tail.

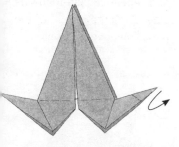

15. Fold over the tip of the head very neatly in both directions and unfold. Crease the folds well.

16. To make the head, open out the neck flap and bend its tip down along the crease made in step 15. Squash the flap flat.

Make a wish and let your crane fly!

Q&A WITH LARA

How did you come across the legend of the paper crane?

I've always had an interest in the things we wish on and what we'd wish for. I hadn't heard of this story before so I was fascinated when I first read about it in an article on the internet. Once, when I was little, I tried to run to the end of a rainbow where I thought I'd be granted three wishes in return for the leprechaun's freedom. I'll let you make up your own mind as to whether I got the wishes. Even now I make little wishes on things all the time; some come true, some are impossible, and some I think I make happen with hard work and determination. Maybe the real magic is inside each of us and we just have to find it...

If you had one wish, what would it be?

Maybe I'd wish for Dorothy's ruby slippers from the movie of *The Wizard of Oz* or I'd help Scooby-Doo solve a mystery. Or I'd wish to find a golden ticket in a Wonka chocolate bar. Those wishes would be fun but really, what I'd wish for most of all is something Becket would wish for too: one more minute with the loved ones I've lost.

What was your inspiration for Becket?

While I was thinking of ideas for book two I kept imagining two boys in an armchair sailing towards an island. At the time I didn't know what their story was or why I imagined an armchair but I knew they were on a journey together and it wasn't going to be plain sailing. As time went on and I began to write things down I realized Becket and Billy had lost their mother. This was to be a story about the journey through loss and I knew it had to be in the armchair as I'd first imagined. By the end I knew Becket and his brother would go through the storm, be stronger for it, move forward in life but never forget.

If you could sail an armchair to anywhere in the world, where would you end up?

Home. No matter where I've travelled, no matter how far, there is only one place I've ever wanted to end up and that's at home with my family. In my books I have named the towns Paradise and Eden because the names suggest they are places of happiness and in each case they are the character's home, surrounded by those they love.

Do you ever wonder what happens to your characters after the end of the book?

Just like in *The Boy Who Sailed the Ocean in an Armchair* it's hard to say goodbye. Part of you wants to hold on to the characters but part of you knows you have to let them go. Eventually I do so accepting they're stronger at the end of the story than they were at the beginning. By the last page, I know that despite what life might throw at them in the future they're going to be happy. That's all I've ever wanted for them.

ABOUT LARA

Lara's debut novel, *A Boy Called Hope*, has been shortlisted for lots of prizes, including the Waterstones Children's Book Prize and the IBW Book Award, and won the Hillingdon Secondary Book of the Year and Hounslow Junior Book Award.

Lara was born and studied in Northern Ireland, before moving to London. To this day, she still makes wishes on dandelion clocks, stars, rainbows and fountains. Meanwhile, her family wishes she didn't go around blowing on garden weeds, staring into the sky, running to rainbows and throwing all her money into the water.

Follow Lara on Twitter @LaraWilliamson

ACKNOWLEDGEMENTS

My heartfelt thanks to the following people without whose help and encouragement I couldn't have written this book:

Madeleine Milburn, my agent, who is dedicated, loyal and supportive always; "Sweet Baby Cheeses! You're ace!" as Becket would say of her able assistant, Cara Lee Simpson; Anne Finnis, Rebecca Hill, Becky Walker, Sarah Stewart, Anna Howorth, Amy Dobson, Sarah Cronin, Katharine Millichope, and Neil Francis at Usborne. They helped in so many ways including reading and editing my work until, like the paper cranes, it was ready to fly. I thank you all from the four chambers of my heart. Special thanks go to Tomoko Nishigaki for help with research. Melissa Roske for being the best writing buddy and making me realise that writing as slow as a snail is okay especially when the snail ends up in the book. Love and thanks to Millie, Graham, Mum and my entire family. If I ever need to sail the ocean in an armchair you're all coming with me.

Finally, Catherine and Billy Peden, this story is for you. We never needed to say goodbye, not really.

Also by LARA WILLIAMSON:

"This book totally blew me away. I love it"
CATHY CASSIDY

A BOY CALLED HOPE

Sometimes
a little bit of hope
can go a long way

LARA WILLIAMSON

Since his dad ran off with the lady from the chip shop, Dan Hope's life has gone a bit strange, what with his sister acting mean and Mum's new boyfriend keeping secrets. And now – even stranger – his dad has turned up as a presenter on TV.

So Dan decides to sort out his messy family, starting with getting his dad back. But as one genius plan after another goes pear-shaped, Dan fears that his wish will never come true...until he starts to realize that your real family aren't always the people you share your name with.

ISBN 9781409570318

Praise for A BOY CALLED HOPE

Shortlisted for **Waterstones Children's Book Prize 2015**
Shortlisted for **Independent Booksellers Week Book Award 2014**

"Warm, heartbreaking and hilarious in turn… a fabulous
book about love, families and making sense of life."
The Sunday Express

"A beautifully written and heartfelt novel that made me
laugh and cry in equal measure."
Waterstones Booksellers' Children's Books of the Year

"*A Boy Called Hope* will tug at your heartstrings and
probably make your eyes all leaky, but it's such a great
book for huddling under a blanket with."
The Mile Long Bookshelf

"Lovely, heartwarming, funny read. I laughed out loud,
and I may have shed a tear or two."
Michelle Harrison, author

#ABoyCalledHope
www.aboycalledhope.com

For more stories to sail away with, go to:

www.usborne.co.uk/fiction